FURNISHING
THE LIBRARY INTERIOR

BOOKS IN LIBRARY AND INFORMATION SCIENCE

A Series of Monographs and Textbooks

EDITOR

ALLEN KENT

Director, Office of Communications Programs
University of Pittsburgh
Pittsburgh, Pennsylvania

Vol. 1 Classified Library of Congress Subject Headings, Volume 1—Classified List, *edited by James G. Williams, Martha L. Manheimer, and Jay E. Daily (out of print)*

Vol. 2 Classified Library of Congress Subject Headings, Volume 2—Alphabetic List, *edited by James G. Williams, Martha L. Manheimer, and Jay E. Daily*

Vol. 3 Organizing Nonprint Materials, *by Jay E. Daily*

Vol. 4 Computer-Based Chemical Information, *edited by Edward McC. Arnett and Allen Kent*

Vol. 5 Style Manual: A Guide for the Preparation of Reports and Dissertations, *by Martha L. Manheimer*

Vol. 6 The Anatomy of Censorship, *by Jay E. Daily*

Vol. 7 Information Science: Search for Identity, *edited by Anthony Debons (out of print)*

Vol. 8 Resource Sharing in Libraries: Why How • When Next Action Steps, *edited by Allen Kent (out of print)*

Vol. 9 Reading the Russian Language: A Guide for Librarians and Other Professionals, *by Rosalind Kent*

Vol. 10 Statewide Computing Systems: Coordinating Academic Computer Planning, *edited by Charles Mosmann (out of print)*

Vol. 11 Using the Chemical Literature: A Practical Guide, *by Henry M. Woodburn*

Vol. 12 Cataloging and Classification: A Workbook, *by Martha L. Manheimer (out of print)*

Vol. 13 Multi-media Indexes, Lists, and Review Sources: A Bibliographic Guide, *by Thomas L. Hart, Mary Alice Hunt, and Blanche Woolls*

Vol. 14 Document Retrieval Systems: Factors Affecting Search Time, *by K. Leon Montgomery*

Vol. 15 Library Automation Systems, *by Stephen R. Salmon*

Vol. 16 Black Literature Resources: Analysis and Organization, *by Doris H. Clack*

Vol. 17 Copyright—Information Technology—Public Policy: Part I—Copyright—Public Policies; Part II—Public Policies—Information Technology, *by Nicholas Henry*

Vol. 18 Crisis in Copyright, *by William Z. Nasri*

Vol. 19 Mental Health Information Systems: Design and Implementation, *by David J. Kupfer, Michael S. Levine, and John A. Nelson*

Vol. 20 Handbook of Library Regulations, *by Marcy Murphy and Claude J. Johns, Jr.*

Vol. 21 Library Resource Sharing, *by Allen Kent and Thomas J. Galvin*

Vol. 22 Computers in Newspaper Publishing: User-Oriented Systems, *by Dineh Moghdam*

Vol. 23 The On-Line Revolution in Libraries, *edited by Allen Kent and Thomas J. Galvin*

Vol. 24 The Library as a Learning Service Center, *by Patrick R. Penland and Aleyamma Mathai*

Vol. 25 Using the Mathematical Literature: A Practical Guide, *by Barbara Kirsch Schaefer*

Vol. 26 Use of Library Materials: The University of Pittsburgh Study, *by Allen Kent et al.*

Vol. 27 The Structure and Governance of Library Networks, *edited by Allen Kent and Thomas J. Galvin*

Vol. 28 The Development of Library Collections of Sound Recordings, *by Frank W. Hoffmann*

Vol. 29 Furnishing the Library Interior, *by William S. Pierce*

Additional volumes in preparation

FURNISHING THE LIBRARY INTERIOR

WILLIAM S. PIERCE
The University Libraries
The Pennsylvania State University
University Park, Pennsylvania

MARCEL DEKKER, INC. New York and Basel

Library of Congress Cataloging in Publication Data

Pierce, William S [Date]
Furnishing the library interior.

(Books in library and information science ; v. 29)
Bibliography: p.
Includes index.
1. Library fittings and supplies. 2. Library planning. I. Title. II. Series.
Z679.5.P53 022'.9 79-25569
ISBN 0-8247-6900-7

MARCEL DEKKER, INC.

270 Madison Avenue, New York, New York 10016

Current printing (last digit):
10 9 8 7 6 5 4 3

PRINTED IN THE UNITED STATES OF AMERICA

PREFACE

In the years since World War II we have witnessed enormous increases in man's need for information and in the amount of information published. A rapid growth in libraries has been the direct result of this information explosion, for libraries are the most important distributors of published information. As library collections grew and as the information organizing, distributing, and interpreting services they provide expanded, new physical facilities for these operations were needed all over the world. Funding was forthcoming from many levels of government, stimulated by new technological information demands. This governmental financial support, in turn, stimulated the expenditure of private funds for libraries. The period between 1960 and 1975 saw a boom in library building that resulted in thousands of new library facilities worldwide.

As the 1970s arrived, however, the pace of new construction began to slacken noticeably. Federal support began to dry up and other funding sources were so affected by inflation that relatively few new libraries were planned during the decade, compared with the 1960s. While it is clear that we cannot expect another period during which funding for new libraries will come as easily as it did during the sixties, there is no question that many libraries, if they are to continue successful operation, must quickly deal with increasing space demands and shortages.

Some libraries were never expanded during the building boom; a few did not need more space so badly then, and some libraries received less new space than they required. Of the libraries needing more space, some fortunate ones will get new library buildings; others will get additions or renovations for existing buildings. Some, unfortunately, will have to make do with the space they have and, without funds for major renovation, will need to rearrange functions and areas to use existing space more effectively. Nearly any library, perhaps with the aid of a competent consultant, can find ways to get more use out of existing space.

During the years of the building boom, some librarians who had significant and varied experience with library buildings tried, through the professional literature, to pass along to future librarians/planners the knowledge they gained. Metcalf's monumental work on academic libraries (1965) and a number of works by Ellsworth and, more recently, Thompson (1977), have covered the issue of library planning thoroughly. These have been supplemented by many journal articles discussing special subjects or individual buildings. The published proceedings of building and equipment institutes conducted just prior to the annual conferences of the American Library Association have been good sources of information and informed opinion about library buildings. Through the years there have been some articles dealing specifically with library equipment and furniture; of particular note are the writings of Frazer Poole. Until now, however, there has not been a book that has attempted to discuss thoroughly the furnishing and equipping of libraries of all kinds.

In this volume we discuss the selection, evaluation, and purchase of furniture and equipment for libraries. We do not cover the planning and construction of library buildings, for these subjects have been thoroughly covered by others. In the first chapter we do discuss the arrangement of the interior to update and illuminate earlier writings and to provide a framework for material in the succeeding chapters. Chapters 2 through 6 cover the kinds of spaces in libraries and the variety of furniture and equipment found in them. Major categories of furniture are described in detail with information about desirable methods of construction and evaluation of materials used. In Chapter 7, we consider the selection, evaluation, and purchase of library furniture and equipment. Chapter 8 discusses the manufacture and marketing of library furniture, and the last chapter describes new developments and recent experience with interior materials and systems. Finally, there is a very important appendix, which includes sample specifications for wood library furniture, seating, and steel bookstacks, accompanied by commentary on the importance of particular requirements in these specifications.

This book could be a good bit more detailed and exhaustive, but it would have become dated much too soon, for both the industry and what it produces are changing rapidly. For the same reason, we have largely avoided naming particular manufacturers and their lines. Although much library furniture produced currently is shoddy, we have not condemned particular manufacturers and their manufacturing methods; rather, we have suggested standards of good practice. If some manufacturers fail to measure up to these standards (assuming that the standards are valid) the conclusion is inevitable. Manufacturers do change their methods of manufacturing and marketing; sometimes they improve, other times they worsen. Thus, use of such standards is appropriate and necessary when evaluating manufacturers.

Books on planning libraries have generally concentrated on one kind of library, for each type differs considerably in function and service requirements. However, in regard to furniture and equipment, the same items are used in all kinds of libraries with few exceptions. Generally, children's rooms with their special furniture are peculiar to public libraries. Carrels are common in academic libraries, but are rarely seen in public libraries.

We have tried to cover these few exceptions and to make the material in the book helpful for those planning and purchasing furniture for all kinds of libraries. Further, we believe that the staff of any library, whether planning a new building, addition, or renovation, or simply adding capacity or new technology, or replacing worn-out articles of furniture and equipment, will find the information in this volume useful. Although only a fraction of all libraries can, in any given year, add to or improve significantly the space available, nearly all libraries will add some equipment or furniture. The material in this book should help those spending even small amounts for library furniture and equipment to do so more wisely.

During the preparation of this book, the United States began to convert to metric measurement, and therefore, the author has converted furniture dimensions into rough metric equivalents. They will be easier for many readers to cope with than will area measurements, for which no metric equivalents are provided.

Aside from the fact mentioned earlier, namely, that no such volume on library planning has been available until now, why else was this book produced? Since the early sixties, the author has been responsible for coordinating the planning, construction, and furnishing of libraries at The Pennsylvania State University, a large multicampus system. During this period he has been involved in all aspects of programming, planning, design, construction, and furnishing 16 complete library buildings, which vary in size from 10,000 to 130,000 sq ft. In addition, he has completed many other projects involving the creation and furnishing of other library spaces within this university system. And he has had frequent opportunities to be a consultant for other institutions. This "on-the-job"training and consulting were supplemented by visits to libraries, furniture factories, showrooms, and exhibits at conferences. As a result of these experiences, the author has acquired a large fund of information about furnishing and equipping libraries. In view of the paucity of information on the subject, it seemed important to the author to make some of this information available in print, to help other librarian/planners.

William S. Pierce

CONTENTS

ACKNOWLEDGMENTS

The author has visited more than 270 libraries and 20 furniture factories in the years since 1960. A list of places visited through 1976 appears in Appendix B. These visits were funded partially by a grant from the Council on Library Resources, which also assisted with photography costs. The author is grateful to the council for this important support.

The author is also grateful to all the librarians who have been patient tour guides and answerers of questions when he visited their libraries. He is also grateful to friends in the furniture industry who have graciously shared their knowledge with him. Of special note here are Bob May, Sam Coston, Henry Hooper, Doug Anderson, and Dick Boyer. The chief administrative officers of The Pennsylvania State University Libraries during this period—Librarian Ralph McComb, Director W. Carl Jackson, and Dean Stuart Forth—have been generous with encouragement and support. Merv Helman, now retired from Penn State's purchasing department, shared his wealth of knowledge about purchasing. Also, thanks are due those Commonwealth Campus librarians and administrators for the pleasure of working with them through the years. Finally, the author owes a debt to his children, David, Rosalind, and Morgan, who put up with his crankiness and need for quiet. The largest debt of all is to his wife, Mim, who has been typist, editor, grammarian, inspiration, and collaborator, and superb in each role.

William S. Pierce

FURNISHING THE LIBRARY INTERIOR

1
PLANNING THE INTERIOR

WHY LIBRARY BUILDINGS FAIL

The truly modern library building began its existence after World War II, although some earlier buildings have strikingly modern features. The more than 30 years since 1945 have seen the construction of thousands of new library buildings, many additions to older buildings, and the development of library areas or rooms within large, multipurpose buildings. These libraries have ranged in size from massive university and central public libraries to small branch buildings and even smaller library rooms and spaces in academic buildings and governmental and corporate structures (see Figs. 1 to 4).

The planning and design of these buildings have drawn upon the professional experience and creative talents of many librarians/planners, consultants, and architects. Many of the resulting buildings have been aesthetically pleasing. Some of them have been merely functional. A few have been both. A detailed critical analysis of the library buildings of this era would help us understand why so few completely satisfactory buildings are found among the great many that have been built. Lack of experience and talent are certainly not the causes. Many of our most creative architects have designed libraries; in some cases, the same man or architectural firm has designed several libraries. While librarians who have the opportunity to plan a library generally do so only once, most of them call upon the services of a librarian/consultant who has worked on many such buildings. Nonetheless, it is true that few libraries built since World War II have been complete aesthetic and functional successes, in the view of this author and other planners/consultants.

FIG. 1 Phillips Exeter Academy, Exeter, New Hampshire. Perhaps the ultimate in secondary school libraries.

FIG. 2 A splendid central public library. Jacksonville Public Library, Jacksonville, Florida.

FIG. 3 A traditional library building moved nearly 100 ft, then added to; the result was this harmonious whole. Salem College, Winston-Salem, North Carolina.

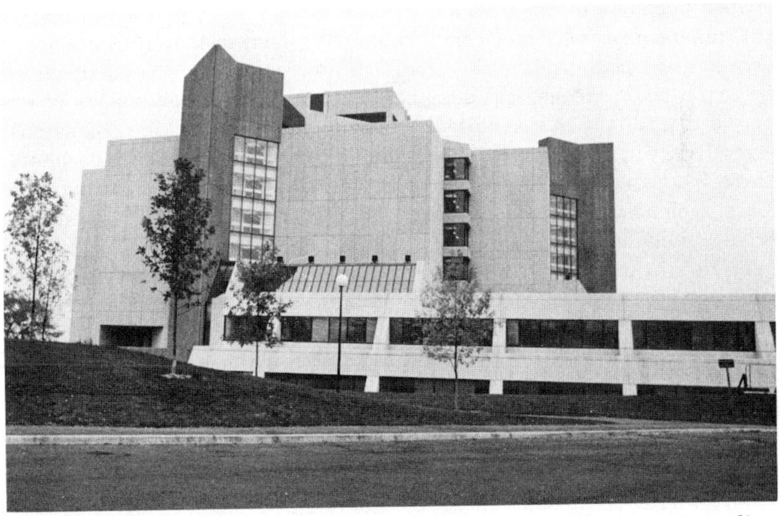

FIG. 4 A most impressive and successful national library. Canadian Institute for Scientific and Technical Information, Ottawa, Ontario.

THE PLANNING TEAM

The process of planning libraries has been discussed voluminously by Metcalf, Ellsworth, and many others. The principles they espouse and the information they present, if accepted and utilized, should have resulted in many more effective and serviceable libraries than in fact, have been built. In this observer's view, a primary cause of most of these unsatisfactory library buildings has been the failure of planning teams to function properly. All the literature on library planning emphasizes that the client institution, the architect, and the librarian(s) involved should comprise a team to discuss and reach agreement on every important aspect of the building plan. In some cases, the librarian will have complete authority to represent the client institution in negotiating with the architect, but often this is not true and frequently there is a somewhat adversarial relationship between librarian and institutional representative. While the person representing the client institution works for the same college or university, municipal government, or other agency as the librarian, there is frequently neither close rapport between the individuals nor great understanding of library problems and operations on the part of the institutional representative, who is often a university planning officer, business manager, trustee chairman, or some other representative of those financing the building. The librarian involved is generally the chief administrative officer of the library, or his representative, who presumably represents the entire library staff and consults with them in regard to their requirements. As staff participation in library governance becomes more prevalent, staff discussion and "input" regarding physical planning become more important. The next essential component of the team are the planning professionals. There will always be an architect, who in turn hires a mechanical designer, and sometimes a designer responsible for the interior. Some architects already employ interior professionals in their offices; in other cases, librarians or governing bodies hire interior designers independent of the architect. The planning team may include other members such as college or university faculty, who can be helpful but often serve only to confuse the issue.

In the view of this author and other consultants, the greatest reason for the construction of unsatisfactory library buildings is the planning group's failure to work and act as a team. In too many cases, an architect overwhelms both client and librarian with his aesthetic sense, and the result is an unfunctional building. Or, in other circumstances, the architect values function but convinces the client that he is more aware than the librarian of functional requirements, with the same result. More rarely, the librarian dominates; he presents his case for function so effectively that aesthetics are given short shrift. Since there are many more aesthetically pleasing libraries than well-functioning ones, it is obvious that the architect "wins" more often than the librarian. The best results occur when a proper balance is struck between the architect's aesthetic concerns and the functional needs expressed by the librarian. How can this be achieved when architects, who possess long experience in designing buildings, are generally very effective advocates of their points of view and are often capable of dominating planning sessions with their personalities and use of technical language? By contrast, most librarians are not only encountering the challenge of planning buildings for the first time, but their education and experience have not covered the process of library planning in any detail. Obviously, it is incumbent upon the librarian first to inform himself or herself about library building planning through the extensive literature available.

LIBRARY VISITS

Visits to good libraries are useful but there is often more to be learned from the bad ones. Appended to the end of this text is a list of more than 200 libraries that this author has visited during the last 15 years. A conscious effort was made to discover which libraries built during the period were of the greatest interest. Some of those visited were widely written about or have won awards for design. Others, though unheralded, were sometimes of more interest and occasionally superior to more highly touted libraries. It is all too often true that the spectacular or award-winning buildings are the most difficult to live with and operate. On the other hand, occasionally an unpretentious building is found that blends beauty with function to an amazing degree.

LIBRARY CONSULTANTS

It is also important to secure the services of a competent consultant with experience and expertise in library planning, one who readily will provide information to the client librarian, along with the necessary balance of power in the planning team, thereby assuring that the library's functional requirements are as effectively advocated as the aesthetic concerns presented by the architect. A good consultant will be thoroughly conversant in the needs of library function and, at the same time, will be knowledgable about the valid aesthetic aspirations of the architect.

CONSULTANT SELECTION

The selection of a consultant is not an easy task; Ellsworth, Metcalf, and others have written about this with feeling and intelligence. Many persons list themselves as consultants in library biographical sources but few have had the breadth of experience necessary to become truly expert in analyzing and solving library physical problems. Many librarians, after going through the long and involved process of programming, planning, and building one library, seem to feel that they have learned so much that they have the expertise necessary to assist other librarians facing the same problems. In fact, while any amount of experience is of some help, it probably takes experience with four or five library planning projects before a librarian/consultant has enough expertise to be truly helpful to librarians facing their first building planning. Enlisting a competent, experienced consultant and acquiring a thorough acquaintance with the literature of library facilities planning, along with visits to a good number of library buildings, should prepare most librarians to act as equal partners in the planning team.

PURPOSE OF THIS CHAPTER

This volume is not intended to be a treatise on library planning or a critique of recent library buildings but, rather, a discussion of the selection, evaluation, and purchase of furniture and equipment for libraries of all types. There is also some material on other aspects of library interiors, for the most part in Chapter 9. However in this first chapter we will talk about some general concepts of interior planning and organization, for some of the material in later chapters can be best understood with the author's general philosophy of interior planning in mind. None of these concepts or comments are original and most planners should agree with nearly all of them.

FLEXIBILITY

"Flexibility" has been a catchword in library planning for years. The concept came about, at least partially, as a reaction to the formalism and use of dedicated spaces for individual functions of earlier library buildings. As libraries began their rapid growth after World War II, it became clear that the buildings to house their changing programs would have to permit easy reorganization and expansion while remaining as functional as the original building. Nearly all the libraries built during this era were intended to meet these requirements, but relatively few have actually done so. Many libraries built soon after 1945 received additions which could not be melded successfully to the original "flexible" building because the latter turned out not to be flexible. Heavy masonry walls were in the wrong places, cores were in the way, or sites were poorly selected or utilized. The location of the collection was often fixed by floors that were incapable of carrying loaded bookstacks. All assignable spaces should have floor-loading capacity to sustain the weight of loaded bookstacks.

Why these failures? Sometimes librarians failed to understand the need for flexible space, discounted the need for ultimate expansion, or were unable to articulate their concerns. But more often, architects who were more concerned with aesthetic considerations and wanted to produce spectacular designs ignored or gave only token attention to their clients' real needs. Recent "spectaculars" like the libraries at Northwestern and New York Universities (Figs. 5 and 6) may have their defenders, but to most knowledgable librarians/planners excesses of this kind are inexcusable. Such libraries are difficult for patrons to use, hard for staff to operate, and incapable of being added to or modified to meet future needs.

FIG. 5 Northwestern University, Evanston, Illinois. This recently completed and controversial library structure is distorted only somewhat by wide-angle lens.

FIG. 6 An impressive but less than completely efficient structure. Bobst Library, New York University, New York, New York.

AESTHETICS VERSUS FLEXIBILITY

There is no question that aesthetic considerations are important in library design. A beautiful building can be a source of pride for staff, faculty, students, and taxpayers and can encourage donor gifts for other projects. But, in library design, function is more important than beauty. A library must perform the function for which it is built, or it fails. It is possible, however, to design and build a well-functioning library that is an aesthetic disaster.

On the other hand, an aesthetically pleasing library that fails to function properly is nearly worthless. Fortunately, if the planning team performs satisfactorily, it is always possible to design a library that is both functional and aesthetically pleasing.

THE IMPORTANCE OF FLEXIBILITY

Why is all this emphasis placed on flexible, functional library buildings? Nearly all library collections have grown steadily and rapidly in recent years and seem destined to continue to do so. Library users and services for these users continue to increase, the result being that library facilities must grow and expand. A few institutions will be able to leave inadequate buildings entirely and move into new buildings designed to meet present and future needs. Other institutions will be able to build additions to existing library buildings, thus providing space that will meet their expansion needs for a time. Hopefully, the librarian/planner will have library space to work with that is capable of being added to, rearranged, or renovated. A competent library/consultant, along with an imaginative architect, generally can devise a plan for more effective utilization of existing space and can design an entirely integratable addition. Fortunately, few libraries built during the last 30 years offer no possibility for expansion and renovation.

ESSENTIALS OF A FLEXIBLE, EFFECTIVE LIBRARY

Earlier it was said that, while the purpose of this volume is to offer assistance in acquiring furniture and equipment for libraries, some discussion of interior planning is necessary to provide background for the chapters that follow. Also, the failure of many recent libraries to be functional, flexible, and expandable structures in the face of advice from both the literature and leading consultants, prompts the writer to restate some of the factors that are inherent in functional and flexible library structures.

Building Orientation

A library floor can best be organized if it is rectangular in a proportion about 3:2, with the principal entry being approximately halfway along one of the long walls, a factor which allows the main traffic routes to be relatively short. Some designers will bring the entrance nearly to the building's center (Oborlin). While other shapes are often more visually exciting, they are harder to organize, furnish, and operate.

Shape and Proportion

An entire library building will organize better and will be more flexible, easier to use, operate and maintain, the more compact its shape. A 3:2 rectangle, 2 to 4 stories high, will be best because it provides the best ratio of assignable area to gross area, allows the most direct traffic and transportation patterns, and is the most easily organized, initially and subsequently. A building so shaped can also be easily integrated with a substantial addition, equal or larger in size, and continue to be a flexible, functional building. Other shapes and proportions are difficult to use without producing dysfunction.

Number of Floors

Number of floors should be the minimum consistent with the requirement that no floor be so large that heavy traffic patterns are more than 100 ft long. Lightly travelled paths can be much longer since they affect fewer people less often. The tower library, a recent cliché in academic libraries, is generally unsatisfactory because it is inflexible, excessively fixes function, is difficult to service and maintain, and offers a very poor proportion of usable library space. The latter is true because each tower floor, however small, must duplicate all the service and transportation functions that are needed on much larger floors, such as space for elevators, at least two stairways, janitors' closets, duct spaces, rest rooms, lobbies, and all the small objects such as drinking fountains and fire extinguisher cabinets that eat up a surprising amount of area in the aggregate. What is left is a depressingly small assignable area, best-suited for only a few bookstacks. Relatively small concentrations of shelving do not use space effectively due to the high proportion of aisle space. And, of course, collections on tower floors organize inefficiently, break at inconvenient places, and are difficult for patrons to follow.

Entrances

It may sound ridiculous to state that only one entrance/exit for public use is necessary and desirable for any library and that the provision of additional ones (except for emergency exits equipped with panic hardware and alarms) is foolish, expensive, and encourages book loss. However, this principle continues to be violated and needs to be restated.

Entrance to the primary floor should be on grade, <u>not</u> up or down steps or ramps, for the benefit of all users, especially handicapped ones. Entrance areas should be clean, uncluttered, and welcoming (see Fig. 7). The use of clear, well-located signs and easily understood directories should orient the reader to the library and its services. Most new and not-so-new libraries completely fail to help the entering user feel welcome, to understand where things are located, and feel confident about using the library.

FIG. 7 Inviting lobby area. Bryn Mawr College, Bryn Mawr, Pennsylvania.

Public elevators and main stairs should be close to the entrance to permit shorter traffic patterns and to avoid adding unnecessary traffic to the "keys" areas.

The main entrance/exit is a most important element of all libraries and is frequently designed poorly. Monumental front (Fig. 8) entrances often have conventional doors that are enormous, heavy, and difficult to open, which pose a particular problem for handicapped or not-too-robust users. There should be some space for milling about in the lobby. Use of some sound-deadening material in the area can help quiet entering patrons so that they are not talking loudly when they enter the library proper. Use of rubber matting outside and inside entrance doors will reduce both noise and dirt. The entrance should be designed so as to avoid drafts and heat loss. Automatic doors used in a few recent library buildings, particularly in Canada, have real benefits in library use, for they assist in keeping drafts and heat loss to a minimum and make life much easier for those entering and leaving the building, particularly handicapped persons. The energy consumption of automatic doors is modest and their success in department stores, supermarkets, and other high-traffic buildings indicate their appropriateness for library use.

FIG. 8 This monumental front is the antithesis of the open, uncluttered entrance. Nonetheless, a rather successful conversion and renovation. Ohio State University Undergraduate Library, Columbus, Ohio.

Organization of Floors

Floors will organize more satisfactorily and traffic patterns will work better if the floor is thought of as a series of concentric circles, with the center being the place where elevators and main stairs or the building entrance are located. The circles closer to the core contain the elements of collection-service points and those functional areas that need the greatest public access (the "high-rent district"), while the outer circles contain those elements that attract lesser numbers of users (the "low-rent district"). Then, thinking of the building three-dimensionally, the same principle holds; that is, the more heavily used elements should be housed nearer to the entrance/exit, vertically as well as horizontally, while the less-frequented collections and functions can be relegated to more remote portions of the building. Space in the "high-rent district" close to the functional center of the building must be carefully organized and utilized, while that in the "low-rent district" can be treated somewhat more casually.

Primary Floor

The floor where the principal entrance/exit is found, or the primary floor, should be the center of library public services. The card catalog or central bibliographic record, information or reference desk with its associated collection, the lending/circulation desk, and the indexes and other bibliographic aids are considered the "keys" to library operation and must be grouped adjacent to the entrance area. It is generally desirable for periodicals and newspapers, along with the closely associated microforms area to be nearby because they are heavily used in all libraries and their use is closely related to the indexes and other reference materials that are found in the "keys" area. The primary floor will hardly ever be large enough to hold comfortably all the functions and collections that ideally need to be there. It should not be smaller than other floors, rather it should be larger, if possible.

The primary floor should generally contain most of the public service areas of the library, along with their staffs. Today's public service functions are changing and new services are added so rapidly that this floor must be flexible enough in order that spaces can be enlarged, reorganized, and moved about. Since these all-important public functions will need considerable space on this level, it should be as large in floor area as any in the library. A building design that makes the primary floor larger than the other floors is almost ideal.

There are some libraries that are more collection-oriented than service-oriented; that is, they have resisted providing significant interpretative service or assistance in research; rather, they have concentrated their efforts on developing, maintaining, and providing access to their collections. These are generally more conservative, long-established libraries with quite large book collections and feel that large public service functions are not needed on the primary floor. But the author's contention would be that the shape of the future, even in such libraries, is not clear and that patterns of operation and service may and probably will change drastically. Nearly all central public libraries have increased the number and variety of their services to the public and most college and university libraries are committing more resources and staff to public service.

The primary floor is hardly ever large enough throughout the life of the library to contain, flexibly arranged, all the essential public service functions that need to be located there along with their associated collections. On this floor the all-too-common location of the technical processes essential for acquiring and describing the collection is difficult to defend in all but the smallest libraries or those with a single floor. The commonest error in library interior arrangement is the location of these processing departments, with their growing space needs, adjacent to public service areas that have their own changing and expanding programs. Having these two vital functions competing for space is a sure way to prevent the effective and economical operation of any library. The usual reason for locating technical-processing functions on the primary floor is to locate them close to the public card catalog, which these departments must maintain and frequently consult. While this need has validity, it is less important than the satisfactory operation of the whole library. It is nearly always possible for these departments to be located just above or below the public catalog with readily accessible vertical transportation. Tasks can be batched so that less frequent trips from department to public catalog are necessary. The increasing use of auxiliary copies of the catalog in book or microform editions or access to it via computer terminal will make such trips even less necessary.

Perimeter Space

Interior walls around the building perimeter are considered prime space, whether used for carrels or other seating, for wall shelving, aisles, or other purposes. These walls should be as straight and uncluttered as

FIG. 9 A delightful interior, though not particularly efficient, that quality was not required here. Alvar Aalto's brilliant Mt. Angel Library, St. Benedict, Oregon.

FIG. 10 Expensive air/light space. Wright State University, Dayton, Ohio.

possible and should not be cut up by unit ventilators, parts of columns, and other protuberances that otherwise prevent their effective utilization. Alcoves, window bays, and other offsets are hard to utilize, reduce flexibility, and interfere with flow and function patterns. Any air supply or return grill or diffuser located on the perimeter affects the placement of reader stations; these stations, in turn, adversely affect the operation of these diffusers and return grills.

Space Stealers

Balconies, air wells, light wells, atria and other space-stealing (Figs. 9 and 10) excrescences continue to be forced by architects on librarians, administrations, and governing bodies. Although these features frequently have architectural and aesthetic appeal, in the hands of some architects they simply do not "come off." They attenuate traffic and transportation patterns, provide inflexible space, separate functions that should be together, make the building hard to organize, are confusing to users, and often are maintenance problems. Most important, of course, they steal space. Librarians in 10- to 15-year-old libraries containing these features are nearly always forced to inquire about extending floors over such openings so that floor area can be added and functional arrangements can be improved.

Security

The security of library materials has become an issue of great importance to librarians in recent years. Electronic detection systems such as those marketed by Checkpoint Systems, Inc. and Gaylord Bros., Inc. are being installed in many libraries and apparently perform pretty much as required. But some libraries were and still are being built with too many exits and other features, such as easily operable windows, that encourage the theft

FIG. 11 End panels of shelves with directory information. The Pennsylvania State University, University Park, Pennsylvania.

FIG. 12 Panel systems (office landscape) can provide some visual and aural privacy and are much more flexible than fixed work areas.

of books. Emergency exits are always necessary but they should be easily viewed and have highly visible exit alarms and signs. All these precautions should help reduce book losses to an acceptable minimum.

Radial Arrangement

In all but the largest libraries, an arrangement of bookstacks and seating areas that radiate from the keys area or central service area can be most successful. In this arrangement a user, after looking in the keys area for the information needed to use the collection, can see before him the bookstack end panels (Fig. 11) directing him to the location of the material desired, go to that stack area, retrieve the needed material, and find seating nearby where he can examine the material. A floor arranged in this manner is easy and comfortable for patrons to use and easy for staff to service and supervise.

Interior Walls

Interior walls should be held to a minimum number and should not be constructed so that they are difficult to change or remove. When absolute privacy and soundproofing are not essential, panel systems that do not go to the ceiling and office landscape systems (Fig. 12) can provide a degree of privacy and noise suppression yet are highly flexible and easily moved, added to, and rearranged. They create offices, service points, functional areas, and work stations. Ranges of single- and double-faced bookstacks with backs can separate functions or areas and form rooms or departmental boundaries. They are easily removed or rearranged and provide useful shelf space. Metal backs are available from bookstack manufacturers, as are other materials with greater acoustical absorption. Ceiling-height metal partitions can be relocated relatively easily and offer excellent privacy. Sound transmission can be held to a minimum if specifications for the partitions are written properly.

Reinforced Concrete Construction

Reinforced concrete construction, popular in recent years for libraries, is too frequently characterized by problems. Interiors are often less flexible and maintenance problems are greater. Leaks seem to be common and interior systems, such as heating, ventilating, and air conditioning are more complicated and trouble-prone. Ceiling and structural systems make partitioning and function changing more difficult, and ceiling and other surfaces must be specially treated for some noise reduction. Finally, more care must be exercised in construction and mistakes, once made, are nearly impossible to rectify.

Use of Glass

The use of glass in exterior surfaces for windows and transparent walls has been much overdone in recent years. Certainly some windows are necessary for psychological reasons and the availability of some operable windows (under staff control) at times when air conditioning is out of order is essential. A modest quantity of carefully designed fenestration is desirable and necessary. However, too much glass wastes energy and prevents effective use of wall areas. Full-height shelving cannot be placed at windows or on window walls—it is unsightly and the sun's rays are very damaging to books. Carrels or table seating often cannot be placed at windows because of glare, unless special, expensive sun-shielding techniques are utilized. Furniture finishes and carpet dyes are often damaged by the sun's rays. Those windows that are to be used should be specially colored to reduce glare and deleterious rays as much as possible. Windows with northern exposures will have fewer problems with solar radiation. As suggested earlier, windows should have operable sashes in case of air-conditioning system failure. They should have removable handles or keys that staff can control and use in emergencies. If public and staff can open windows as they wish, air-conditioning systems will be "out of balance" and energy will be wasted.

Elevator Inadequacy

Another common failing in recent library buildings is that too few elevators are available to carry the vertical traffic. Elevators are expensive, but if substantial service areas and collections are more than one storey above or below the primary floor, two or more elevators are required. Highly useful is at least one oversized elevator with openings into staff and service areas among which books and other materials must be transported. Elevators are more efficiently utilized when concentrated in one area rather than spread throughout the building.

Electrical Outlets

All too often there are not enough electrical outlets in a library. Outlets are comparatively cheap if included in the initial building, but become quite expensive when added later. Provision of too many is not extravagant, but having too few is disastrous!

Electronic Distribution Systems

The capability of distributing electronic signals in libraries is important and must be considered when planning construction or renovation. The shape of the future is uncertain and exact planning is not possible. However, blank conduits in columns will certainly be useful and many ceiling systems permit use of conduits. Cable trays can be placed on walls to provide for such future developments. Under-floor duct systems will be indicated in some applications. The point is that some foresight during the planning stage can save considerable trouble and expense later.

Heating, Ventilation, and Air Conditioning Failures

Most of the libraries built in the last 30 years have had heating, ventilating, and air-conditioning (HVAC) systems to provide comfortable temperatures year-round. In the author's years of visiting libraries, he has heard as many complaints about air conditioning as about any other single problem in library buildings. Sometimes poor design is responsible; other failures are the fault of poor maintenance or operation. A frequently found combination of circumstances is an overly sophisticated system coupled with poorly qualified maintenance personnel. While librarians must rarely be conversant with such systems, they should be cautioned against overly complex designs and be prepared to operate during periods when these systems are out of service.

Concluding Remarks

Finally, again, a good library building is akin to a warehouse or loft building. It should be as open and flexible as possible with a minimum of permanent walls. The services and collections of a library are organic and changing and the building that houses them must allow easy change and growth. A plain box, flexible and expandable, furnished with attractive, functional, and durable furniture and equipment is eminently preferable to an architectural monument that will not work properly.

2 HOUSING THE USER

INTRODUCTION

Today, when library service is so actively promoted, it is hard to realize that the concept of making libraries serve reader needs is a very recent one. Until recently, the housing of collections was the primary reason for a library's existence and user requests were serviced only grudgingly. Even today, only public libraries and most academic libraries cater actively to reader needs, while national and most specialized libraries limit direct access to their collections as much as possible.

EVOLUTION OF READER AREAS

When we think of libraries through the centuries, the general impression is one of high-vaulted rooms, lit at first only by natural light and later by individual reader lamps (Fig. 1). Readers sat on straight, often ornately carved wooden chairs at long tables that were arranged in rows reminiscent of a prison dining room (Figs. 2 and 3). Upon request, library employees retrieved books from protected sanctuaries and such staff as were in evidence seemed to be more concerned with surveillance than service. Indeed, the monumental library buildings of the day could hardly have permitted a different kind of service even if the librarians had wanted to provide it. It was not until after World War II that a few young librarians in academic libraries began advocating open stacks and divisional reading rooms. The new libraries they built, along with the newly burgeoning public library branches, began the present trend of mixing books and readers, a prospect only dimly perceived before the war. The succeeding years have seen enormous growth in the variety and number of user stations in libraries of all kinds. This trend shows no sign of slackening, though some librarians

FIG. 1 Reader tables of 70 years ago with individual lamps. Deering Library, Northwestern University, Evanston, Illinois.

FIG. 2 Large, high-ceilinged room with long slope-topped tables. New Jersey State Teachers College, Trenton, New Jersey.

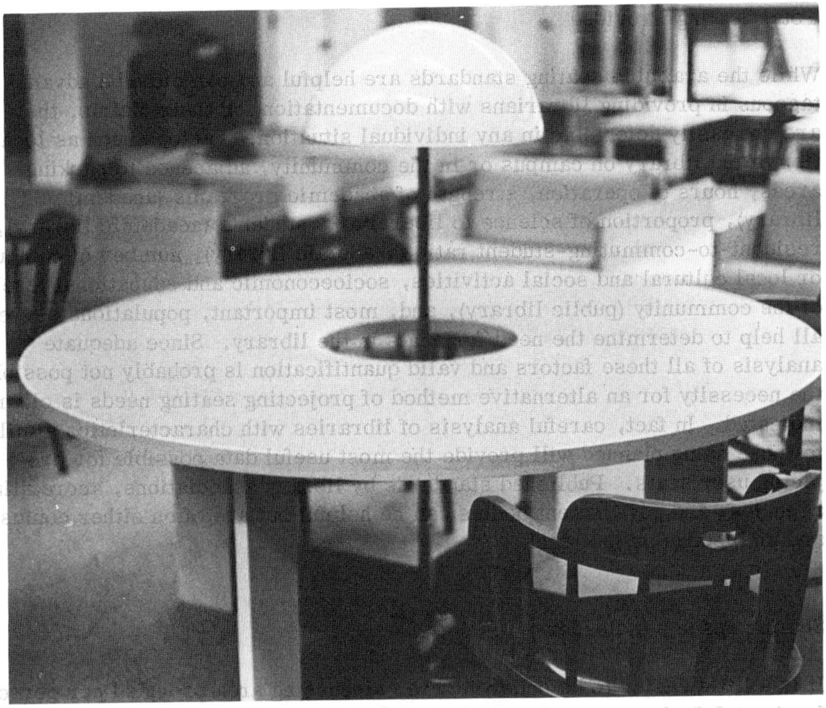

FIG. 3 Modern use of lamps on reading tables, now called task lighting. Williams College, Williamstown, Massachusetts.

occasionally exhibit twinges of nostalgia for the old days of closed stacks, when books stayed on the shelves. This chapter attempts to examine the various kinds of user accommodations in libraries today and makes suggestions for using the space effectively and furnishing it for efficient use.

PLANNING SEATING CAPACITY

This book is not intended to be a guide to library planning, for the issues of concern to those planning libraries have been treated voluminously elsewhere. Metcalf (1965) has discussed the subject of seating capacity exhaustively in his magnum opus. Here we will comment only briefly on the amount of space needed for library users.

Total Seating Provided

While the available seating standards are helpful and can often be advantageous in providing librarians with documentation for their claims, they are not easily defensible in any individual situation. Factors such as location of the library on campus or in the community, adjacence to parking areas, hours of operation, strength of academic programs (academic library), proportion of science to liberal arts students (academic library), resident-to-commuting-student ratio (academic library), number of campus or local cultural and social activities, socioeconomic and educational level of the community (public library), and, most important, populations served, all help to determine the need for seats in the library. Since adequate analysis of all these factors and valid quantification is probably not possible, the necessity for an alternative method of projecting seating needs is clearly indicated. In fact, careful analysis of libraries with characteristics similar to those being planned will provide the most useful data possible for projected user seats. Published standards by library associations, accrediting agencies, and government bodies can be helpful but are often either confusing and ambiguous or too rigid.

Seating Space per Reader

It is a little easier to be concrete when discussing area provided per person. In view of the larger number of individual seats, increased use of lounge areas, and greater emphasis on research in higher education, it is evident that the average area for each student seated should be 30 sq ft, though some college and university libraries have provided less. Public and school libraries, on the other hand, can probably provide amply for their users with 25 sq ft per reader in view of the lesser need for individual seating there than in academic libraries.

SEATING AT TABLES

Although very large reading tables, 10 ft (3000 mm) or more in length, are seldom found anymore except in the few remaining monumental reading rooms (New York Public Library, Library of Congress, Duke University), tables seating more than one reader (usually four or six) are still used and purchased by all kinds of libraries, despite the popularity of individual seating at carrels or individual study tables. The group table constitutes nearly all study seating in public libraries and generally makes up the majority of seats in academic libraries.

SEATING ECONOMICS

Table seating is the most economical form of seating suitable for libraries both in terms of space consumption and initial cost. The initial cost of a user area 2 × 3 ft (600 × 900 mm) in a single carrel is about twice the cost of the space for one user at a 4 × 6 ft (1200 × 1800 mm) table. The cost differential per person is less between four persons seated at the same table or at a four-place carrel, facing and side by side. In its use of space, the four- or six-place carrel also is as economical as a four- or six-place table. In addition, table seating enables students to study together; less mature students often feel that study should be a social experience and find that the table, where they can be next to or across from a friend, is perfect for that purpose. Of course, persons seated at tables can be easily monitored.

TABLE SIZES AND SHAPES

Most tables seating two or more users have flat tops with unobstructed working surfaces, though some occasionally have sloped tops. Tables used in libraries have many shapes and sizes, but rectangular tables seating four or six, and round tables, seating four, are most common. Other shapes used less often are the square and trapezoid.

For years the sizes of rectangular tables used most frequently were 3 × 5, 3 × 7, or 3 × 8 ft (900 × 1500, 900 × 2100, or 900 × 2400 mm), the first seating four, and the second two sizes seating six. These seemed to provide adequate user space in most situations. In recent years, however, planners of many college and research libraries have felt that readers need working areas of at least 6 sq ft and they have specified that tables seating four be 4 × 6 ft (1200 × 1800 mm). Not many years ago tables of these dimensions were considered "specials" by some manufacturers and, consequently, were considerably more expensive. Today these large sizes are standard in most manufacturers' lines and are not priced as custom or special items. At least one manufacturer calls the 4 × 6 ft (1200 × 1800 mm) table the "university" table.

Obviously, users of college and university libraries have more room on 4 × 6 ft (1200 × 1800 mm) tables to spread their materials and appreciate the larger size. Further, some architects and psychologists suggest another point in favor of using tables of this size; that is, the likelihood of utilization of all four seats at these tables is greater than at smaller ones. Studies have shown that personal space (the amount of open area surrounding a person in any situation) is very important. Apparently, sitting at a four-place table with three other persons is comfortable when the table is 4 × 6 ft (1200 × 1800 mm), but not when it is smaller. My personal observations in many libraries have confirmed this fact countless times. Obviously, four persons seated comfortably at a 4 × 6 ft (1200 × 1800 mm) table will utilize floor space more effectively than three persons seated at a 3 × 5 ft (900 × 1500 mm) table. Thus, those planning academic libraries should hesitate in buying tables of less than 4 × 6 ft (1200 × 1800 mm) to seat four. Public libraries probably need not be so concerned about using larger tables since their users generally do not remain in one seat for as long a time as those using academic libraries, and thus do not need to provide as much space for spreading material. There may be exceptions to these situations, but these observations can be generally accepted as true.

The round table, the square table, and tables of other shapes will always have appeal to those designing library interiors. They are attractive because their shapes offer visual relief in an area full of rectangular shapes. Also, these shapes and sizes are frequently more appealing in themselves. The person planning a library interior will surely be wise to consider using some such tables to break up and add variety to spaces, but must be careful to use them in only a small percentage of the total table seating. All of these odd table sizes and shapes (round, square, triangular, etc.) are inherently wasteful of floor area, are expensive commodities, and do not provide sufficient working surfaces for the number of users they are designed

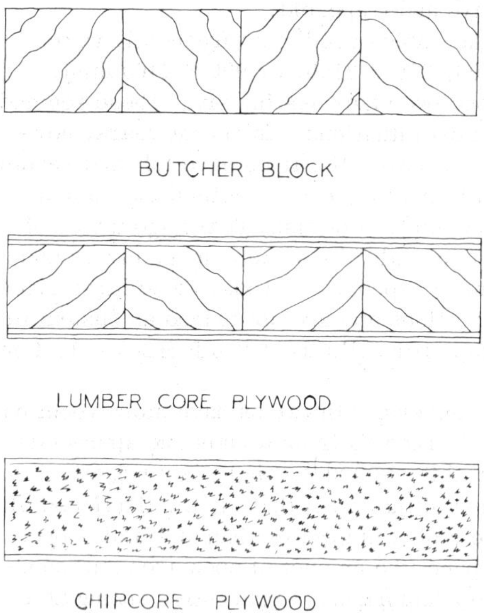

FIG. 4 Note differences in construction of (a) Butcher block; (b) Lumber-core plywood; and (c) Wood-composition-core plywood (particle board).

to seat. They are best utilized in "casual use" areas such as current periodicals and browsing areas or spaces surrounding new-books displays.

Table Height

The average table height for library areas with adult users seems to be 29 in. (725 mm) and in public library children's rooms or elementary school libraries the height is generally 26 in. (650 mm). This allocation provides a differential of 11 in. (275 mm) between the working surface of the table and the 18-in. (450 mm) seat height that seems comfortable for most adult users and the 15-in. (375 mm) seat height for children. Another important consideration is the clearance between the underside of the table edge and the chair seat. While substantial aprons (structural members or panels connecting legs on long sides of tables) are not common today, many tables used in libraries are made with a stretcher or frame member connecting the legs for reasons of structural rigidity or aesthetics. Aprons should be avoided, for they affect the clearance of knees and chair legs, as well as user comfort. When armchairs are used, lack of clearance can damage the arms.

WOOD TABLE CONSTRUCTION

Tops

Tables were made of solid wood at one time, but this is very seldom true nowadays. Real solid wood is almost unavailable in those species of wood that make satisfactory table tops. "All-wood" tables are available, but the tops are not made of one solid piece of wood. Rather, they are, in order of descending cost, (a) butcher block; (b) lumber-core plywood; (c) conventional plywood; and (d) woood-composition core (Fig. 4).

The first wood type mentioned, butcher block, utilizes relatively long and thin pieces of wood, glued and laminated together under pressure and heat. Butcher block became quite popular in the 60s although it is known to have been used previously (John Crerar Library). It is quite expensive and difficult to manufacture butcher block in the quality required for library tables. The wood slabs (individual pieces) utilized must be end grain or side grain rather than flat grain (Fig. 5) because wood expands or contracts with changes of temperature and humidity. However, edge grain or end grain changes size much less than does flat grain; thus flat grain affected by temperature and humidity is more likely to delaminate or separate at the glue line.

A butcher-block top is the closest to a solid wood top available today. If made correctly, it rates high in appearance and its ability to bear loads.

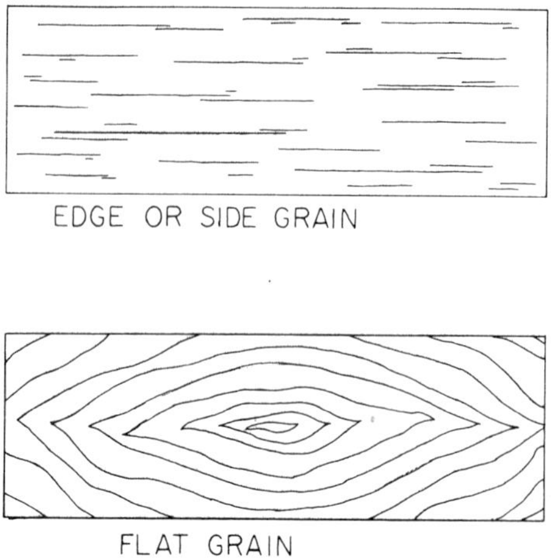

FIG. 5 Edge or side grain versus flat grain.

It needs no separate top or edge banding and can be assembled into an outstandingly rigid and durable table. The main disadvantage of butcher block is its cost.

Lumber-core plywood is used in the tops of the best standard tables of the finest library furniture manufacturers. It requires separate top and bottom surfaces and edges. In fact all table tops, other than butcher block, depend entirely on the tops and edges for their appearance since the core is entirely covered by the tops and edges along with the balance sheet on the underside. Lumber-core tops are excellent for load bearing and are easily "worked" and assembled. They are also now increasingly expensive and more difficult to obtain.

Conventional plywood is still used in some better-quality table tops. It is nearly equal to lumber core in most respects with a little less load-bearing capability. It, too, is becoming more expensive and harder to come by.

Wood-composition core, called chipcore, particle board, etc., has become the most commonly used core in library furniture manufacture. It is readily available, comparatively inexpensive, and obtainable in different weights and a wide range of quality. It is easily worked, but seems somewhat inferior to plywood and butcher block in screw-holding power. The main weakness of this material is its weight-bearing capacity, which is not equal to solid wood or many of the plywoods. Wood-composition core is not acceptable in table tops sized 4 × 6 ft (1200 × 1800 mm) or larger without substantial longitudinal reinforcement. Standards for composition-core materials therefore should be carefully specified.

As stated earlier, the various plywood and composition cores must be covered with separate tops, some sort of banding around the edges, and backing sheets. The top provides an attractive, durable, and functional working surface; the edge banding protects the table from impact damage and protects objects (chairs) and persons moving or striking against it. The backing sheet is necessary in all types of laminated (plywood or composition-core) construction to balance the top surface. The latter is generally made of a composition material such as Masonite.

Tops have been fabricated from all types of materials, including marble, slate, tile, linoleum, and leather; but the materials most generally used today are wood veneer and high-pressure laminates. Veneers are thinly sliced wood surfaces which are glued to the core under pressure and heat. They are generally of the same wood species as that used in the table legs and other members, but sometimes are of a more expensive wood. For instance, many libraries own tables that appear to be walnut, with the grain characteristics of that species on the top. Actually, the legs, apron, and keel are of dark-stained maple or birch, and only the top is made of walnut. The veneers used today are very thin; the walnut currently available is generally 1/32-in. thick. When veneers are this thin, they must be worked and finished very carefully. Obviously there is little chance of sanding down and refinishing a gouge or scratch in a veneer-faced top. Planners selecting furniture for libraries where heavy use or occasional abuse is expected should hesitate before selecting veneer working surfaces for tables, carrels, and other furniture.

High-Pressure Laminates

High-pressure-laminated plastic (HPL), frequently called Formica, is the most commonly used top surface in library furniture today. Actually Formica is the trade name for a high-pressure laminate manufactured by American Cyanamid Co., but many other companies produce similar materials, some of which are Parkwood, Textolite (by General Electric) and Wilson Art. This material, which consists of printed paper sandwiched between layers of melamine plastic, offers a combination of features which make it highly acceptable for table-top surfaces. It is durable, available in many designs and textures, absorbs neither grease nor stains, is easily cleaned, can be replaced relatively easily and inexpensively, and is non-reflective when specified in matte or dull finishes. At one time, HPL tops often looked shiny and artificial; today they are made to be much more natural looking; indeed, in some of the wood-grain finishes, it is almost impossible to detect the difference between HPL and genuine wood. HPL is very difficult to damage. However, it has two relatively minor weaknesses: (a) some people believe it is cold to the touch; and (b) it can be used only on flat surfaces. All in all, HPL is the most generally useful material available for tops of library tables. Incidentally, when specifying furniture with both HPL and matching natural wood surfaces, it is easier to arrange to have the wood match the HPL rather than the other way around. The reason for this is that HPL comes in a relatively limited number of colors and finishes, while skilled wood finishers can easily match any wood-grain HPL. Of course, laminates can be specified to contrast with natural wood finishes instead, and the result is often visually pleasing.

The specifier should be cautioned about using top finishes that are too light or too dark. The too-light top is uncomfortable to the eye of the user and difficult to keep clean; the very dark top provides too great a contrast to paper; thus is uncomfortable to the eyes. Also, when selecting table tops, it is important to remember that many users will be writing on paper; wood grain or other texture can make this difficult. Finally, it is important to avoid finishes that have significant reflectiveness or potential for glare; this is most uncomfortable to the user and can easily be avoided by the specification of dull finishes on wood or high-pressure laminates.

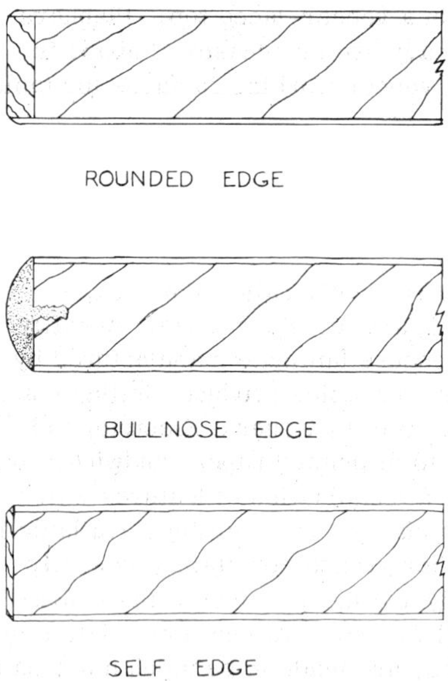

FIG. 6 Three varieties of edge banding: (a) Rounded edge; (b) Bull-nose edge; and (c) Self-edge.

Edges

The edge of a table is extremely important to its long life and continued good appearance. It must be slightly resilient so as not to be easily damaged. A rigid edge with no "give" to it may separate from top and core or crack under severe impact. A crack may introduce moisture to the core where it can quickly cause deterioration and ultimately the destruction of the top. Further, a resilient and slightly rounded edge will cause less damage to things that hit against it, such as chairs. Incidentally, maintenance personnel frequently are to blame for damage to library furniture, by striking it with mops, vacuum cleaners, and other equipment. The most satisfactory materials for wood-table edge bands are: (a) slightly rounded solid-wood strips; and (b) vinyl bull-nose edge banding (Fig. 6 (a) and (b)). They are both resilient yet resistant to damage and, if properly applied, should last as long as the table. Under no circumstances are library tables with "self-edging" suitable (Fig. 6 (c)). This technique involves applying a narrow strip of HPL on the edge by gluing it to the end of the table core. Because the core is rigid, the laminate quickly becomes loose under impact, thus exposing the vulnerable ends of core plies to moisture and other damage. It is somewhat cheaper than the wood or vinyl edge described above, but is never satisfactory for library use in public areas.

Table Frames

The other frame elements of wood tables should be made of solid wood, since these elements are of smaller dimensions than the top and more easily available. They can be, and frequently are, made from species of wood other than the "show wood" of the top, since their dimensions are such that their grain is not apparent. They can easily be finished to match the appearance of the top. Actually, it is beneficial to use table legs of dark-stained birch or maple if a dark-finish top is used, since these wood species are the toughest, most damage-resistant woods used in library furniture manufacture. Oak tables will be made entirely of that wood since oak is both tough and has a very attractive grain.

Assembly

The manner in which wood library tables are assembled is extremely important. Librarians expect long life and continued good appearance from these tables, which receive continuous use and abuse from patrons and maintenance personnel. We have pointed out just previously the importance of first-class components in the table top and its supporting structure. Of at least equal importance are the methods with which these elements are assembled. Present table design trends, maintenance consideration, and our desire to keep patrons' feet on the floor have resulted in today's library table design, which has nothing showing beneath the top except legs or a pedestal base. It is extremely difficult and expensive to construct a completely solid table structure which rests only on four legs. Many of us have seen large, vintage library tables which have been in use for many years, but these older designs generally used aprons and stretchers to achieve structural rigidity. Today some current designs compound the problem still further by placing the legs on the very corner of the table where it is even more difficult to brace them properly. To make matters even worse, the carpeted floors found today in most new and renovated libraries provide a rough surface over which it is most difficult to push or pull a table without damaging its frame. Since such shifting does occur, a table's structure must be extraordinarily strong to withstand it.

The most important considerations in assembling the table structure are as follows: (a) the legs should be firmly attached to the top so that there is no movement or wobble; and (b) the larger tables should have no deflection (sag) under load. The latter problem is relatively easily managed by placing one or more keels under the length of the table, fastening them both to the underside of the top and to end stretchers which connect the legs on the narrow ends of most tables (Fig. 7); keels can be made of wood or metal. However, the former problem is a little more difficult to solve, for a table leg cannot be fastened directly to the table top. Some intermediary element, such as a metal plate, or as in some designs, an end rail, must be fastened both to the underside of the table and to the leg. Such a leg plate should never be screwed directly into the core of the table top. It can too easily work loose under lateral pressure. Good designs have utilized (a) receptors for bolts implanted in cores, with bolts threaded through metal plates into these receptors; or (b) pinned bushings placed within top structures. Leg plates are generally fastened to legs with pinned bushings. In addition, an end apron or rail is frequently fastened directly to the leg to provide additional rigidity. It is essential that the leg plate and all metal fasteners be of generous dimensions and high quality. The best leg plate we have seen provides for additional fasteners to the side of the leg and to the end apron for further strength.

TABLES OF OTHER MATERIALS

Tables made of materials other than wood or, at least partially constructed of metal and plastic, are relatively common in libraries. Actually, it is a rare wood table that does not contain components of metal or plastic. Tables with wood tops and metal frames are rather common. Tables of metal and/or plastic offer a number of advantages: (a) they are generally less expensive than the all-wood table of good quality; (b) they can be con-

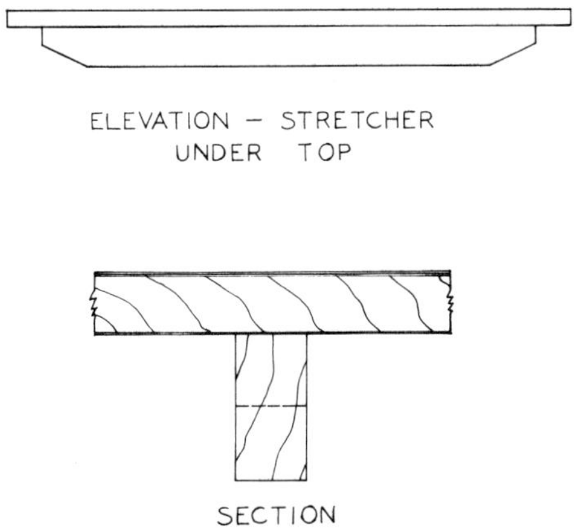

FIG. 7 Stretcher, or keel, longitudinal support for table tops.

structed to be more rigid than the strongest wood table; (c) they are, when properly constructed, virtually indestructible in ordinary use; and (d) they are capable of more diverse design possibilities than wood, which is relatively limited in this regard. Indeed, the possibilities of imaginatively designed plastics have scarcely begun to be realized. A look at the Italian magazine Abitare suggests some of these possibilities.

Yet, with all the advantages and possibilities of metal and plastics in library furniture, we continue to use mostly wood furniture in current libraries. Is this due to innate conservatism on the part of librarians and designers? Not really—rather, the real reason is that furniture of metal and plastic generally looks "tired" after a few years of use, while good wood furniture retains its appearance much longer. Some wood furniture looks better after a few years' use than it did when first purchased. The tired look that seems characteristic of metal and plastic furniture does not affect its long life; indeed there is no question that good furniture of this type will outlast wood furniture of the same quality. The only problem is its appearance. If furniture looks tired and worn, it invites abuse, not only to itself but also to other objects surrounding it. The atmosphere for study and research is thereby impaired. In short, manufacturers and designers of metal and plastic furniture must improve the long term appearance of their products before they can achieve wide acceptance in libraries.

SPACE ALLOCATIONS FOR TABLE SEATING

As mentioned earlier in this section, four- or six-place tables with 6 sq. ft per reader assure efficient use of floor area, provide adequate research or study areas, permit comfortable use of all seats, and prove

FIG. 8 Attractive butcher-block tables with ends close together. Kent State University, Kent, Ohio.

reasonably flexible if rearrangement is desirable. Such tables should be arranged so that they avoid a "prison dining room" appearance. Some can be arranged at right angles to the general orientation. Carrels can be interspersed in areas of tables to break up the monolithic look. A few round tables can break up the monotony.

On the average, a 5-ft (1500-mm) clearance is desirable around each table, but if space is at a premium it is possible to "steal" some space from the ends of some tables by putting two or three tables almost together and thereby reducing the number of aisles (Fig. 8). Tables generally seem more useful in the middle of an area rather than on the perimeter. Carrels seem to utilize perimeter space more effectively, particularly when placed against a wall with an aisle separating them from stack ranges.

SPECIAL TABLES

Tables have been given all sorts of special treatment and features in some library applications. When library reading rooms had high-vaulted ceilings, individual reading lights or banks of lights down table centers were essential. Although these should be unnecessary with modern lighting techniques and lower ceilings, they are still seen occasionally. Designers now call this task lighting. Some libraries have used dividers of various heights to provide private space on tables. Indiana University used single study tables with low profile rear dividers. These study desks were fastened together in different configurations to form tables or were used singly as individual study tables; also, with the addition of Plexiglas dividers, they became carrels.

Another table with a long history is the slope-top table, which is particularly helpful for use of large volumes such as atlases, though some readers

FIG. 9 Attractive slope-top table in children's room. (Library Bureau.) (Garfield Photo.)

find it preferable for using any type of material. These tables should be designed with a lip at the lower edge to prevent material from sliding to the floor.

Other tables are sometimes supplied with electric outlets so that various audio-visual hardware can be used on them. Occasionally, equipment such as record players, audio tape decks, and cassette players are built into table tops.

Tables for children's rooms in public and elementary school libraries are not as high or large as tables for adult use. Frequently bright colors are used on tops and frames are lighter, since they do not need the strength of larger tables. Slope-top tables are especially popular in these libraries (Fig. 9).

INDIVIDUAL SEATING

The first library furniture of which we have pictures are individual cubicles (carrels ?) used in monastic libraries during the Middle Ages. While seats at long tables became the norm for library reader accommodations during the next few centuries, many libraries provided individual cubicles or tables for some users. When the great expansion in college and university libraries took place after World War II, some libraries began making extensive use of individual study units, and a type of individual study table with high partitions at the back and sides to provide privacy became popular. This has now become known as the carrel, a name that causes great confusion. Until recently, <u>carrel</u> has been a widely used name for a small enclosed study <u>room</u> used by one person for study or research, and Metcalf (1965) calls it such. Thompson's recent excellent work (1974) also reflects this usage. However, for our purposes here, a carrel is a separate item of furniture, either movable or built in, which has, at the least, a work surface and some kind of high divider at its back to provide privacy for study or research (Figs. 10 and 11). A separate room used by a single person is called a <u>study</u> in this book (Fig. 12). Individual study tables used by one person for study or research are smaller. They differ from carrels in that they do not have high dividers at the back and sides to gain privacy (Fig. 13). They may have low dividers at the back and sides to prevent material from falling on the floor. It is unwise to use individual study tables in large quantities in any one area because (a) they give a schoolroom appearance to which some librarians and planners object; and (b) they must be separated to provide privacy and access aisles. Because separation for privacy is desirable, they are generally less efficient in their use of floor space than are carrels, which can be placed immediately adjacent to each other because of the high dividers separating the units. Nonetheless, individual study tables are used in some libraries and are well-suited for certain situations. For instance, they are occasionally used in single-file rows along edges of

FIG. 10 Attractive double carrel with full returns. Light-colored laminate interior provides better light with less contrast. (Library Bureau.)

FIG. 11 Carrel with locker can be assigned. York University, Toronto, Ontario, Canada.

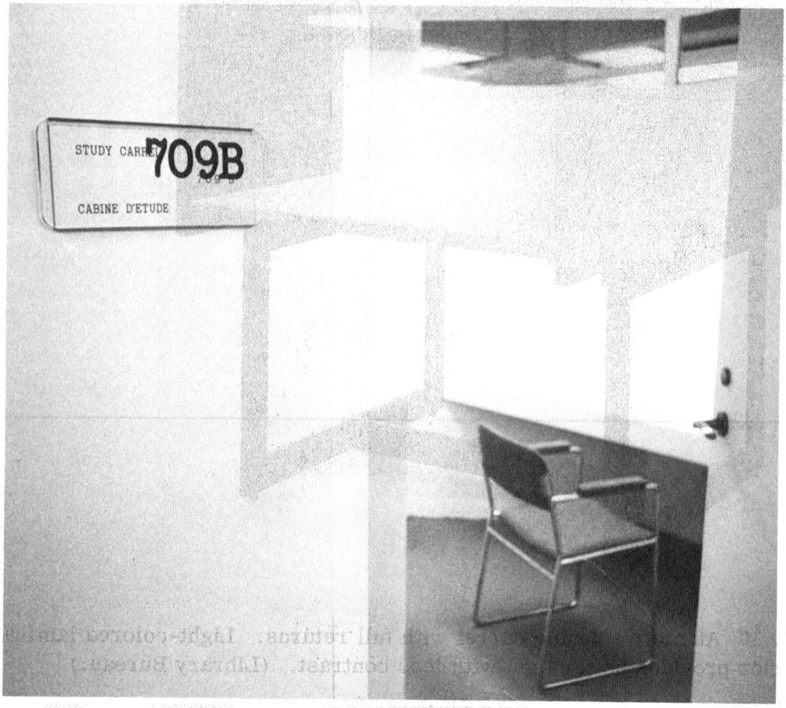

FIG. 12 Study, sometimes called carrel. Canadian Institute for Scientific and Technical Information, Ottawa, Ontario, Canada.

FIG. 13 Individual study tables. These built-in ones are somewhat inflexible. Williams College, Williamstown, Massachusetts.

balconies or light-wells, where their height is more pleasing than that of carrels. They have been used to provide visual relief in areas full of carrels or multiple-seat tables. Mature student users having a choice between an individual study table and a carrel nearly always will choose the latter.

CARRELS

Carrels are extremely popular in libraries today. While they were first widely used in college and university libraries, they are found today in public and school libraries and in special libraries of all kinds (Figs. 14-18). They are used not only for study of printed material but also for viewing video tapes; gaining access to computers; watching and listening to slide or cassette programs; doing programmed learning; listening to music on records, tapes, or cassettes; using dial-access learning systems; using calculators; typing reports; reading microforms; and on and on. Carrels

FIG. 14 Carrel built for two. Seeley G. Mudd Learning Center, Oberlin College, Oberlin, Ohio.

FIG. 15 Carrel train. University of Massachusetts, Boston, Massachusetts.

FIG. 16 Built-in carrels with concrete returns. State University of New York, Fredonia, New York.

FIG. 17 Some public libraries use carrels. Boulder Public Library, Boulder, Colorado.

FIG. 18 Attractive, very modern carrel. ('Carola' by Risom.)

may contain book shelves, lockers for personal belongings, coat hooks, lights, electric outlets, separate tablet arms, screens for visual presentations, earphones, telephone dials, and built-in hardware of almost any description. Carrels come in single units, double units (face-to-face or side-by-side), four-place units (side-by-side, facing side-by-side, or "pinwheel"), and in configurations seating five or more people in almost any grouping imaginable (Fig. 19). Users prefer carrels in almost every situation where they are offered a choice between that and other kinds of seating accommodations.

Carrel Variants

All carrels have a work surface (top), legs, and a visual barrier at the back. They also generally have a visual barrier called a return along the sides, or at least part of the way to the front edge (partial return). Many carrels have returns all the way to the front edge of the work surface (full return), or even beyond. The return provides the complete privacy many readers require. Full returns are almost mandatory when carrels are used in multiple, side-by-side arrangements. Partial returns are preferred by users not requiring the degree of privacy afforded by carrels with full returns. Single carrels with partial returns, if not used in heavy concentrations, are quite acceptable and generally more aesthetically pleasing than carrels with full returns. For users needing privacy from visual and aural disturbances, carrels with full returns are vastly preferable. To provide relief from visual disturbance, which can be as distracting as noise, the height of the back must be at least 52 in. (1300 mm) from the floor; otherwise, a male user of average height will have both insufficient visual privacy and bothersome eye contact with the person seated in a facing carrel. To hold books and other objects, nearly all carrels have a shelf which usually extends across the back and is fastened between the side returns. This shelf also serves to tie the carrel together structurally. Such a shelf is sometimes found along one side where it functions both as a shelf and book-locker top (Fig. 20). A locker is sometimes desired as part of a carrel so that the carrel can be assigned to a graduate student or faculty member.

Other features common in carrels are study lamps and electric power outlets. To supplement the general lighting in the area, many carrels have a fluorescent light fixture fitted under the shelf at the back of the carrel. Since carrels are often placed along wall perimeters or in stack areas, where general illumination may be marginal, such an individual study lamp is often necessary. Also, as the cost of electric power increases, the provision of adequate illumination only when needed becomes imperative. If carrels are to be used for non-print hardware, electric outlets connected to sources of electric power are essential.

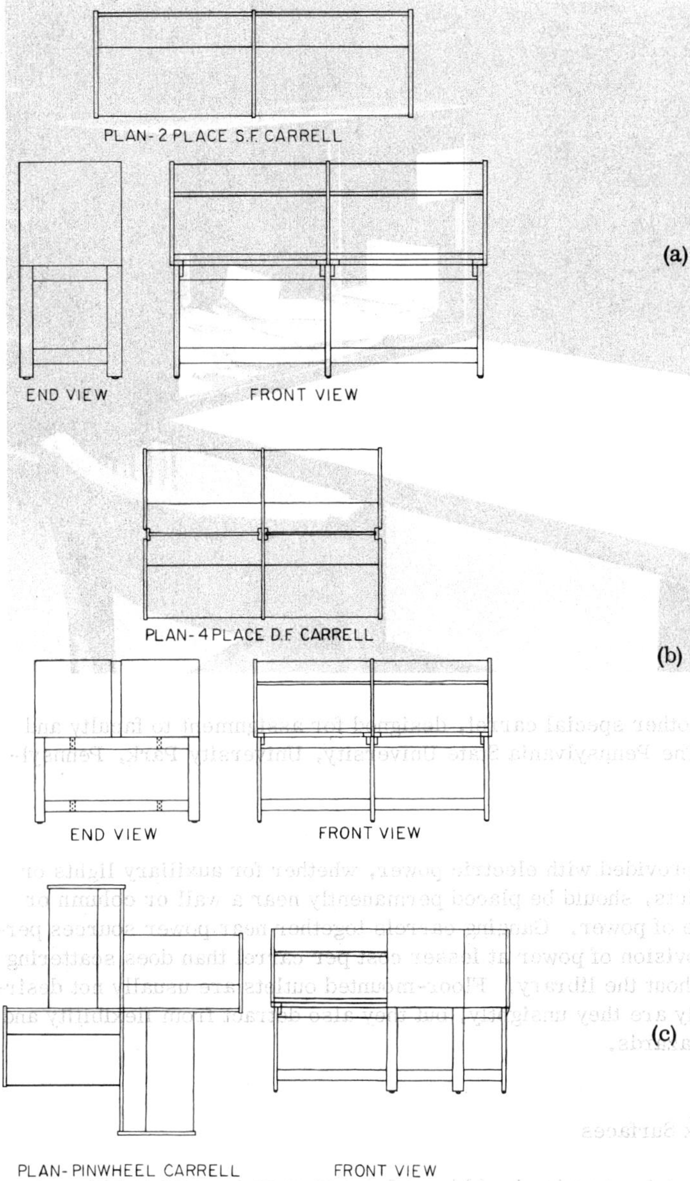

FIG. 19 Common carrel configurations: (a) two-place, single-face; (b) four-place, side-by-side, facing; (c) four-place, pinwheel or swastika.

FIG. 20 Another special carrel, designed for assignment to faculty and students. The Pennsylvania State University, University Park, Pennsylvania.

Carrels provided with electric power, whether for auxiliary lights or electric outlets, should be placed permanently near a wall or column or other source of power. Ganging carrels together near power sources permits the provision of power at lesser cost per carrel than does scattering them throughout the library. Floor-mounted outlets are usually not desirable; not only are they unsightly, but they also detract from flexibility and are safety hazards.

Carrel Work Surfaces

Work surfaces in carrels should be at least 24 × 36 in. (600 × 900 mm), the minimum size for almost any user. Carrels used by graduate students, faculty, art and music students, and those for use of any kind of nonprint hardware, typewriters, large calculators, or microform readers will need to be much larger. The Pennsylvania State University uses research carrels with work surfaces 37 × 30 in. (925 × 750 mm) and they are none too large. Also at Penn State, microform reading carrels are 45 × 30 in. (1125 × 750 mm), a size which seems adequate but not excessive.

Equally appropriate for carrels are the recommendations regarding table work surfaces made earlier in this chapter. Table-top color contrast with paper, writing surface texture, and degree of reflectivity must be carefully considered. Some planners have used lighter-colored materials on back and/or side panels of carrel interiors so that the reflectivity of these materials will improve the illumination level. Edge banding on carrels is particularly important, because students sitting in the privacy of carrels often seem to pick absentmindedly at anything loose and, if an edge banding is loose, a student may loosen it still further.

Assuring Carrel Quality

High-quality construction is no less important in carrels than in tables. Carrels should be of heavy construction, with good-quality components joined together with the best techniques, and have durable finishes. (For more details, see Appendix A.) Indeed, in evaluating for purchase, the problem of separating good from poor is greater for carrels than it is for tables. Generally, only manufacturers of complete lines of library furniture will try to manufacture and sell library tables. Carrels are quite another matter. Due at least in part to the recent increased interest in the nonprint media, the carrel, which is heavily employed as a user station in media systems, is now offered for sale by a great many manufacturers who have no interest in the library business. These carrels are often of very marginal quality and not at all suitable for a library. Thus, carrels must be specified very carefully and the buyer should seriously consider grouping them in a bid with the remaining technical furniture and tables in a library, so that no manufacturer of cheap carrels can take a bid for carrels only and perhaps provide the library with shoddy merchandise.

Carrel Configurations

As suggested earlier, carrels are frequently ganged, or used in multiple units in one area. They may either be purchased in groups joined together or single carrels can be arranged in multiple groupings. It is less expensive per unit to use carrels that are manufactured in multiple units. They are available in these standard configurations: two-place, either facing or side-by-side; three-place, side-by-side; and four-place, either facing and side-by-side or pinwheel. Other quantities of seats in various arrangements are available as special orders. Single carrels, on the other hand, can be arranged in any of the standard configurations or in any other arrangements desired. Single carrels can easily be moved around at will, while the large multiple carrels are so unwieldy that they can be shifted only with difficulty.

Carrel Placement

Carrels are now so universally accepted that nearly all college and university libraries of recent vintage have large numbers of them. Carrels number from 20 to 80 percent of university and college libraries' total number of seats. They are found in all parts of these libraries, including microform rooms, media areas, typing rooms, reference and periodical areas, as well as in reading rooms. They are frequently used singly against perimeter walls behind stack areas; they are ganged in areas in reading rooms where they can also be interspersed among tables in order to provide visual relief and to prevent concentration of tables so large that they become "noise generators." Carrels are frequently placed near columns when electric power is required. They are increasingly popular with students and no library ever has enough of them!

LIBRARY CHAIRS

Chairs are the hardest used and among the least-appreciated items of furniture in libraries. Chairs used at library tables must be attractive, inexpensive, comfortable, and never need repair or replacement. Few chairs manufactured are capable of standing up under the kind of use the average library study chair receives. Even fewer are aesthetically pleasing. It must be remembered that hardly any seating, except perhaps that in airline terminals, gets as much heavy use for long hours as does the library chair. Other seemingly heavily used seating in academic institutions, such as that used in dormitory rooms, dining rooms, and classrooms, is only in use for a few hours a day, while most libraries are open and their seats are occupied from 12 to 24 hours a day. Thus it is absolutely essential that library chairs be attractive and usable for long periods of time. Many older libraries have heavy, all-wood chairs that have been in use for 30 or more years, and library chairs in today's lighter designs should nevertheless last at least 15 to 20 years with hard use. Chairs of ordinary commercial quality are not adequate. Such chairs are frequently specified for commercial offices where new installations of furniture are possible every few years. Most libraries are elements of nonprofit organizations who must obtain furniture that will last most of the life of the building. Hence library furniture, and seating in particular, must be of such design, material, and construction that it will have a life expectancy of many years.

Study Chair Types

Many kinds of seating used in libraries include lounge units, secretarial or clerical chairs, executive chairs, high swivel chairs for circulation desks, benches, stools, conference chairs, and a variety of special-purpose seating for other applications. However, the chair of the greatest importance and the one purchased in the largest number is the study chair for use in seating at tables and carrels as well as in other applications throughout the building. This chair will receive the greatest use (and abuse) and, though generally the least expensive chair in the building, it must be highly durable and retain its good appearance for a long time. While it is reasonable to replace lounge units, executive chairs, or secretarial chairs occasionally, the expense of replacing large quantities of study chairs is not reasonable. They must be well-selected and meet the highest standards of quality.

The principal materials used in constructing study chairs are wood, metal, plastic, and upholstery materials. The chairs may be all wood, wood with upholstered seats and/or backs, metal with upholstery, all plastic, plastic and metal, with or without upholstery, wood with metal or plastic or both! (See Figs. 21-23.) In short, the possibilities are infinite. Traditionally, the best and most durably attractive chairs are of all-wood construction. For example, for many years the Sikes Chair Company of Buffalo, New York, now unfortunately defunct, produced large and handsome "captain's" chairs which were used in many library reading rooms (Fig. 24). A number of these, after 35 years of the hardest use, are still in use at Penn State and other libraries and are holding up beautifully. Several firms still make all-wood chairs which are sturdy, attractive, and suitable as study chairs.

All-wood chairs are not so popular today as they once were and have been largely displaced by wood chairs with upholstered seats or backs or both. These chairs add color, much desired by designers and others so concerned, and are supposedly more comfortable. The comfort contention, however, is open to question. Comfort is a very individual thing. While comfort in seating has received some investigation, few clear-cut conclusions are possible. However, it does seem reasonable to make the following assumptions: (a) proper design and dimensions to fit the body contribute much more to long-term comfort in seating than does soft padding on a seat; (b) a study chair should be designed to support erect seating; and (c) a chair that permits fairly frequent position shifts is more comfortable for lengthy use than one that constricts movement.

A chair of improper dimensions or poor design with a padded seat and back will be less comfortable than an all-wood chair with a properly shaped seat and good dimensions and design. It is also true that the chair that feels comfortable at first is not nearly so comfortable over a period of time as the chair that initially feels less comfortable but encourages posture

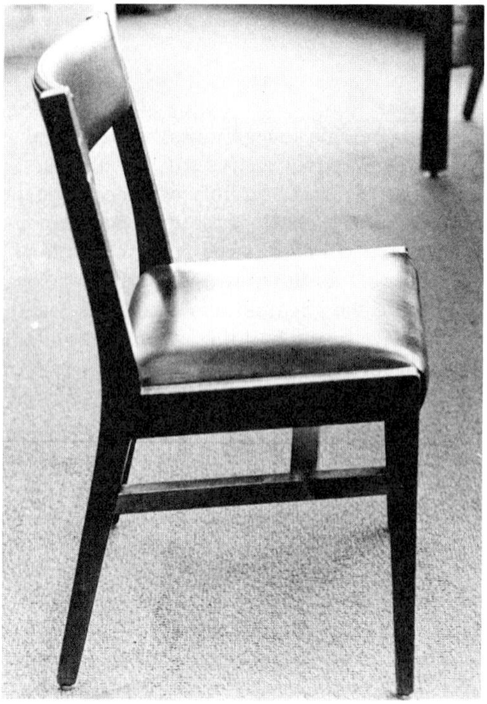

FIG. 21 Side chair of high quality. (Gunlocke.)

FIG. 22 Distinctive all-wood arm chair. Williams College, Williamstown, Massachusetts.

FIG. 23 Very attractive metal/plastic chair. University of New Hampshire, Durham, New Hampshire.

FIG. 24 Thirty-five-year-old chair by Sikes Chair Company (now defunct) has outlasted many chairs manufactured much more recently.

that provides long-term comfort. For the greatest comfort, the best solution is to use an upholstered chair of proper design and dimensions with good-quality and correctly applied upholstery.

Upholstery

Selecting upholstery that will hold up well over a long period for heavily used library study chairs is very difficult. Worn or dirty upholstery will detract greatly from the chair's appearance even when the wood components look "like new." This writer does not believe that fabric upholstery that will retain its appearance and color and remain in like-new condition when used in library study chairs is available today. In visiting more than 200 libraries in the last 15 years, fabric upholstery has not been seen that has held up well under such use for longer than 4 or 5 years. Obviously some fabrics perform better than others and chemical treatments such as Scotchgard can add to the useful life of such upholstery. Nonetheless, vinyl or leather, while retaining their appearance, will provide upholstery covers that last much longer.

Why the emphasis on appearance retention? Those who are interested in this problem have frequently observed that user abuse accelerates rapidly when like-new appearance is gone. That is, when library furniture begins to look tired or dirty, even if its condition in other respects is unchanged, patrons are much more inclined to be careless in their treatment of it. We have discovered that when upholstery, or for that matter, frame elements are damaged by scratches, punctures, or slits, the chair affected should be withdrawn from use and promptly repaired, or other chairs in the vicinity are more likely to receive equally cavalier treatment.

If fabric must be used in study chairs, light or solid colors that show dirt quickly should be avoided in favor of more subdued colors and tweeds. Tight weaves and tough fabric such as nylon are preferred. The fabric must be fire-retardant for use in most institutions and planners of any library should insist on fabric that meets such standards.

Although fabric of any description is not recommended for study chairs, its use for lounge seating or secretarial and executive chairs is quite another matter. Secretarial chairs, because they are used by the same person for long hours, should always have seats of fabric because it is porous, breathes, and feels warm. Vinyl, even the newer expanded variety, is cold to the touch and induces perspiration by the user. Leather, while possessing greater breathability, is cold and slippery to the touch. Neither vinyl nor leather is satisfactory in either a secretarial or office chair seat. On the other hand, vinyl and leather are far superior to fabric for covering seats in upholstered study chairs. Both will last longer under heavy use, retain their appearance, and are available in a variety of colors. Of the two, leather is somewhat more expensive but decidedly superior; it looks more natural and generally looks more attractive as it ages. Vinyl, on the other hand, looks soiled as it grows older. Also, it slits more easily and does not wear nearly so well as leather. Leather is cooler to sit on because it has tiny openings (hair follicles) which permit some breathing. The range of colors available in leather is not so great as in vinyl, but the colors are more subtle and natural looking. Although leather is considerably more expensive, the difference may be less painful in quantity. One company, to our knowledge, sells leather upholstered chairs for a relatively small price differential over vinyl. In selecting vinyl the heavier weights, 40 oz or greater in expanded vinyl, are recommended.

CHAIR DESIGN AND CONSTRUCTION

Both design and construction are extremely important if wood chairs are to be comfortable for the user and remain useful and attractive over the years. We mentioned previously that good design is important if users are to be comfortable. Proper design also is essential if wood chairs are to last for many years. Several years ago another agency purchased for Penn State a chair that was improperly designed, with an inadequate joint at the all-essential junction of back post and side rail. Failure was predictable and since then we have lost about half of the more than 850 that were purchased for us. Since we had to replace as many as we could afford with properly made side chairs, this improperly designed chair, which we were forced to accept, ended up costing a considerable sum.

The design of a properly constructed wood chair is an art. Because wood is a natural material, possessing the natural imperfections and differences found in nature as well as expanding and contracting according to atmospheric conditions, it must be used in chair construction in such a way as to emphasize its strengths and permit it to expand or contract naturally. An all-wood chair seat 18 in. (450 mm) wide may expand $\frac{1}{2}$ in. (12.5 mm) in warm weather and may contract the same amount if the weather is cold and dry.

Joinery

The way the chair elements are joined together is a very critical factor in long-term durability. The best joinery for all-wood chairs involves glued joints with dowels (two or three per joint) to provide a maximum bearing surface for the glue. Metal fasteners are not adequate for joining wood elements because of the differing rates of expansion and contraction of wood and metal. A well-done glue joint will be stronger than the wood it connects. When possible, such glue joints should be further strengthened with corner blocks.

Chair Size and Configuration

It is important that study chairs be large enough for the comfort of today's users, many of whom are larger than their parents. Backs of study chairs should form with the seat an included angle of approximately 97° so that the user may sit erect comfortably. Study chairs with back to seat angles of 100° or more do not support the back adequately.

Studies have shown that library users in study chairs shift their positions to some degree with great frequency. A chair that is large enough or that has design elements that encourage shifts in position will be more comfortable to users than a chair which does not permit many variations in seating posture. Arms on a study chair provide additional support elements that encourage position changes. Nearly everyone will find the support of arms helpful in sitting, reading, or writing comfortably. Armchairs used for study do have certain drawbacks. They are more expensive and the arms are susceptible to impact damage from table or carrel edges and aprons. Difficult to make is a study chair of correct seat height, 18 to 19 in. (450 to 475 mm), with an arm of correct height to support user arms, that fits under the apron bottom of a table or carrel so that the chair arms will not get banged up regularly. Of course, the human arm that grasps the front of the chair arm to pull the chair in or out must have some clearance. All this is not to say that armchairs should not be used, but rather that they can be used if the dimensional relationship between armchairs and the tables or carrels at which they are used is planned before commitment to purchase.

In specifying study chairs another factor to be considered is the use of chair legs of "wall-saver" design. If the back legs curve to the rear instead of being a straight continuation of the back post, both user comfort and chair durability are enhanced. First, the chair back is not against the wall when the legs are; thus avoiding back damage. Second, a user cannot easily rock back on the chair's back legs; therefore preventing potential damage to the chair and injury to its user. For additional details to be considered in specifying wood chairs, see Appendix A.

Metal and Plastic Chairs

Chairs of metal and plastic in various combinations of these two and other materials are presented for use as library study chairs. A few are of good quality and quite suitable for the purpose, while others are not at all satisfactory. Wood library study chairs are often specially designed for use in libraries and meet their needs very well. Most metal/plastic chairs are designed for mass production for other purposes and are not really suited for use as library study chairs. In addition, chairs of this kind with quality comparable to first-class wood study chairs, will generally be more expensive than the wood ones.

The most common objection to metal/plastic chairs for library study chairs is their appearance. Chairs of these materials seem to lose their new appearance quickly and appear tired and worn. This does not affect their durability but may adversely influence the treatment given adjacent units of furniture, and this loss of attractiveness will certainly displease those who purchased the chairs and must live with them. If metal/plastic study seating is used, it would be well to select colors and finishes that show neither dirt, discoloration, nor loss of luster so easily. Those wishing to avoid the appearance of too much metal should consider using polished finishes which pick up color from surrounding materials such as carpet. Plastic materials have great potential for use in seating, particularly casual seating, but library study chairs, being essentially straight and offering little latitude for the kind of imaginative design possible with plastic, will probably continue to be constructed of wood.

LOUNGE SEATING

Seating for casual or lounge use in libraries is much more open to imaginative design and use of materials other than wood. Lounge seating is almost always upholstered, though some unusual plastic chairs with no upholstery can be classified as lounge seating and are appropriate for occasional use in libraries. Lounge seating appropriate for library use comes in all prices from $30 bean bags to $1000 Barcelona chairs. Almost any library will have at least one casual seating area and larger libraries will have a number of casual areas. These areas provide eye relief by breaking up otherwise repetitive groupings of tables and carrels. They are preferred by users for more casual reading of books or magazines or for listening to music, and they are beloved by architects and designers for the contrast in color, line, and texture they provide in relation to other more functional library furniture.

Lounge seats are lower (16 in. or 400 mm) with backs that lean back further, thereby providing larger included angles (110° or more) than those in study chairs. They generally have more generously sized seats than do more upright chairs. They customarily have arms and offer more room for position shifting than do study chairs. A study (Serig, 1975) recently conducted by a Penn State psychologist in a library lounge demonstrated that (a) students preferred seating that permitted the greatest amount of position shifting; and (b) the majority of students using lounge chairs in the area actually spent most of their time in positions that were more horizontal than vertical.

As stated earlier, lounge seating offers great opportunity for use of imaginative design and unusual materials (Figs. 25-27). Lounge seating is generally not used in large quantities and contemplating replacement or repair is easier for a few lounge seats than for large numbers of study

FIG. 25 This 'conversation pit' is a popular student seating area at the University of Akron, Akron, Ohio.

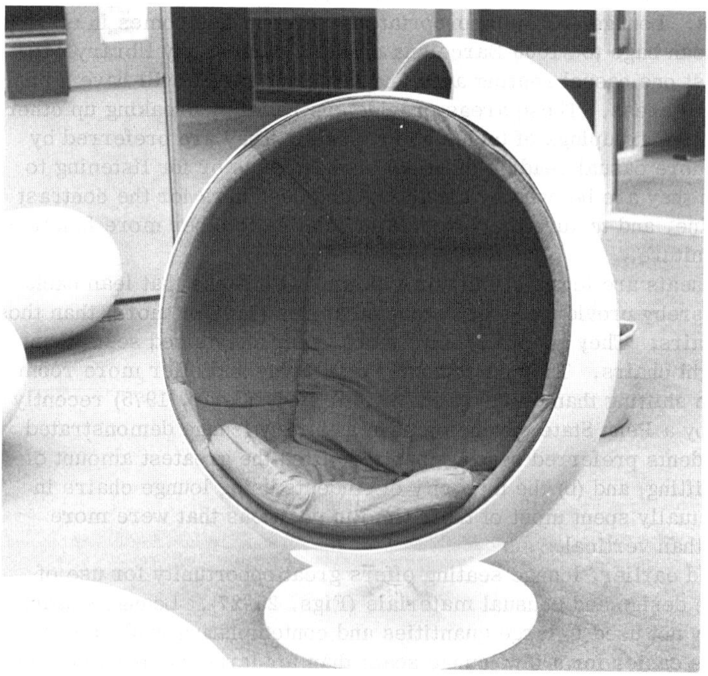

FIG. 26 Every library needs one! ('Egg chair' by Stendig.) University of Denver, Denver, Colorado.

FIG. 27 Another approach to seating (?) students. Oberlin College, Oberlin, Ohio.

chairs. Fabric upholstery is frequently used for lounge seating where life-expectancy need not be so great. Upholstered arms are unsuitable, for they get dirty very quickly; use of lounge chairs with all wood arms or arm caps of some sort is recommended.

When purchasing groups of chairs for a library, unit cost is less if all of a given class of chair, i.e., study chair, lounge chair, conference chair, is purchased from a single vendor or manufacturer. Significant quantity discounts are common when purchasing seating. Nonetheless, in specifying seating for lounge use, it is often desirable to get a few pieces that are different from the lounge chairs bought in quantity. A few chairs of dramatic design can add greatly to the visual impact of library space and the cost in a good-sized furnishing budget is hardly noticeable.

Couches are sometimes purchased for library lounge areas but defending this practice is difficult. They utilize space inefficiently, for they are usually occupied by only one person whom other users are reluctant to join, even on a three- or four-seater. Frequently couches are used for sleeping. Occasionally they are occupied by a couple, but then the ensuing activity may be distracting to nearby readers. In short, we see few advantages in the use of multiple-seat units, but many disadvantages. If there is an area in the lobby or other nonstudy area where conversation is encouraged, a couch or two may be appropriate.

GROUP STUDY FACILITIES

Small group facilities for library users have been popular in all types of libraries for years. The old seminar in academic libraries—a room which a class or academic group used regularly as a sort of headquarters and where a separate book collection was maintained—is not used much today. Rooms called seminar rooms, where smaller classes using library materials may hold sessions, are quite common. Such rooms, seating no more than 10 or 12 people and not exceeding 300 sq ft can be very useful in some academic libraries. They can function as conference rooms for library staff or others. A seminar room should have a chalk board, small bulletin board, coat hangers and possibly a pull-down projection screen, along with chairs and two or three tables. One table large enough for a group this size is unduly expensive and two or three tables can be arranged in different configurations, depending on the group.

It is usually unwise to include full-size classrooms 500 to 600 sq ft in college and university libraries, at least within the controlled area. The administration undoubtedly want to schedule them as regular classrooms and the resultant noise, confusion, and queuing problem at the exit-control point will be highly disagreeable. A single such classroom can be helpful for use in library instruction programs but when the administration, looking for classroom space, is tempted to absorb your classroom, you may have difficulty opposing it. Some libraries have designed 200 to 300 sq ft seminar/conference rooms adjacent to one another with movable walls or partitions. Movable walls prevent sound transmission better than movable partitions, but are more expensive. This arrangement, of course, allows the two rooms to be used separately or combined into one larger space.

Other smaller rooms for groups are used in many libraries. Rooms of 100 to 150 sq ft are popular for small conference or group study rooms. These will seat four or six people comfortably at a table. Another popular space in academic libraries is the study seating one or two users in a room of 50 to 75 sq ft. With a table or desk, chairs and shelves, these can be assigned for a period of time to faculty for research (not offices) or may be available for assignment to one or two students who need the space temporarily.

Other special-purpose rooms made available to library users include typing rooms, rooms for various audio-visual presentations, and smoking rooms. Typing rooms may be for one person each or may hold several users at typewriters. Power will be needed at each typewriter and some sort of sound-absorbing treatment is helpful, particularly in rooms holding several typewriter stations. Typewriters can be placed on typing tables with steno chairs for seating.

Rooms for audio-visual presentations will be discussed in Chapter 6. Smoking rooms are separate reading rooms with tables and chairs or casual furniture where people may smoke without disturbing nonsmokers.

The use of interior windows in small rooms used by groups or individual library users is a subject of some controversy. In academic libraries, where use of such rooms is most common, some institutions have felt that the use of large glass surfaces on the wall facing the library proper, or at least, glass or half-glass doors is important for supervision. Other college and university libraries reject this premise on the basis that today's student cannot nor should not be supervised in this way. While students may accept these viewing windows or walls, faculty generally will not. We have visited many libraries where faculty have covered these windows with posters or other decorative devices to achieve privacy. One acceptable compromise is to use a glass peephole small enough so that no one feels that they are under surveillance, but large enough so that the presence of a user is apparent.

These rooms will almost certainly on occasion become administrative problems. Nonetheless, their value to the institutional program is considerable and they can be administered in such a way that difficulties are held to a minimum. Careful issuance and control of keys will provide responsibility in their use. Studies assigned to faculty or groups should have time limits with renewal privileges so they do not become unused status symbols. At least one institution issues keys to faculty assigned to studies each time the study is in use and collects them as faculty leave. This may be hard to achieve politically speaking, but it certainly enables the library staff to know which studies are unused.

All these small rooms, except the assigned faculty studies, are valuable adjuncts to a libraries' nonprint media program. They readily lend themselves to a number of activities, i.e., small group or individual viewing or listening, and previewing of audio-visual materials. They may be appropriate locations for terminal access to various data bases or can be assigned to students who want to use their own or library-owned calculators. They should have convenient power along with pull-down screens and, if possible, dimmers on light switches. They should be light and pastel-colored rather than bright and primary-colored so that the rooms seem larger. Air-handling systems should be individually controllable for such rooms and there should be supply and return air in each one. Doors with louvers for return air are not satisfactory because of noise transmission.

Finally, a few libraries have provided lounges (Penn State) or even reading rooms (Cortland) with refreshments in vending machines and other libraries (Indiana, Toronto) have installed cafeterias. This type of facility can cause all sorts of problems, but the number seems to be growing, so they must obviously be needed in some situations.

3

HOUSING SERVICES AND STAFF THE "KEYS" AREAS

INTRODUCTION

When libraries were considered as collections of books to be guarded from the desires of importunate readers, service points as we think of them today were represented by a guard post from which a staff member could observe the library's users to see that no book was removed from the room. Since then, our concepts of service have changed markedly and it is a small library indeed that does not have multiple points for active service to readers. This change in service, along with the attendant enlargement of collections of books and other materials, has greatly magnified the need for library staffs, and consequently has increased the requirement for space to house them and the materials they service.

Today's libraries have a great variety of public-service areas where readers with differing interests and information requirements can have access to the services they need. These service areas include general information desks or areas; reference areas; bibliographic and card catalog areas; circulation or lending areas; periodical and newspaper rooms or areas; children's and young adults' rooms; rooms or areas for public documents, microforms, and maps; subject or divisional service areas such as music, art, or literature rooms; local history rooms; service areas for audio-visual materials; and rare book rooms. There will almost always be staff work spaces or offices adjacent to these public-service areas. In this chapter we will discuss these service areas with their accompanying staff areas as well as other operational areas occupied by staff where direct public service is not provided.

REFERENCE AREA

Nearly every library has a central service complex which will introduce the user to its services and collections. It will almost certainly include the card catalog or an equivalent means of access to the collections, along with a manned reference desk, and in a few large libraries, a catalog information desk where those using holdings records can receive assistance. The reference department, in addition to assisting readers to use the catalog, will also be responsible for helping readers locate materials and services in the library and will assist readers in finding answers to specific questions or pursuing research in their areas of interest.

Another activity of the reference department is instruction in use of the library for groups of users, a recent trend of increasing importance in some libraries. To help them provide information, reference staff will have at hand a collection of reference resources, including dictionaries, encyclopedias, indexes and abstracting tools, bibliographies, and a great variety of statistical summaries, almanacs, works of collective biographies, and other volumes containing concentrated information. These materials are shelved near the center of the reference service areas, with those most heavily used being shelved adjacent to the reference desk. These desks will be sized in proportion to the library's size and volume of use. Some small libraries combine reference and circulation (lending) in one station while larger libraries will often have a separate large counter/desk, behind which a number of staff can work (Fig. 1). The reference function sometimes is housed in a separate room and in some libraries it occupies a part of a larger area which may include functions such as periodicals, public documents, maps, or perhaps a separate bibliographic center.

The essential furniture elements in a reference area include (a) the inquiry point (desk or counter); (b) seating space for those using reference materials; and (c) means for housing the collection. Usually the card catalog and other holdings records are here or close by, but they will be treated separately.

Reference Desk

The inquiry point may be a desk or desks of regular sitting height (29 in. or 725 mm), behind which one or more staff members sit ready to handle reference inquiries. There will be one or more telephones at hand. Constantly needed items and personal effects may be kept in drawers. Some shelving will be behind or near the desk for the most often-used sources of reference information. Often the desk top has a glass cover under which work schedules, telephone lists, and other notices of concern to the staff can be kept visible. Some larger libraries use an enclosed counter, perhaps in a square or circle, behind which several reference librarians can

FIG. 1 Large general information/reference desk. Kent State University, Kent, Ohio.

stand and provide service. Such a counter can provide under-counter space for reference materials. A desk, the height of which requires that the reference staff sit, may be viewed as a disadvantage, for some staff have a tendency to become so engrossed in reading or work that they are not alert to users needing assistance. Also, an inquirer may feel uncomfortable asking help from a staff member seated behind a desk. If a desk-height unit is chosen, it would probably be desirable if staff spent most of their desk time on their feet to appear more approachable and aware of user needs. If a standing-height counter (39 in. or 975 mm) is used, there should be no such problem. In any case, the desk should be so oriented that persons entering the library are immediately aware of it as their first point of contact. Some libraries do not make the reference desk obvious and visible; this is inexcusable.

Other Furniture in the Reference Area

Along with the most heavily used reference materials (ready-reference collection) which are immediately next to the desk, many large reference departments will maintain a separate card catalog of their own collection. This is convenient to both reference staff and users, who need not then constantly consult the much larger catalog to the entire library or system. Larger libraries will also frequently have a shelf directory to the reference collection, to assist readers to find needed materials easily. Since larger reference collections generally shelve certain groups of materials out of classification order for convenience (telephone directories, indexes, abstracts, encyclopedias), such a directory is often essential. To help readers use the library more effectively, a recent innovation in reference departments has been the provision of self-instruction programs which may use audio or video cassettes, or slide shows with sound or computer terminals. Carrels to house these programs can be located close to the reference desk.

In any reference area, some materials are used much more frequently than others. Generally, the reference books getting the most concentrated use by readers (encyclopedias, periodical indexes, etc.) will be housed on index tables or on counter-height shelves relatively close to the reference desk. The work surface of the index table and, to a lesser degree, the counter top of low shelving units, will provide a writing surface for note taking. Because index tables contain heavily used materials, seating at them should not provide such comfort that users are inclined to stay there, for queuing problems can result. Hard wooden stools 18 to 19 in. (450 to 475 mm) high will provide adequate seating for short periods of time. Anyone needing the books for longer periods can take them to nearby tables; thus freeing the index table seats for other users.

Housing the Reference Collection

Reference books used less frequently can be housed on regular book shelves of 12-in. (300 mm) depth somewhat further removed from the reference desk; users can take them from shelves to nearby tables or carrels for consultation. In some libraries, an intermediate category of access is provided by housing some materials on steel shelving frames with carrel units hung between the brackets and shelves hung above the carrel. This seems to be a reasonable solution to shelving reference books more compactly than on two-shelf-high index tables, but with work surfaces for note taking closer to the books. One alternate way of compacting storage density on index tables is on three-shelf-high tables; these are large, unwieldy, not particularly pleasing to the eye, and quite expensive, but they will provide greater shelving density than the two-shelf-high models most commonly used.

When reference books are housed on full-height shelves, user access can be made more convenient with the addition of pull-out reference shelves. Other libraries place carrels, and even tables, right in the stack sections of reference areas. The use of tables in stack areas is quite wasteful of space but carrels can be placed at intervals along perimeter walls without excessive use of space. Other reader seating in reference areas will be at tables and, occasionally, at carrels within open areas adjacent to reference stacks and areas housing index tables. This seating is primarily for the use of persons using reference volumes for longer periods of time. Many users of reference materials, especially the larger, heavier volumes, will appreciate the availability of one or more slope-top tables. These are particularly helpful in consulting atlases.

Seating Space

A few words on the size of the reference area and its seating capacity may be useful. Metcalf (1965) feels that reference areas in large libraries are often larger than they need to be. It is certainly true that, since reference areas generally provide the first general seating one finds when entering most libraries, there is some tendency for users to settle in these seats to study their own material, especially in academic libraries. If seats are modest in number, there may be more inclination on the part of non-users of reference materials to go further into the library to find seating more suitable for quiet study. Certainly a busy reference area does not (and should not) provide the best atmosphere for quiet study. Staff must escort users throughout the area, instructing them in the use of the reference collections. The author feels strongly that the reference area should be a vital, somewhat noisy place, rather than a quiet study area where an inquiring reader is afraid to ask a question for fear of disturbing all the readers in the room. Seating for 125 to 150 persons should be adequate for almost any reference area.

Collection Size

There is no set ideal number of books in a reference area. Metcalf (1965) feels that 10,000 well-selected volumes will meet most needs in large central reference collections. He pointed out that this number would increase perhaps by 50 percent if bibliographies were included in the reference area. Actually, the production of both reference books and bibliographies has increased so greatly in the last few years that this optimum collection number has since increased considerably. For a large academic library providing research assistance and housing a substantial bibliography collection, a collection size of 25,000 should be contemplated.

Other Furniture

Other furniture found in many reference areas includes dictionary stands, atlas cases, new book displays, CBI tables (specially designed tables for housing this unwieldy and heavily used set), vertical file cabinets and a variety of other items of specialized storage and display furniture and equipment.

Recently some academic libraries, in their concern for providing adequate instruction in use of the library, have greatly stepped up their programs of formal and informal instruction. Some have made media presentations and lectures available to classes and interest groups. For such libraries it may be desirable to provide a classroom where instruction and media presentations can take place. This should be acoustically separate from but immediately adjacent to the reference area for convenience in using reference books and for ease in combining classes and tours in one area. Normally, classrooms should be kept out of libraries, for they steal needed library space and cause regular disruption of the library's atmosphere when classes change. If, however, such a classroom is in the midst of the main library service area and clearly a part of the library's instruction program, it should be possible to restrict its use to library programs only.

Staff Space

Adequate work and office space for the reference staff should be provided adjacent to the reference area. For the department head there should be an office of at least 100 to 150 sq ft with standard office equipment (desk, chair, shelving, file cabinet, and one or two guest chairs), plus a table with chairs, either formal or informal, for small meetings. Each librarian should have a small office or work station in a larger room. A small conference room (200 sq ft) in this complex will be most useful. A small workroom (200 to 250 sq ft) will be most helpful to house staff other than librarians and the processing functions that take place in this department. Some reference staffs will prefer one large work/office area with separate work units or desks for each staff member.

Finally, since many libraries are providing access to machine-readable data bases for their users, some reference departments will need to provide carrels or small tables with computer terminals. These will be placed near the reference desk for easy instruction and supervision. In some cases, small closed rooms (60 to 100 sq ft) will be desirable for these terminals so that staff may confer with terminal users.

CARD CATALOG

The reference area with its reference books and indexes, and the card catalog and other facilities for bibliographic access are the "keys" to the library and its use. They should be immediately visible to the user entering the library. The staff member providing assistance in using the card catalog, whether reference librarian or catalog information specialist (North Carolina State, Pennsylvania State) should be next to the catalog, facing potential inquirers.

The card catalog units are probably the most important and heavily used items of furniture in the library and should be very carefully selected. In the author's experience, only those catalogs made by old-line library furniture manufacturing concerns can be depended upon, and even among these there may be fairly significant differences in quality. The recent adoption of plastic drawers (although generally with wood fronts) has slightly reduced the needed high standard of cabinetmaking in card catalog manufacture. Even though use of these plastic inserts has reduced the importance of close tolerance in tray manufacture, standards for card catalog manufacture must still be high because of the heavy loads and use these cabinets will have to take. The spacers between drawers receive constant impact and should be of densified wood. If wood drawer inserts are to be used, they should be very carefully specified so that they will work smoothly and quietly and will hold up under years of use and abuse.

Card catalogs for small- and medium-sized libraries are frequently purchased in 60- or 72-drawer units (Fig. 2). These cabinets are generally approximately 41 in. (1025 mm) wide, 17-$\frac{1}{2}$ in. (440 mm) deep, and 60 in. (1500 mm) high. When there are 6 drawers across and 10 rows of drawers, the top and bottom rows can be comfortably reached by nearly any adult using the card catalog. Adding 2 extra rows to produce the 72-drawer catalog makes the top and bottom rows somewhat more difficult for some people to reach, while a 90-drawer catalog (occasionally used, but not really recommended) is even more difficult for many users to use. On the other hand, if the minor inconvenience can be tolerated, the 72-drawer has 20% more capacity than the 60-drawer; or put another way, five 72-drawer catalogs will hold the same number of cards as six 60-drawer catalogs. Where floor space is at a premium, and it is almost everywhere, 72s should seriously be considered.

Catalog drawers are usually purchased in 15, 17, and 19-in. (375-, 425-, and 475-mm) lengths. The 15-in. drawer does not hold enough cards to utilize floor space efficiently and the 19-in. length is heavy and unwieldy for some users (and staff). The 17-in. length seems to be about right in

FIG. 2 Sixty-drawer card catalog. (Risom.)

weight and density of storage, for it holds 1000 medium-weight cards when the drawer is about 70 percent full, a good working capacity.

Number of Catalogs

The ultimate size of the public card catalog is, of course, dependent on the size of the collection to be described. It is suggested that 72-drawer units be purchased but that planning capacity be based on 60-drawer units because the difference in cost is modest and most planners' estimates will have been too conservative. Based on 4 cards per volume with each drawer about 70 percent full, each 60-drawer unit will provide space for a collection of 15,000 volumes. If 72-drawer cabinets are purchased, the top and bottom rows can be left empty until that unhappy day when your collection is larger than your building was planned for and your catalog has exceeded the capacity originally planned.

Smaller libraries or those that can house the card catalog more spaciously, often use smaller cabinets (30 to 45 drawers) or low-profile cabinets sometimes called rancher units. These smaller cabinets are more aesthetically pleasing and easier to work around than the larger units. In the other extreme, larger libraries have used larger individual catalog units (i.e., 144 drawers) or built cabinets into walls. These lack flexibility and do not belong in modern libraries.

Location and Direction Information

We pointed out earlier that the card catalog must be near the entrance to the reference area/bibliographic center and readily apparent to users entering the library. Since the card catalog area must be in the midst of patterns of heavy traffic, it should be arranged so that users can readily see where needed cabinets are located; easily find assistance, whether printed or by staff contact; locate needed drawers without delay; and have at hand a flat surface on which to consult catalog cards in a drawer and make necessary notes. Signs will be needed to (a) give basic instruction on catalog use; (b) identify holdings of cases (and, if necessary, rows of cases); and (c) identify drawers by portion of alphabet covered.

Numbering drawers consecutively and color-coding rows of drawers will assist users or staff in returning drawers to their correct positions. Graphic presentations in this heavily used area will get dirty, tired, or worn very quickly so they should be checked and replaced regularly. Incidentally, if drawer fronts on the bottom two or three rows slant upwards, they will be much easier to read. The staff concerned with assisting readers in use of the catalog and the patron needing help should be visible to each other. The catalog area should be arranged with this in mind.

Using Catalog Drawers

Finally, standing-height surfaces upon which catalog drawers can be placed and notes written are essential. A separate catalog reference table or table top hung between two catalog cases is the best answer. Pull-out shelves in the catalog cabinet itself are often used to hold catalog drawers as they are consulted, but persons using them interfere with patrons wanting to use other drawers. This same objection holds true for using the top of low profile catalog cabinets as consulting surfaces. Catalog reference tables should have working surfaces at a comfortable height for persons standing (39 in. or 975 mm) and racks or containers for call cards or slips.

They must be of very high-quality construction to achieve maximum durability. Because such tables receive very heavy use, the working surfaces should be of high-pressure laminate.

Since these heavily used tables are not only higher than normal tables, but also long and narrow, their under-structure must be exceptionally strong and rigid. Some libraries provide high stools (27 in. or 675 mm) for those using these tables. More information about the details of construction of card catalogs, consultation tables, and stools will be found in the specification in Appendix A. Other furniture in a card catalog area may include a table or two where users can work with catalog drawers for longer periods of time, where an instructional program on card catalog use may be viewed and/or listened to, or where computer terminals or other machine-readable data-base output may be consulted. A small table or stand will be needed for the Library of Congress list of subject headings. If there is to be a catalog information librarian in the complex, a desk and chair, or better yet a high desk or table, and an upholstered chair will be needed. A telephone is essential and some large libraries have provided telephone jacks at intervals on uprights between card catalog sections so that a catalog information specialist can plug in a telephone headset near the drawer needed to answer a telephone inquiry.

FUTURE OF THE CARD CATALOG

What of the future of the public catalog in card form? For the forseeable future, most small libraries will retain it. Nontheless, at this writing there are now and clearly there will be many more libraries with catalogs in machine-readable form with access via book catalog, computer printout, COM (computer-output microform)-produced microform, and computer terminals. It is not yet certain whether many libraries will be willing to terminate additions to their card catalogs or, indeed, to discontinue them altogether. In the first of these alternatives, no more cards are added to the card catalog after a selected date and a machine-produced catalog then begins operation. Within a few years, the card catalog contains older, less-needed material and perhaps then it can be relegated to a less strategic location or phased out entirely. An advantage of this approach is that it saves the very high cost of adding the pre-machine-readable part of the collection to the machine file. On the other hand, it means that many catalog users must use two files, in quite different formats. The second alternative, discontinuing the card catalog, will soon be carried out by some larger libraries, where the size and cost of catalog maintenance have become so great that phase-out of the card catalog has become a necessity. Of course, this has been true of our largest libraries for some time now, but only very recently have they felt that machine-readable catalogs are becoming adequate and dependable replacements. Libraries that are not yet experiencing these difficulties with catalog maintenance are very reluctant to consider discontinuing their card catalogs. The catalog on cards permits almost unlimited access at any one time, while cost and space considerations generally preclude large numbers of access points to catalogs via computer data bases. Other problems with catalogs in machine-readable formats include (a) difficulty with updating in some formats, such as book catalogs; (b) high cost of presenting all the information that printed cards contain; (c) unsatisfactory or inadequate subject access; and (d) serious human engineering problems such as visual differences among users. The plight of a wearer of bifocals trying to use COM-produced, high-magnification microfiche on a reader or to read the readout on a computer terminal is painful to behold. Nonetheless, as further improvements in access to machine-readable catalog files are made and catalog maintenance and space for card catalog cabinets become greater problems, more large libraries will be forced to give up their catalogs on cards.

REMOTE CATALOG ACCESS STATIONS

One of the chief advantages of the catalog in machine-readable form is the remote-access capability; that is, a duplicate of the entire catalog or a desired portion can be made available to any location. It is possible now to place catalog duplicates in locations in stacks and at service points and branches and, indeed, in departmental or individual faculty offices; in short, almost anywhere. These duplicates can be in several forms with each having different implications for the space planner. Book catalogs, at least for a library of any size, occupy a considerable amount of space and require some sort of shelving or large table with shelves. A catalog remotely available in microform will take up less space than a book catalog. The general configuration of such a station utilizing microfiche is a chair and small table on which is placed a microfiche reader and the file of fiche (often in a ring binder with pockets) and a printed index along with instruction on use of the remote access station. Other systems use closed-roll film viewers which can be placed similarly on small tables. The user will be able to view the screen of such microreaders more readily if the surrounding area is somewhat darkened and a table lamp is available to light any writing or reading done in association with using the catalog data on the screen. The only utility needed is electric power for the fiche reader and lamp.

If access to the machine file is through computer terminal, a small table with chair, similar to that for the microreader above, will serve to seat the terminal user. In both cases, the table should be large enough to hold the microreader or terminal and provide some writing surface for note taking. Terminals need both a source of electric power and a wired connection to the computer. This computer connection can be via telephone line or by direct line, sometimes called "hard-wired." If access to remote-data bases (out of town) is to be available at a terminal which is not likely to remain in place permanently, the use of telephone lines is necessary and, of course, there is a continuing monthly charge for this. On the other hand, if terminals can remain in place indefinitely and need only be connected to a nearby computer, it is generally less expensive in the long run to use the hard-wired method. Terminals should be used in areas where ambient light can be reduced, for their screens are generally not easy to read for long periods of time, and glare and reflecting light should be held to a minimum.

Book catalogs and microfiche readers can be used by most readers with a minimum of assistance; usually good, clear printed instructions nearby will suffice. Computer terminals, on the other hand, present enough difficulties that they should be located close to service points, where staff can easily assist readers in their use.

CATALOG PRODUCTION STAFF

Public catalogs, card or other, must have associated staff space and this may well be the staff area with the largest number of personnel in the library. In this book we will call it "technical processing" although it goes by different names in different libraries. This term recognizes that in many forward-thinking libraries the processing of library materials is a continuum and that rigid departmentalism of functions does not encourage efficiency or staff morale. The old distinction between acquisition (acquiring library materials) and cataloging (describing them so that they may be easily found) seems to some an artificial division. Certainly in almost any library it is desirable to place acquisition and cataloging functions in one large area, so that materials flow easily and differing work loads or changes in methods of operation in the two functions can be recognized by exchanges of space allocation within the area. If it is necessary to separate some of the technical processing functions, it may well be more satisfactory to split them by materials handled; that is, serial versus monograph, rather than by whether material is being acquired or cataloged. In each case the process is continuous from selection to placement in use. Conversely, the difference between the two types of material in their acquisition and description for use as well as the kind of use received is sufficient that separation is not bad and may even be advantageous.

LOCATING THE TECHNICAL PROCESSING STAFF

We discussed in Chapter 1 the inevitable "elbowing" for space that takes place near the library's service center, the place where catalog, reference and bibliographic center, and materials distribution center (lending or circulation) are located. It is generally considered most desirable to locate the technical processing area as close as possible to the card catalog, thus saving steps for technical processing personnel and enabling them to be more productive. Frequently, then, technical processing is given space in this "high-rent district" near the card catalog, though this space is hardly ever enough because of the need to house the important "keys" elements here. Soon more space is required to house departments expanding to process a growing collection. Inevitably, there is competition for space with the public catalog, reference, and lending functions, all of which must also grow with the library.

The result too often is an overcrowded area or floor with none of these essential departments having sufficient area in which to operate satisfactorily. Or perhaps it is necessary to split up technical processing to gain space for other functions, with consequent loss of efficiency. In many cases, it is far better initially to assign to technical processing ample, expandable space on a floor above or below the public catalog, with good stair or elevator connection between them. A number of academic libraries have done this effectively, and technical processing staff quickly learn to batch work that must be done at the public catalog or in the specialized bibliographies available in reference or the bibliographic center. As more remote access to bibliographic records becomes available, this separation becomes easier to accept.

ORGANIZING TECHNICAL PROCESSING AREAS

Technical processing is in the midst of a revolution, with many institutions becoming part of shared cataloging networks and others utilizing machine-readable catalog files in various formats under development (Fig. 3). While no approach has received universal approval, other than the apparent acceptance of shared catalog networks, it is abundantly clear that physical facilities for technical processing must be as flexible and capable of housing new techniques and hardware as possible.

Any new technical processing area should utilize a large unbroken space for its operation with a minimum of acoustically private offices. All furniture should be easy to move and rearrange. Work stations might well be of the modular office landscape type units rather than more traditional desks. These modular units provide efficiently designed work and storage space, a degree of privacy that encourages productivity, as well as providing a modicum of status enhancement, and make better computer-terminal stations than do ordinary desks. The textured back and side panels common in such units offer noise absorption, opportunities for use of color and texture, and provide surfaces for tacking up pictures and notices. In short, the use of large areas for technical processing with office-landscape-type work units permits flexibility of space allocation,

FIG. 3 Terminal providing access to Ohio-based shared cataloging network (OCLC). The Pennsylvania State University, University Park, Pennsylvania.

provides desirable aesthetic and sound-absorbing qualities, and allows organization of work flow to meet changing needs.

Of course, private offices for department heads and a small conference space are necessary for discussion of personnel and other private matters. These can be best furnished with conventional desks and chairs. These offices should be small but light and well-decorated so that they are pleasant for the occupant. Some department heads prefer a large glass window so that they can survey the area under their supervision. This can cause problems when personnel matters must be discussed. Drapes can be drawn but, of course, this only serves to draw attention to a situation.

FURNISHING THE AREA

Other than work stations or desks, the furniture and equipment in technical processing will be mostly conventional office and library furniture, as well as card catalog files to serve a variety of functions; vertical and horizontal files; work tables for sorting, mending, marking, and other functions; book trucks; tab files; other specialized record-keeping devices; and, of course, shelving. Shelving used in technical processing areas should be regular library shelving rather than the more inflexible storage shelving. In larger processing areas, shelving serves usefully to separate areas and delineate functions. Backs can be added to improve the separation when needed. Shelves can be moved around fairly easily as areas need to be expanded or relocated.

Book Trucks

Book trucks (called trolleys in England and elsewhere) are essential equipment items in all library operations but are particularly concentrated in TP (technical processing) departments. They are the principal materials-handling devices in technical processes. They are used as materials-batching devices at individual work stations, conveyors of materials in process throughout the area, and distributors of library materials to other parts of the library. The other primary function of book trucks is in moving books to, from, and within bookstack areas, but they will also be found in all parts of any library. They must be very well constructed for they are expected to perform well for years under the heaviest kind of use and abuse. The most commonly used trucks have two or more shelves, flat or sloped, fastened to two ends, by which they are pushed in the desired direction on wheels fastened to the truck base. The trucks most commonly available today have four swivel wheels, one on each corner. Another popular arrangement uses two swiveling and two fixed wheels, a variation which some users find easier to maneuver. Trucks may be of wood or metal, and either type will last many years if well made initially (Fig. 4). There are two sizes commonly used: a two-shelf unit generally 36 in. high × 30 in. long × 16 in. wide (900 × 750 × 400 mm) and a longer, higher three-shelf unit approximately 40 × 34 × 15 in. (1000 × 850 × 375 mm). In either size the shelves may be flat or sloped. Trucks with sloping shelves generally have a divider down the longitudinal axis. Rubber bumpers are frequently specified for trucks so that impact damage to them and to other surfaces they move against is reduced. Until recently metal trucks were offered only in a few subdued colors, but lately trucks have been made available in a variety of bright colors with accent colors on end panels. Trucks to be used in carpeted areas should have wheels of larger diameter, at least 4 in. (100 mm), so that they roll more easily. Truck wheels are available with locks so that they may be kept still when appropriate. At least one manufacturer markets oversized trucks (Porta-trucks by Bro-Dart, Inc.) which are especially well-suited for some tasks such as shifting book collections. Others market extra-narrow trucks that can be used in narrow stack aisles.

A loaded book truck, particularly a large one, is a heavy and unwieldy object and, improperly operated, can be a safety hazard. The models with

FIG. 4 Wood book truck, with flat and sloping shelves. (Worden.)

four swiveling wheels are easily steered but are none too stable, while models with two fixed wheels are more stable but the large turning radius causes problems in tight quarters. A truck with swiveling wheels can also be moved sideways, a dangerous practice which causes accidents. The University of North Florida specified trucks with six wheels in its new library. The wheels in the corners swivel and there are stationary wheels halfway along each side. As a result, the truck can turn in its own length, cannot be pushed sideways, and is more stable than four-wheeled trucks. Unfortunately, such a truck is not available from any manufacturer as a standard item. A customer purchasing a number of wood trucks could possibly have two additional wheels added for a modest additional cost. In metal, the additional cost would probably be prohibitive.

Modular Work Stations

We have already mentioned other specific items of furniture, including modular work stations (office landscape), desks, chairs, and files. Of these, the newest concept is the modular unit, although some have remarked on its remarkable similarity to the roll-top desk. Nonetheless, office land-

FIG. 5 Attractive, efficient work stations for libraries can be made with office landscape systems. University of Toledo, Toledo, Ohio.

scaping has been the "hottest" thing in commercial interior design for several years now and it seems likely to sustain its popularity for some time to come. Basically, the concept calls for the construction of large-area office space instead of space broken up by individual offices. The larger area is then broken up into work spaces by use of upright panels and work stations. The primary advantage is, of course, the flexibility realized when work stations can be rearranged almost at will. The panels and work stations are high enough to give some privacy and acoustic protection, but low enough to permit air movement and light distribution throughout the area. The panels provide visual barriers, color, and space for decoration or signs. Work stations are generally more versatile than desks because available component units including drawers, files, and shelves can be arranged for the convenience of each user (Fig. 5). Individual lights and power outlets are customarily available as components of these units. These systems provide admirable work stations for many commercial applications and they have important potential for some library applications.

Of course, libraries have utilized a kind of office landscape for years in planning interior arrangements of modular libraries by using bookstacks and banks of carrels to break up large interior expanses into more liveable spaces. They have used this technique to make the library's interior more aesthetically pleasing, to organize the interior space into different functional and service areas, and to provide vertical separators that will absorb sound. However, use of office landscape in library work areas is quite new. Penn State has used it in a systems development or computer area within the library and for the acquisitions area. The Canadian Institute of Scientific and Technical Information, a new building which is Canada's national science library, uses office landscape for all its staff and work stations. The University of Toledo has work space for nearly all its technical processing and public service staff in one large area with office-landscape work units for each person. Other libraries are making some use of this approach.

At present these systems are not available from those firms which are best-known for the manufacture of library technical furniture. However, names of some firms which manufacture such systems are familiar to librarians because they are large firms who manufacture some library furniture, steel book shelving, or office furniture. Examples are Interroyal, Steelcase and Risom.

Evaluating these systems for purchase involves some considerations that may be unfamiliar to librarians. Of course, most important is whether the entire unit and its individual components are suitable for the library functions to be performed. Since flexibility and adaptability are important selling points for such systems, components should be easy to add, remove, and rearrange. Work units should be well constructed and durable, and soft-surfaced components, which quickly wear and become dirty, should be easily replaceable. A list of firms that currently manufacture such systems will be found in the annual issue of Contract magazine that features office landscape or open-plan offices.

Desks

Desks will be found in library work areas, service points, and offices, with wood desks generally used in private offices of top management and steel desks used elsewhere. Conventional office desks are sometimes used at service points but generally are not well-designed for this purpose. Available from manufacturers of library technical furniture are desks that are specially designed for use as reference desks or circulation desks (for small libraries), but none of these will suit everyone. Desks used at service points will generally be made of wood because of the greater variations in design available and for aesthetic reasons. On the other hand, metal desks of standard configuration will generally fit the functional needs of technical processing personnel and wooden desks will often be too expensive to use in the quantities needed for comparatively large processing staffs.

Metal desks are available in a wide range of quality. While all are reasonably durable, the cheaply made ones will look tired and worn long before they become unserviceable. Work surfaces should be made of high-pressure laminate rather than metal or linoleum. The edge of the work top should be slightly rounded or of vinyl or similar absorbent material in order to absorb impact damage. A most important consideration, and one neglected in the manufacture of poor-quality steel desks, is the use of good drawer suspension. As the only moving part of a desk, the drawer must go through many thousands of cycles during the desk's life. If the metal in the suspension is sufficiently heavy and firm and if the bearings are adequate and of good quality, the feel of the drawer in motion will be smooth when the drawer is new and will remain so after thousands of cycles of opening and closing.

For most library applications, the storage capacity of two pedestals in a desk will be welcome and most users will want also a center drawer for additional storage. Many manufacturers offer some choices in the number, location and kinds of drawers (i.e., box drawers, file drawers, or pencil drawers) and in the types of inserts available for the drawers (stationery units, 3 × 5 in. card compartments, hanging files, etc.). For library use, one file drawer large enough to hold suspended letter files will nearly always be useful; these are also frequently used for purses and other personal effects. In processing areas library staff who are not primarily typists will generally be well-served with a double pedestal desk with a file drawer and one box drawer on one side and with three box drawers on the other, with the center drawer having an insert for items such as pencils, paper clips, or rubber bands. At least one of the box drawers should be compartmentalized for 3 × 5 in. cards, the ubiquitous mode of library communication and record keeping. Pull-out writing shelves in each pedestal, just beneath the working surfaces, are most desirable. Unfortunately, many desks with "modern" lines no longer provide these; therefore desks that offer this much-used accessory must be carefully sought out.

A double-pedestal desk will need to be at least 60 in. (1500 mm) wide in order to provide adequate space for pedestals and a large enough opening for the users' legs. A modesty panel across the front of the opening is nearly always desirable. The depth of the desk can be as little as 30 in. (750 mm), for the rear of the desk top is difficult to utilize adequately if the desk is deeper. Addition of a desk back unit at the rear of a desk can be most useful (Fig. 6). Such a unit will provide additional storage space, will cut down on casual conversation, and will confer upon workers some sense of privacy and status. It also provides a good surface for the kind of decoration that is common in technical processing areas.

For some tasks, it will be helpful to get a desk with a return on one side for additional work or storage space or as a place for ready accessibility to some office machinery, such as adding machines or computer terminals. Returns of 26 to 27 in. (650 to 675 mm) high are available for typewriters; returns of 29 in. (725 mm) high for the continuation of desk tops, though these are less popular than compartments in desk pedestals that can conceal typewriters or separate typewriter stands. Although the typewriter compartment

FIG. 6 Desk-back units like these provide the occupant with storage space, privacy, and a sense of status. The Pennsylvania State University, University Park, Pennsylvania.

within the desk pedestal conceals the machine when not in use, it does take useful storage space away from the desk. The separate typing stand is particularly handy for a typewriter that is sometimes needed by more than one user. Still another way of housing a typewriter at a work station is in a well in a single-pedestal desk. This is only appropriate for someone who does typing only, for such desks have little remaining space for work or storage.

When evaluating steel desks for purchase, the quality of the finish and appearance of the places where different surfaces and materials meet are important indications of good construction. It is common for poor-quality desks to have sharp edges or metal burrs which can ruin hose and other clothing and, consequently, staff morale. Visiting installations of steel office furniture and furniture showrooms, and checking the evaluations of such furniture that periodically appear in Library Technology Reports will assist in the selection of metal desks.

Wood desks are frequently purchased for use as service points, such as reference desks, and as executive desks for library administrators.

They are often used as public service desks because of their good appearance and the fact that wood desks can be customized or specially designed for library functions; whereas it is prohibitively expensive to customize metal desks. The reasons for the desirability of wood desks for executive offices are principally aesthetic. A standard configuration of drawers and sizes will usually please their prospective occupants.

The same concern for good-quality suspensions and finishes holds for wood desks as for metal desks. If wood desks are to be at all heavily used, the tops should be of high-pressure laminate, for the thin wood-veneer tops provided nowadays (1/28- to 1/32-in.) will not stand up to any abuse. If wood tops must be used, a tempered-glass cover with edges and corners carefully smoothed will protect the top. Some wood desks have metal frames and legs and these can add structural rigidity as well as prevent the kind of damage that maintenance personnel and others occasionally cause to wood legs. Some lines of wood desks currently available have end panels rather than legs; these almost seem to invite damage.

As we suggested above, wood desks can be purchased in many sizes and configurations, with numerous accessories. One Knoll International desk has an oversized working surface and a raised front platform on which patrons can fill out charge cards and behind which cards and other small objects can be stored. It has both drawers and shelf space in its pedestals

FIG. 7 Reference desk with consultation stations at either end. Davidson College, Davidson, North Carolina.

and can be an effective reference desk in some situations. The desk illustrated in Fig. 7 was designed for Davidson College and has space for two reference librarians behind it and on each end there is a specially designed area where each can consult with patrons. Nearly any concept of service or special functional need can be provided for with specially designed wood desks. Particularly useful for many service desks is the addition of a return unit which forms an L-shape and provides extra space for work, storage, consulting with patrons (more comfortably if the return top has an overhang), or even conducting small meetings, as well as a convenient place for constantly used card files or other records.

Incidentally, these returns will not be too satisfactory without proper knee space. They can, of course, be specified for attachment to either end of the desk, thus providing left- or right-hand returns, depending on room configuration and layout. Returns can be attached to single-pedestal desks only. Such specialized wood desks are available from manufacturers of library technical furniture as well as from suppliers of conventional office desks.

Chairs

Chairs for library work areas are most commonly of the same sort as commercial and office seating, and are available through office furniture suppliers and other sources of contract furniture. However, library side chairs, sometimes purchased from suppliers of library technical furniture, are often used as guest chairs and in other applications. Nonetheless, the office seating most often found in library staff areas is of conventional, commercial design with metal or wood frames and bases, and is almost always upholstered, with or without arms. Such chairs generally swivel, tilt, and are on casters.

Overall quality, durability, and comfort are the most important considerations in considering such chairs for purchase because of the long years of continuous service to which they are subjected. Since they are almost constantly occupied by a single individual for long periods each day, comfort is exceedingly important. Seats and backs should be large enough to support the person adequately. Chairs should have adjustable seat height (to suit occupants of differing heights) and back tension (if the chair frame is flexible). The so-called posture chair offers more adjustment and, therefore, more comfort for the user than the chair with seat and back connected by a nonflexible frame. Chair seats should have sufficiently firm padding, and upholstery padding should be made of fabric rather than vinyl for seating comfort. Casters should be large enough ($2\frac{1}{2}$ in. or 62.5 mm dia.) to move easily and smoothly on all kinds of floor surfaces. The conventional wheel-type caster seems to hold up better under heavy use than other casters. Wheels should be $\frac{3}{4}$-in. (18.75 mm) thick and have spindles at least 2 in. (50 mm) long. When floors are carpeted, chairs and casters will last longer and chair users will be able to move around their work stations more easily if chair mats are purchased for use under each desk. These variously shaped mats of Masonite, acrylic plastic, or vinyl allow chair casters to move over a smooth surface, away from the rougher carpet underneath. If armchairs are to be selected, the arms should be made of wood or covered with vinyl rather than fabric, which soils quickly when so used.

Files

File cabinets are used throughout all libraries. Although frequently file cabinets are taken for granted, some attention to the selection of the right ones will pay off in better function over a longer life span. The so-called vertical file is deeper than it is wide, with the material filed in drawers from front to back through the depth of the cabinet. Interestingly enough, Library Bureau, Inc. first developed and marketed the vertical file during the last century. The newer, increasingly popular lateral or horizontal file is wider than it is deep and has material filed over the width of the cabinet. Vertical files are familiar to most people, fit better into some confined spaces, are generally cheaper, and are easier to use than some lateral files. On the other hand, lateral files have greater storage density (more documents can be filed per square foot of floor space), are generally more attractive, and are much more versatile than vertical files. Whichever of the two types are used, the use of hanging files on frames is strongly recommended. While the initial investment of these frames is greater than for conventional manila folders, their long life and the consequent ease in filing and handling more than justify the higher initial cost.

With vertical files, it is not generally possible to file to the entire depth of the drawer and materials near the end of the drawer are hard to reach. Lateral files, available with drawers like those of vertical files (Fig. 8) or with shelves which slide out (Fig. 9), are easy to use. The latter type has flap doors which lie flat and can be used for holding material to be filed. The flexibility of lateral files is exemplified by their common incorporation in office-landscape work stations where the face is used for files and special inserts such as telephone or dictating stations, secondary work stations, etc., and the back side is used as a divider or as a location for a tackboard or chalkboard. Many of the inserts available in lateral file systems are particularly useful in library work station applications.

Vertical and horizontal files are generally available in two-, three-, four-, and five-drawer heights. The two- and three-drawer units are usually placed beside the desk of a person who has a modest filing requirement. Four-drawer files are those most commonly used, though five-drawer files are well worth considering for the 25 percent greater capacity

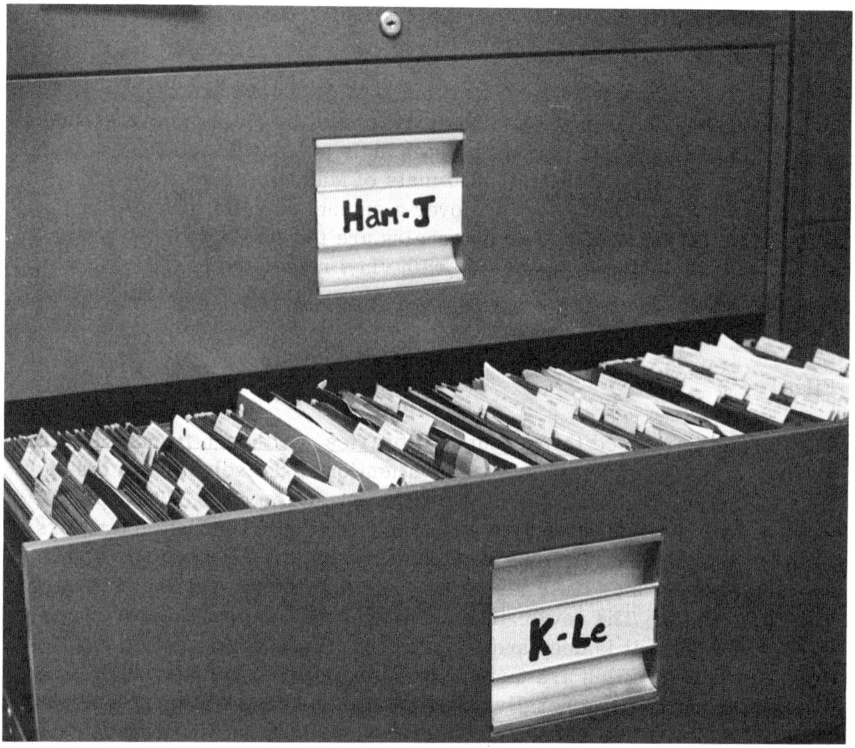

FIG. 8 Lateral file, drawer-type, is less convenient for most purposes than shelf-type.

FIG. 9 Lateral file, shelf-type ('Montisa' by Browne-Morse.)

they provide for a modest additional cost. Both types of files are available in letter and legal size; that is, the interior of the file space is designed for file folders holding sheets either $8\frac{1}{2} \times 11$ in. (212.5×275 mm) (letter size) or $8\frac{1}{2} \times 14$ in. (212.5×350 mm) (legal size). Letter-size vertical file cabinets are approximately 15 in. (375 mm) wide and legal-size are approximately 18 in. (450 mm) wide. The depth of vertical files is generally 29 to 30 in. (725-750 mm), and of lateral files about 20 in. (500 mm). Lateral files are available in 30-, 36-, and 42-in. (750-, 900-, and 1050 mm) width, though the 36-in. (900 mm) is most common. Two-drawer files of both types are usually about 29 in. (725 mm) high, or about desk-top height; three-drawer files are generally about 40 in. (1000 mm), approximately the height of a standard circulation desk. A dimension critical to the space planner is the overall depth from the front of a fully open drawer to the back of the cabinet. For lateral files the overall depth, when opened, is approximately 36 in. (900 mm), and in vertical files, approximately 52 in. (1300 mm).

In evaluating files for purchase, it is important to examine the overall finish and hardware, but the most important factor is the drawer suspension, which must operate smoothly for thousands of cycles. Opening a fully loaded drawer with a poor-quality suspension is most difficult and such cabinets will not last long. For more information and evaluations of particular files, as well as of desks and chairs, Library Technology Reports can be most helpful.

THE LENDING FUNCTION

The circulation or lending function is a most important aspect of almost all library operations. All but the few libraries where materials are only available for use in the building will have one or more stations where library materials are loaned to patrons. These stations vary in complexity from a single desk, perhaps used for many purposes, where a single card file holds the library's total circulation transactions, to one or more large public lending desks, compartmentalized into sections where various circulation functions take place with a large, separate work area nearby.

In the most up-to-date libraries, a computer in the library, across town, or across the country may be an integral part of an individual library's lending or circulation function. One noncomputerized circulation system in a large public library with which the author is familiar had separate, manned work stations for book return and fine collection, personal reserves, registration for library cards, and two stations for charging books. There were perhaps 20 people, some professional, required to operate this large and complex department. Most circulation departments are smaller than this and consist of a single, large circulation desk with a work area and probably an office close by for the circulation librarian. The office and

FIG. 10 Circulation file for manual system.

work area will be quite similar to those in technical processing. Larger, noncomputerized departments will sometimes have a large mechanized or rotating circulation record file of some sort (Fig. 10), depending on the system used.

Lending Desk

The circulation desk itself is a quite distinctive item of furniture and requires some discussion. It is generally large and of such height (39 to 40 in. or 975 to 1000 mm) that the patron being served and the staff performing the service are standing. High stools, often upholstered, frequently are provided so that staff may sit when appropriate. These desks are usually large enough that they can house a number of functional work units (Fig. 11) and also so that the counter surface can provide space for the various public lending services. The desks are generally backed by a wall separating them

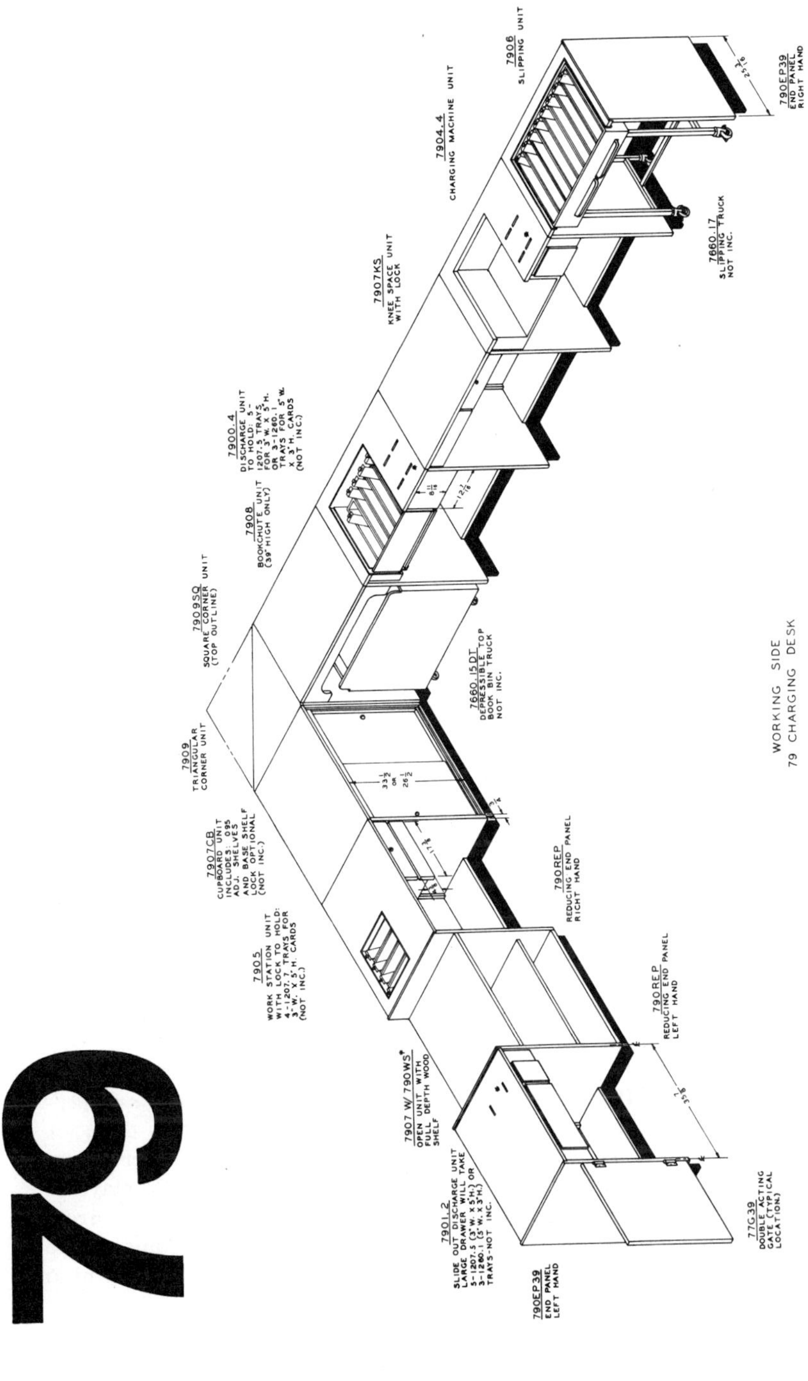

FIG. 11 Circulation desk with its components showing. (Library Bureau.)

from the circulation work area, with shelving arranged on or near the wall. The desk itself is often of monumental size, ranging from 20 to 40 (6000 to 12000 mm) long and its sides extending 15 to 30 ft (4500-9000 mm) from the wall behind. Such desks are frequently rectangular with rounded or angled corners, although they have been produced in every imaginable shape. To avoid having to truck large amounts of material across public spaces, they should be backed up against a work area or stack area where sorting can take place.

Architects will often consider the circulation desk an opportunity to display originality in use of shapes, materials, and other concepts. Unfortunately, such designs often result in structures that may please aesthetically but fail completely to meet the functional requirements of the library. It is essential that custom-designed circulation desks be planned with careful consultation among architect, librarian, and representatives from a reputable library technical furniture manufacturer. All such firms offer library-circulation-desk components as standard items in their lines. These component modules, usually 36 in. (900 mm) wide by 26 in. (650 mm) deep by 39 in. (975 mm) high, are designed to meet demonstrated functional needs of circulation departments and, as such, are very well-suited to these needs. Any number of these modules may be grouped together in any desired arrangement to form a most satisfactory circulation desk of any size or shape. Different shapes are achieved by combining these functional models with corner or end units in different shapes and angles. As functions and procedures change, the units within such a desk may be switched around or be attached to additional units. This does happen and has occurred, for instance, at two of Penn State's smaller libraries. Architect-designed circulation desks, on the other hand, are nearly always inflexible and sometimes even unfunctional. A most acceptable compromise can often be achieved by housing standard circulation-desk inserts made by a library furniture manufacturer in a desk with a custom-designed front and work surface. Such a desk can easily realize the architect's aesthetic concerns while giving the librarian a functional desk that is easy to live with. If this solution is attempted, careful coordination is required between furniture manufacturer, architect, and librarian.

These circulation desk modules or inserts are available in a number of configurations to perform a variety of tasks as shown in Fig. 12. Among the most common are (a) book return units, used for concealing depressible book trucks to receive books returned through a slot in the unit's front; (b) charge units, where books may be charged, fines collected, etc.; (c) truck ports, in which a work-top covers an opening where book trucks may be kept; (d) open-shelf units, in which reserved books, cassette players or other items can be kept; and (e) discharge units, where files of circulation records on cards are kept. Further information on available components for circulation desks is available in the catalogs of library furniture manufacturers.

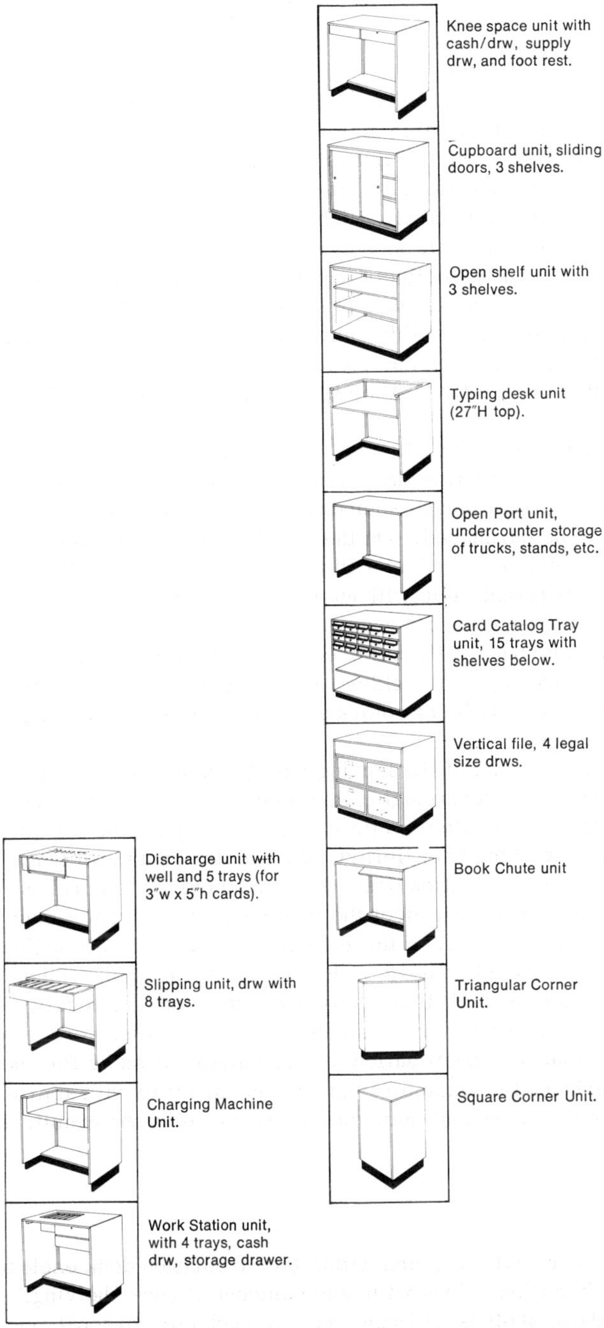

FIG. 12 Components of a circulation desk. (Library Bureau.)

The top of a circulation desk receives extremely heavy use and it is essential that it be of a highly durable material. Linoleum was once very common but, while it wears well, it lacks aesthetic appeal. Wood is not suitable, for it wears much too rapidly. Marble has been used, but its porosity and cost make it impractical. High-pressure laminate is a good and reasonably priced material. It does eventually wear but can be replaced relatively easily, and it can be routinely supplied by manufacturers of library technical furniture as a standard top. An interesting material used occasionally for desk tops is a slatelike material of cement-asbestos that is impervious to almost everything and comes in several subdued colors. Several firms manufacture it; Johns-Manville, Inc. for instance, calls it "Colorlith."

Any architect could specify one of these surfaces for a custom top. Incidentally, if modular circulation-desk units are bought in order that the configuration may be rearranged someday, separate tops rather than a continuous one should be purchased. On the other hand, if a custom top and front with inserts manufactured by a library manufacturer is chosen, the inserts should be rearrangeable without affecting the top or front. The front of the circulation desk does not receive quite the amount of heavy wear suffered by the top, but it will suffer considerable impact and scratching damage from brief cases, belt buckles, and other items. In view of this factor, desk fronts should be of colors and materials that do not easily show nicks and scratches.

Since the efficient operation of the lending function is essential to any library, a well-designed and functional circulation desk is extremely important. As we pointed out earlier, while it is certainly possible for an architect or designer, working with library staff, to design an efficient, flexible, and long-lasting circulation desk, it is much easier to purchase a desk made up of components that meet the functional needs from a manufacturer of library furniture. Any of these firms will work closely with an architect or designer to provide a desk of the specified colors and finishes which will work satisfactorily. It is unlikely that a desk of equal quality or efficiency can be manufactured by a "millwork" house. Therefore, we strongly recommend that the specification of a circulation desk be for one produced by an experienced manufacturer of library furniture with appropriate special design or component materials as required by the architect.

Lending Operations

In larger libraries, there will be space within the circulation desk enclosure for one or more work stations along with some amount of book shelving. In some libraries, these shelves will hold reserve books or personal reserves being held for patrons. In other libraries some sorting of books prior to reshelving takes place here.

Today, in order to control book circulation, circulation departments employ a variety of mechanized systems, from relatively simple mechanical systems such as those marketed by Bro-Dart and Demco, to highly sophisticated on-line computer-centered systems utilizing terminals and light pens for input. The input-station portion of these systems all fit into the confines of the circulation desk complex, thereby generally becoming an integral part of the desk itself. In some cases, the modification of standard circulation-desk units will be required and some system components (i.e., terminals or minicomputers) may be placed behind the desk on stands or tables. Additional work space for record storage or processing or, in some cases, microform readers will be required elsewhere, generally in the adjacent circulation work space. Computer facilities for circulation systems utilizing them will sometimes be in the library, but may be part of time-sharing systems operated by a college, university, or municipality, or indeed, by a cooperative center or commercial firm located half a continent away. In short, the appearance and size of the circulation area, both the portion visible to the public and the behind-the-scenes portion, will be little affected by the kind of circulation system in use; the complement of furniture and equipment will utilize conventional elements, other than the hardware of the particular system concerned.

Since the aim of this book is to provide principles and general information to assist librarians and library planners in evaluating and selecting furniture and equipment for purchase, we have chosen to touch lightly on rapidly changing technologies, such as circulation systems. Developments are occurring so rapidly in this field that a system alluded to as current today might well be obsolescent by the time this work is in print. Library Technology Reports and the current library literature will provide awareness of recent developments in this area and the section on evaluation in Chapter 7 should also be helpful.

Exit Control

The exit-control function is an essential element of almost all libraries and customarily is administered as part of the circulation function. Only small or specialized libraries can manage to retain their collection relatively intact without checking people and their effects as they leave the library. In some libraries, mostly small ones, traffic patterns are organized so that patrons must pass by a portion of the circulation desk where staff on duty can observe them as they exit. Alternately, when they come to a point at the desk, their books, briefcases, or purses are checked manually or electronically before a turnstile is released and permits them to pass. This system utilizes staff more economically, but may cause a queuing problem at a busy circulation desk with consequent reader unhappiness. Most large libraries operate control points remote from circulation desks, right at the building exit (or, sad to say, exits). Since most large libraries have a sizeable lobby or, at least an open area for traffic passage between circulation desk and exit point, the distance between these may be 50 to 100 ft (1500 to 3000 cm), or more.

In most instances, these exit-control points are manned by one or more guards, often uniformed, who examine books, packages, briefcases, and other objects that could conceal library materials. Readers are generally funneled past these exit stations by traffic-control devices, such as theater cord (posts and ropes). Frequently, turnstiles are part of such stations and they are generally controlled by the guard. They are frequently provided with counters, which are most helpful. Some feel that the turnstiles add a jarring note to the lobby, with suggestion of regimentation; others feel that they are essential to collection security. Guards are often behind high desks (40 in., approximately) which provides a better height for inspection, though regulation desk-height stations are also used. Guards may have to stand, particularly for inspection of briefcases, but should have a high upholstered stool or chair with back. The desk, whatever its height, should be shallow, no more than 24 to 28 in. (600 to 700 mm) deep so that the guard can easily reach objects to be searched. The guard should have a telephone readily at hand so that assistance or information can be easily obtained.

Exit Security Systems

In recent years, the problem of loss of books and other library materials has become so severe in some libraries that they have had to install electronic security systems to prevent patrons from walking out of the library with library materials concealed in their clothing or in packages, cases, or other objects. In such systems, library materials are treated by adding or attaching to them some sort of object that will respond to a transmitter signal or activate a field. When this treated object is taken through a gate or past a sensor, the system alarms and patrons are prevented from leaving the library with unrecorded library material. These systems can significantly reduce book theft, although none of the systems seems to be foolproof.

A number of firms market such systems (Fig. 13) and they differ in the type of activating element and sensing hardware utilized. Some are magnetic in principal; others use radio sensing. In evaluating these systems for purchase, special attention should be paid to the solvency and experience of the vendor. This field has seen a number of firms begin operations and quickly go under. Another factor that many consider important is the incidence of false alarms; this is, nonrelated objects can sometimes activate such a system with the possible result of false accusations. Still another economic factor some librarians feel is important is the cost of installing the activating pieces or strips. These systems are offered in

FIG. 13 Exit-control system by Checkpoint.

two configurations, one (sometimes called "full circulating") permits unattended operation of the exit point, while the other (often called "bypass") requires the continued presence of an exit guard who handles all declared library books and material. The full circulating system costs more but offers the possibility of saving the cost of exit clerks. The bypass system provides better control inasmuch as it requires that each visible library book be physically handled, enabling guards to check for due date, etc. Both kinds of systems are available from leading manufacturers. Library Technology Reports presents additional information on these systems in its evaluation reports.

PERIODICALS

The areas considered thus far in this chapter have been those surrounding the library entrance/exit, the areas considered the "keys" to the library's service, along with their accompanying staff or work areas. While the areas already discussed (reference, circulation, card catalog, and bibliography) must always be in close proximity to each other, at least one other area, that of periodicals and serials, should be close by. In Chapter 1, we discussed the desirability of arranging the most heavily used library areas closest to the entrance so that heavy traffic patterns will be short. Periodicals are very heavily used in all libraries, and the area in which they are housed should be close to the entrance. In addition, periodicals must be close to the "keys" mentioned above because the bibliographic tools located among the catalog and reference areas relate so closely to them. In smaller libraries, a significant portion of the reference staff's time will be spent with periodicals. If periodicals cannot be located near the bibliographies and indexes, considerations of good service will require duplicating these tools, which is an expensive proposition.

The functions and areas associated with periodicals are one or more reading areas; a service desk; a periodicals/serials record; work areas where such functions as periodical check-in, cataloging, bookkeeping, ordering and renewing, and bindery preparation must take place; and, of course, the collection itself. Libraries will organize these functions differently. For instance, some libraries catalog serials along with monographs in a catalog division; others, particularly larger academic libraries, will have a separate serials division where functions dealing with all serials, including periodicals, take place. Incidentally, we include newspapers in this serials section, though they are often separately organized and housed.

Reader Space

The reading area for periodicals and newspapers does not differ greatly from other reader spaces. It will have index tables to hold such tools as the <u>New York Times Index</u> and <u>Reader's Guide to Periodical Literature</u>. There also should be a list of the library's periodical holdings available for patron use. This may be in a card file, visible record, or computer output; it should list periodical name, location, and holdings.

Reader seating will be mostly at tables and chairs; however, lounge chairs are particularly useful here for casual readers. Carrels are not especially well suited for these areas. Sloped-top reading tables are particularly welcome for those using newspapers and large periodicals. Some large public libraries use nearly vertical sloping surfaces to which newspapers are fastened so that the pages may be easily turned but the newspapers remain in place.

Service Point

The service area will be similar to a reference service point except that a comprehensive serial record must be close at hand. There should be some shelf space here for periodicals being held, in process, or that need some sort of special treatment or protection. The serials work area should be adjacent to the service area for maximum staff utilization and easy access to materials and records. Many libraries have nearly all their periodicals on open stacks, freely available to users. Others, often due to severe losses, keep some portion of their collection in closed areas, from which they are retrieved for use by the periodicals service staff. If such is the case, the closed area should be near the service area for maximum efficiency.

Staff Processing Area

Periodicals/serials work space will differ little from that for technical processing. There will be a large shelving requirement because of the amount of material in process or being held for binding. One or more large tables on which material may be sorted or organized will be very useful. Files and work stations will generally resemble those in technical processing with the one important exception of the master serials record, which will be found in some form in almost all libraries.

This record may be located in the serials work area or, particularly in smaller libraries, it may be right at the periodicals service desk. If it is in the serials work area, it should be convenient to all periodicals/serials operations. In this file are listed all serials with their holdings and the location of all issues, along with payment records, dates of receipt of all issues, and change of title and binding records. It may be necessary to use more than one file to obtain all this data, but most departments will have one master file in which all this information is held. Most libraries use for this purpose a periodical check-in record (often called visible card files) of the type illustrated in Fig. 14. These files have space enough on both sides of their entry cards to record all the necessary information about each serial title for several years. When selecting such files, it is important that the device holding the entry cards be removable or that new pockets can be interfiled so that it is not necessary to move a large number of cards to interfile new ones. It is anticipated that such records can be successfully replaced by computer-controlled serials operation, which will record this data more efficiently and automatically perform some periodical-related routines, such as claiming missing issues and initiating the binding of completed volumes. Experimental systems are operational but none are yet universally available.

Housing Periodicals

The housing and display of the periodical and newspaper collection is, of course, the central issue for the periodicals function. In some libraries, particularly larger ones, periodicals are located in different parts of the

FIG. 14 Visible filing systems are essential for library record keeping. (Kardex, Sperry Rand. Photo by UPI.)

library for a variety of reasons. If the library is organized by subject division, such as science, business, or fine arts, periodicals are often part of these divisional collections rather than being shelved in a general periodicals room. Having bound periodicals classified and shelved in subject divisions is particularly advantageous in that current periodicals are close to the bound ones. Periodicals are also decentralized for the benefit of various user groups, i.e., children (public libraries) or undergraduates (academic libraries). Some periodical titles are relocated because of special security problems and many libraries will separate the most popular periodicals from those of more specialized interest. Finally, almost all libraries separate bound and unbound periodicals.

Periodical reading rooms generally display and store periodical issues for the current year or volume and often have a separate display for the current issues of popular magazines (Fig. 15). The latter are often placed in binders with transparent plastic fronts that show the covers. These binders help to keep the magazine clean and upright on the display shelf, and make it somewhat more difficult to steal.

When adequate floor area is available, wood or steel shelving that displays each current issue on a sloping shelf, with back issues for the current year or volume stored on a flat shelf directly below, is a popular and attractive means of housing unbound periodicals. The slanted shelf can be either fixed or able to be lifted up to show the concealed back issues. This approach is reasonably expensive both in terms of initial cost and space consumed. Many library planners do not care for these shelves or cannot afford to expend the space they require. For those libraries, one solution is a combination of relatively compact storage for back issues of the current volume, separate from the display of the most recent issue. Storage of the current volume is generally on some kind of steel library shelving, modified for the purpose. Among the possible arrangements are (a) shelving issues flat on inverted-bracket flat shelves (Fig. 16); (b) storing issues upright; (c) on their sides on divider shelves; or (d) in Princeton files on regular book shelves. Possibility (a) permits quite compact use of display space, for as many as 60 titles can be stored per single-faced section, though 45 is a more reasonable number; it assumes that files will be no more than 3 in. (75 mm) deep before binding. A very few weeklies (i.e., Engineering News Record, Newsweek) will probably require two or more spaces for a year or volume's issues. Option (c) permits files of more issues but fewer titles per section of shelves. Current issues can be displayed on separate display racks with all these methods. If space will not permit separate display of the current issues, they may be set on top of the other unbound issues.

Bound volumes of periodicals are generally housed on steel library shelves, often along with the library's books (monographs). Depending on the library's philosophy and practice, bound volumes may be classified

FIG. 15 Current periodical issues are conveniently displayed on this rack. (Gaylord.)

FIG. 16 Flat periodical shelves. The Pennsylvania State University, University Park, Pennsylvania.

and housed with the library's book collection or separately, perhaps near the current issues and arranged alphabetically by title. The library staff's perceptions of how the collection is used will determine which scheme is preferred. Shelves used for bound volumes of periodicals should be at least 10 in. (250 mm) in depth.

Although unbound and bound periodicals are generally housed separately, some libraries place both on the same shelves with unbound issues on their sides or standing in pamphlet boxes, Princeton files, or supported by shelf dividers. However periodicals are housed, clear, readable labels are essential; unfortunately, many libraries fail to provide clear markers.

Newspapers

Because of their size and frequency, newspapers cause peculiar problems in service and housing. The most recent issue of each newspaper received is generally displayed for easy access, usually on special newspaper rods

FIG. 17 Newspapers are often mounted on sticks, then hung from open-topped tables. (Library Bureau.)

which hang from special racks (Fig. 17) or hang within book shelves. Sometimes they are laid flat on slanted newspaper shelves, with hinged clear plastic covers to hold them in place. Often, current issues other than the latest are shelved flat on newspaper shelves (16 to 18 in. or 400 to 500 mm deep). These issues pile up quickly and most libraries find it necessary to discard them soon. Few libraries bind newspapers today because it is very expensive, the poor paper deteriorates rapidly, the newspapers take up exorbitant amounts of space, and they are difficult to read and handle. Most back newspapers are found in microform areas, the next area to be discussed.

MICROFORMS

Microforms are an essential segment of nearly all library collections today and their importance is increasing rapidly. As libraries of all sizes and types run out of space, more of them are making heavy commitments to microforms as one way to stretch their available space. We pointed out in the last paragraph that the only rational way to house a newspaper collection of any size is on microfilm. Although newspapers are not easily read in this format, there is really no viable alternative. (But worse is to come!) More libraries are beginning to place significant portions of their periodical collections on microforms and this trend can only accelerate, given increases in binding costs and the number of titles available on microform, and worsening space problems everywhere.

Indeed, for many of the new libraries that have begun operations in the last few years, the microform edition of newspapers and periodicals has been the only edition obtainable. In addition, enterprising microform publishers are offering collections of related research materials that cover many areas of scholarly interest. Examples of these are Library of American Civilization, Human Relations Area Files, and Landmarks of Science. Many of the items in such collections are not available to most libraries in any other format and a sizable research collection can be acquired by purchasing a number of these collections. Although the lack of adequate bibliographic access causes problems to those using and servicing these materials, it is clear that their production and use will continue to increase. More and more libraries are making serious commitments of space, staff, and budget toward developing major microform collections in order to save space that will be needed to house library materials on paper.

In some libraries microform readers and materials are located in the periodicals area, whose staff services them. Other library departments with significant bodies of material in microform often have smaller subsidiary microform service areas. Many larger libraries have established separate microform departments with large numbers of reader stations (Penn State has about 60, for instance), housing for large microform collections, associated bibliographic materials, and staffed service areas. In those libraries where microforms are decentralized, the feeling is that material on a subject should remain together, whatever the format. On the other hand, libraries that have brought microforms together in one area feel that economical utilization of equipment and the availability of trained assistance in a microforms department outweigh the advantages of bringing together similar subject materials in differing formats. Whether physical facilities for microforms are decentralized or in one area, the rapid rate of collection growth must be accounted for when space allocations are made. Even optimistic estimates will probably be exceeded. Areas that can expand into neighboring space are preferable to closed rooms where expansion cannot easily take place.

Microform areas characteristically have a few shelves and perhaps an index table to hold the necessary bibliographic aids, a service desk, and a card catalog. However, the furnishings most characteristic of microform areas are the cabinets or shelves for storage of different microforms and the reader stations which house the readers used for viewing microforms.

Microformats

Microforms are available in several formats and all but the smallest collections will need a variety of readers and storage facilities. The most common format is roll film, with 35 mm being the most popular size and 16 mm increasing in popularity. The latter is often incorporated in reader systems using cartridges, and lends itself to automatic-retrieval systems. Another film type is the microfiche which consists of sheets of film in different sizes (generally 3 × 5 or 4 × 6 in. or 75 × 250 or 100 × 300 mm) and which contains 50 or more page images on each. Recent advances in technology permit use of very high reduction rates on fiche, which may contain as many as 3000 images per sheet. Techniques such as this offer great possibilities for really compact storage of some kinds of material. A third basic format of microform is the opaque card with photographic image from which light must be reflected for viewing. This type, called microcard or microprint, has the inherent weakness that light cannot be projected through it; therefore the image produced is not as bright as that projected directly through film. Still another format is the aperture card in which a single-page film image is located on a machine-sortable tab card. This has very few library applications. All these various types of microform utilize different readers though there are multi-purpose readers that will view roll film and fiche (with a fair amount of adjustment) and at least one that views both opaque and transparent sheets.

Storage

Roll film requires one kind of storage case or shelf, while sheet formats require a different kind. Roll film is sometimes stored on special shelving, either wood or metal. It promised good space utilization, but when it was tried at two different Penn State campuses, it proved less than satisfactory; it is hard to retrieve material from high or low shelves, the shelves are very expensive, and boxes of film are easily knocked off. Also, their storage density is not as great as that of some closed cabinets now available.

Steel cabinets with compartmented drawers have been the traditional storage for roll microfilm. Earlier models often had reservoirs for the addition of water so that humidity could be maintained. Modern libraries generally have humidity control adequate enough so that no additional moisture is needed. A variety of steel and some plastic cabinets are found. They should be evaluated for purchase on the basis of estimated durability and quality of workmanship, quality and smoothness of the drawer suspension, and amount of film boxes able to be stored per square foot of floor area. Price should be evaluated on the basis of dollars per film stored per cabinet. At this writing the most satisfactory cabinets are double-height units in which a cabinet with 5 vertical drawers sits on another cabinet with 11 horizontal drawers. Although tall, the top drawers can be reached by relatively short persons and the fully extending drawers mean that the cabinet's entire depth can be utilized. The top unit can be purchased separately and used atop any sturdy cabinet with horizontal drawers.

Microforms on flat sheets are generally filed in steel cabinets, although 3 × 5 in. (75 × 250 mm) fiche can easily be filed in small card catalogs or cabinets. Fiche are occasionally boxed and placed on shelves. The most universally satisfactory solution is probably steel cabinets. These are used in different sizes for many office and commercial applications, and are readily available and not expensive. It is essential to control access to fiche and cards by using lockable cabinets or placing them in closed areas, for they can easily get out of order when not retrieved and refiled carefully. When out of place, the sheets are essentially "lost" because their format makes it difficult to distinguish one from another. Much less a problem is roll microfilm which is not easily misplaced because of the size (4 × 4 × 1 in. or 100 × 100 × 25 mm) of the boxes.

Microform Reader Stations

Although microform readers have been used extensively in libraries for many years, along with reader stations of various kinds, there has been no real standardization of reader station configuration as there is for other library artifacts as card catalog cabinets and atlas cases. At this writing, only one manufacturer offers an "off-the-shelf" station and new libraries visited recently show a great diversity of designs. Several years ago Donald C. Holmes, with the aid of a Council on Library Resources grant, investigated this subject in some depth and published his conclusions in a volume entitled Determination of the Environmental Conditions Required in a Library for the Effective Utilization of Microforms (1970). In this report, he suggested an ideal reading carrel in which a platform within a carrel could raise, lower, tilt, or swivel, thereby permitting the user to change his position to provide muscle relief and to compensate for microform readers of different sizes and viewing-screen angles. There were also pull-out slides on either side of the viewing position so that either left- or right-handed users would have a proper writing surface as well as a Tensor lamp to light it. For several years planners at Penn State

FIG. 18 Custom-designed micro carrel by Library Bureau. New York University, New York City, New York. (Stanley Seligson Photo.)

FIG. 19 Attractive wood micro carrel with built-in reader and accompanying storage unit. (Carrel by LM & M. Storage cabinet by Sjostrom/Gunlocke.)

FIG. 20 Micro carrel at Penn State with writing tablet, carpeted walls and Tensor lamp.

worked with manufacturers to produce such a carrel but the technical difficulties in the platform mechanism made the carrel very expensive for general use. Library Bureau, Inc. has produced a modified version of the carrel for New York University and it seems to work well (Fig. 18).

A number of new libraries have custom-designed reader stations (Fig. 19) that attempt to make microform use easier. Penn State now uses a carrel (Fig. 20) that has a working surface large enough to house comfortably the largest reader, carpeted walls to absorb noise generated by reader motors and blowers, and a Tensor lamp. A tablet arm arrangement is supplied, either left- or right-hand, so that users can write comfortably while sitting close enough to the screen to read it satisfactorily. Since we were unable to provide the moveable platform mentioned earlier, it was hoped that the possibility of easy movement of the microfilm reader on the smooth work surface, as well as the use of a posture chair that the patron could adjust, would permit comfortable use of the microform readers. These reader stations have been well accepted and are heavily used. Other libraries have used tables, either individual or long. Carrels are preferable to tables because (a) ambient light and reflected glare are reduced; (b) sound reduction is possible; and (c) privacy is provided.

Environment

Areas where microform readers are to be housed should have means of controlling the level of ambient light and a number of power sources. Often it is desirable to gang together a number of carrels, each having a double convenience outlet so that a continuous power channel connects the group to a single power source. Although this arrangement is inflexible, the special power and light control requirements of microform areas generally dictate that they have dedicated space. Indeed, microform areas should be planned so that reader stations can be added in substantial numbers. As to the light level, the room should not be dark, for this provides too much contrast, but the light level should be substantially reduced, perhaps to 10 to 20 foot candles on table tops. Individual lights at each reader station will provide adequate light for the user who is reading or writing but will not cause the distracting glare that bright ceiling lights produce. The chair at the reader station should be lightweight and easily moved but comfortable. Well-suited for this purpose is a good-quality steno chair, which provides for easy change of position and is adjustable for users of different sizes.

Microreaders

Machines for microform use come in a great variety of shapes and sizes. The range of applications and the number of formats and sizes of microform available, along with the design considerations emphasized by different manufacturers, are responsible for this diversity. Attempts at standardization have not been conspicuously successful; indeed, at times the trend seems to be in the opposite direction. Moreover, the market for microforms and their readers is largely commercial and library applications represent a tiny part of the sales of those firms in this business. Thus, the available readers are tailored to what these firms believe to be the needs of business and industry and the needs of libraries are not considered to any great extent. The result, of course, is readers that are not designed for library users and their needs. Also, the readers most heavily used in libraries are still those utilizing 35 mm reel film, for the largest use of microforms made by most libraries is of newspapers and periodicals which are commonly available in this format. Industry and commerce make comparatively little use of roll film and new developments for these customers are mostly in other formats. Further, when business and industry, such as banks and manufacturers, utilize roll film, viewing is generally momentary and image quality is not so essential as it is in library applications where users must sometimes read film for hours at a time.

Many librarians feel that the MPE-1, last manufactured many years ago, has not been surpassed in performance since Recordak, Inc. stopped making it. When the neck strain involved in prolonged use of this machine is considered, the sad "state of the art" of roll film readers is apparent. Many of the roll film readers produced in the last few years seem to have such disadvantages in library use that many librarians considered them unsatisfactory. Just recently, however, new roll film readers seem to be somewhat better-suited for library needs by offering such features as turret lenses with several magnification ratios and better design for long-time use. Today's buyers may well find one or more models that meet their requirements.

Purchasers of readers for the format second most commonly used in libraries, the microfiche, will find the available machines more suitable to their purpose. Due to the considerable commercial sales of these machines, the technology is steadily improving and a number of good machines that lend themselves to library use are available. A remaining problem with the format is that magnification ratios vary from 18x to 150x Dual-range lens assemblies help here somewhat, but libraries with larger collections of fiche must have available a number of fiche readers with different ratios. This problem has been compounded recently with the availability and strong promotion of the ultramicrofiche which uses ratios up to 150x or more. While this system permits much greater economy in utilization of storage space than previous ratios, entirely new software and hardware are required and access is most difficult when hundreds of images are on a single fiche.

Evaluating microform readers for purchase is not easy, due to the relatively complicated technical problems involved and the fact that most of the firms in the business are primarily or entirely concerned with the nonlibrary market. Only the two or three largest firms in the business make much effort to sell to the library market and most librarians are unaware that hardware of considerable merit is available from other manufacturers. Several periodicals, such as Administrative Management, The Office, Information and Records Management, and Reproduction Review offer occasional articles surveying available microform products or listing new developments, as well as carrying advertising from many companies wanting to sell their microform hardware or peripherals.

However, for the best introduction to the industry and its products, a visit to the annual conference of the National Micrographics Association (NMA) is recommended. Here one can see displayed a comprehensive selection of microform readers and other hardware, some software and peripherals. Also displayed are a number of closed retrieval systems, some of which can have application in libraries. It is recommended that potential buyers take along samples of microfiche and roll film from their collection so that they can comparison-test them on different machines under somewhat controlled conditions.

As stated earlier, only a few of the firms in the microform business have names familiar to librarians. Those few are large firms who market aggressively and provide some degree of service for their products. Other smaller, lesser-known firms are often innovative and develop new machines and systems before they become available from the giants, but the mortality rate among such firms is high. Also, there are other large firms, whose products would be encountered at the NMA show, who are not familiar names to librarians, but whose products are well accepted by other buyers. Here is an example: the storage and reproduction of engineering and architectural drawings is essential to many firms. The originals of such documents are large and when they are reduced, they must be restorable to their original size and reproduced to the highest fidelity. To assure the quality, larger formats are often used, frequently 105 mm, in contrast to the 35 mm and 16 mm familiar to librarians, and these are mounted in aperture cards, which are actually tab cards with film inserts. Aperture cards can easily be sorted by machine and can be used for very large files of single drawings. The hardware for such systems is quite large and expensive but often provides superb quality for reading and reproduction. The firms manufacturing such hardware are generally unfamiliar to librarians although a few libraries have purchased these large expensive readers. Such machines are available to handle film of the sizes used in libraries, but again, they are very expensive and better suited for use in commercial applications rather than for seated library users.

Reader-Printers

Finally, we come to the subject of hard-copy reproduction of microforms. The development of machines to reproduce hard copy for library users remains a long way from perfection, in the view of this observer. Newer reader-printers utilizing so-called dry (electrostatic) processing can produce copy superior to that generated by older wet processes, and the dry process is certainly neater and easier to operate. However, this writer is still waiting for development of a microform-reader-printer that consistently produces high-quality copy at a reasonable price without requiring high volume and trained operators. A user should be able to sit in front of a motorized film reader, view a high-quality image of adequate size and, when coming to a needed page, insert a coin (receiving change if appropriate), press a button, and receive an excellent copy. This goal is close, but not yet achieved.

For more detailed information about microfiche hardware and software, Hawken's book, Evaluating Microfiche Readers, is very useful. Library Technology Reports evaluates hardware on occasion and these evaluations are helpful. The technology in this field changes fairly rapidly, so while the above books and reports are helpful, personal investigation will be required to get the best values in the most modern hardware.

THE INTERLIBRARY LOAN FUNCTION

The areas discussed in this chapter are those which Ellsworth and others call the "keys" areas; that is, those service areas that are located closest to the entrance/exit where the majority of library users will find the information they need or will be directed to other library areas where materials they need are located. Two other functions often take place in this "keys" area—interlibrary loan and the service and housing of reserve books.

The interlibrary loan function is often located within the reference department or the lending department, or both. The borrowing function in interlibrary loan involves requests by a library's clientele for materials that must be borrowed from other libraries. The primary elements of this process are bibliographic verification (pinpointing the exact material needed) and locating a library that has the desired item and is willing to lend it. Obviously much of this operation utilizes reference materials and techniques. On the other hand, the lending function in interlibrary loan utilizes techniques that are part of a library's circulation (lending) function, that is, verification of ownership and availability for loan, retrieval from the collection, and transmittal to the requesting library. Some libraries split the functions between reference and circulation departments; others, particularly larger libraries, establish an interlibrary loan division which performs both functions.

Such a division should be located in the "keys" area because of the need for constant access to the card catalog and bibliographic aids. The division will also generally be responsible for providing libraries requesting them, photocopies of both printed and microform material some of which will be found in the nearby periodicals and microforms areas. The area for interlibrary loan need not be large compared, for instance, to the area for reference, but there should be perhaps 150 sq ft of work area per staff member with adequate shelving for bibliographic aids and material in process. Records of past transactions are especially important here and the record keeping function, whatever the method used, should be carefully planned. One or more microform readers and whatever copy machines are necessary must be provided. Departments in larger libraries will generally acquire one or more computer terminals to gain bibliographic access to their own or other collections as such access systems become more common.

RESERVE COLLECTIONS AND SERVICE

Most academic libraries, as well as libraries of other types, maintain collections of reserve materials which are housed separately from the rest of the collection. In these collections are library materials which must be specially handled so that the maximum number of users may use them over a brief period of time. Such materials are generally loaned for very short periods—several hours, overnight, or for a day or two, and sometimes use is permitted only within the library.

To guarantee availability, reserve materials are often kept securely in closed-shelf areas. In smaller libraries they are often housed behind the lending desk and serviced by that department's personnel. Many larger libraries have separate reserve book rooms, in some cases with open shelves but with security at the exit point. The facilities used in these areas include seating, shelves for housing the collection (open or closed to users or both), and a circulation desk with some associated work space. Some academic libraries have arranged their library interiors so that reserve rooms can have separate outside entrances/exits and maintain longer hours of opening than the remainder of the library.

UNDERGRADUATE COLLECTIONS AND SERVICE

In recent years, many universities have established undergraduate libraries in separate buildings or in separate areas within large university library buildings. In their establishment is the assumption that the library and information needs of many undergraduate students, particularly those in the first two years, can be met more satisfactorily by carefully chosen smaller collections of materials and the appropriate reserve books. The use of nonprint material can be of particular value to these students and undergraduate libraries often make considerable use of nonprint hardware and software. The basic premise of such libraries is that many beginning college students are not experienced users of libraries and their introduction to library use will be more comfortable in an undergraduate library than in a large, necessarily complex research library. Implicit in this approach is a very active program of instruction in the use of the library.

Seating in undergraduate libraries is similar to that in other libraries but with a larger emphasis on informal or lounge areas. Separate group and individual study rooms are common. The nonprint media are frequently very heavily used in these libraries with many user stations available.

Wired listening and television systems are common. Classrooms and seminar rooms for instructional purposes are often available. The reserve collection and its service is, of course, an important element in any undergraduate library, although nearly all such libraries have also a basic collection of nonreserve library materials appropriate to the needs of undergraduates. These will vary in size from 20,000 to 200,000 volumes. Basic reference service and a collection of heavily used periodicals are often provided but these are only necessary if the undergraduate library is in a separate building. Recent increased emphasis on the instructional function in academic libraries would seem to bode well for the continued popularity of such libraries; however, in view of today's straitened budgets, many library administrators are beginning to raise serious questions about the cost-effectiveness of these libraries which duplicate existing collections and services.

4

HOUSING SERVICES AND STAFF IN OTHER AREAS

"KEYS" AND "NON-KEYS" AREAS

In the previous chapter we discussed service areas that are considered "keys" to the library, along with their associated staff or work areas. These service areas, as previously stated, are those where the needs of most patrons are served; they should be close to the library's entrance/exit so that the traffic flow of most readers is kept as short as possible. Also, since most of the library's public service staff is needed to service these areas, concentrating them will often result in better staff utilization. Finally, the interrelationships of these critical services are so important that their concentration in one area will make provision of superior service much easier.

There remain a number of service areas that, while not found in all libraries, are important elements in many libraries, or in some cases, only specialized libraries. These include lobby areas; public document areas; maps areas; fine arts, music, and other subject-division areas; special collections, rare books, local history, manuscripts, or archives areas; children's or young adult areas (mostly in public libraries); auditoriums and meeting facilities; and galleries and exhibit areas.

LOBBIES: THE LIBRARY'S INTRODUCTION

Nearly all libraries have lobbies of some sort, ranging from vestibules with single sign boards to the very large, monumental, multistorey lobbies characteristic of our older, large public and university libraries, and indeed, some of the newer ones (Fig. 1). While these grandiose building introductions are still occasionally built, modern library lobbies are generally simpler, smaller, and less rococo in keeping with today's architecture.

FIG. 1 Monumental lobby. New York University, New York, New York.

Today's planners generally feel that it is more important to welcome and orient users than it is to awe or impress them. Readers of this book, whether librarians or not, will almost certainly recall entering some large- or even medium-sized library and being appalled and confused by its complexity and lack of locational information. Unfortunately, once we become accustomed to our own libraries we lose sight of this problem and fail to see them through the eyes of the first-time visitor.

The lobby provides most libraries with an opportunity to welcome visitors into a pleasant atmosphere and to instruct them about the complexities of the building. A good architect should be able to produce the desired atmosphere of warmth and welcome with his design of spaces and use of color and textures. Artwork and decorative objects will also help to achieve this desired effect. Of even greater importance is the development of adequate locational information, which introduces the user to the building and its component parts. Libraries have tried to do this in a number of ways, including graphical presentation, three-dimensional models, or audiovisual presentations.

In visiting more than 200 libraries of all types and sizes during the past 15 to 20 years, less than a score of the libraries the author has seen have had first-class locational information in the lobby. The most successful approaches have used two-dimensional graphical presentations, which basically are improved versions of architectural plans with high-quality lettering, color coding, and plenty of white space. At Penn State such a locational display is used, which is based on a similar display devised for the Carnegie Library in Pittsburgh. In this presentation a white plastic sheet hung vertically in a glass case shows plans of each library floor with red lights (actually light-emitting diodes) in each public area. Below and in front of this sheet is a control panel for the display, set on a wood table resembling a dictionary stand. The control panel has numbered push buttons which correspond to the lights in the public areas on the floor plans. An alphabetic list of public areas on the control panel next to the push button indicates which numbered button to push to activate the light in the corresponding service area. Also on the display panel are (a) an exploded three-dimensional view of the library to explain further spatial relationships in a complex building and (b) a map of the university campus with red lights for the main library and branch libraries which can also be activated by the numbered buttons. Such a presentation would not be suitable everywhere and can be expensive, but the importance of providing a good graphical introduction to the library and its components and services justifies almost any reasonable investment.

Lobbies also may contain exit-control points, exhibit facilities, building directories, some seating or "meet-your-friends" space, entrances to public toilets, bulletin boards, public lockers, coat rooms, and information desks. Seating in lobbies should be the sort that is comfortable for only short periods of time, as when waiting to meet someone, and should be of very durable material and construction (i.e., wood benches). Often found in lobbies are very hard floors, which are chosen because they wear well in this heavily trafficked area, as well as for aesthetic reasons. Marble, stone, brick, terrazzo, concrete and tile are examples of the materials used. Use of some of these materials results in some amount of noise but since this space must always be acoustically separated from the remainder of the library, some noise is acceptable. Others feel that carpet should be used in lobby areas to add warmth and color to the space as well as for reducing noise. If carpet is used, it should be very durable and easily cleaned. The installation should be planned for easy replacement of carpet in traffic lanes. As in all purchases of carpet for library installations, a quantity of extra carpet, probably five percent of the total bought (in each color, fabric, pattern, etc.), should be purchased at the time of the original carpet contract so that replacements and repairs can be made with identical carpet from the same dye lot. More discussion on carpets and floors will follow in Chapter 9.

Incidentally, all wall surfaces and furniture used in the lobby should be of very durable material because of the heavy use they receive.

Directories

Building directories and space for posting notices will often be found in lobbies. Although a good graphic locational display, as described earlier, is essential for assisting persons to find their way around the building, a building directory kept up to date is a valuable supplement and is the most effective way of directing users to library staff by name. To display official notices of library-related events or to allow students or community groups to display notices and messages, many libraries provide either closed or open bulletin board space or notice boards in lobby areas. Some libraries provide what amounts to a forum space in their lobbies where a sizeable pinup surface is made available to students and others in the community, and student gathering is encouraged here or at nearby seating. The result will not be pleasing aesthetically, but many feel that the value of attracting student interest to the area outweighs this problem. Other libraries provide a notice-posting space which they control by limiting notice size or duration of posting or even by locating notices behind a glass door.

Other Lobby Facilities

Public toilets must always be provided even though they are frequently problem causers. In libraries of any size, the law requires that they be provided on each floor. However, since the largest number of building occupants will usually be found on the principal floor near the keys areas, the largest rest-room facilities can be located in the lobby. To discourage loitering, rest rooms should be no larger than necessary and materials used for them should be hard, smooth and impervious to damage and grafitti.

Lockers and coat rooms are occasionally provided in library lobbies. Lockers provide space for patrons to deposit personal effects they do not wish to carry into the library. Coat rooms, attended or unattended, are occasionally provided so that patrons need not carry wraps with them; in fact, a few libraries mandate their use so that patrons intending to steal library materials will have fewer garments under which to hide them. Unmanned coat rooms are security and maintenance problems and therefore many patrons are reluctant to use them. Manned coat rooms, however, are expensive to operate and difficult to justify unless funds are almost unlimited.

A few large libraries operate an information desk in the lobby where locational information is provided by trained personnel. This is not defensible except in the largest libraries and a good graphic locater display is much less expensive and provides more consistent information. When such a desk is provided, patrons will often also want answers to reference questions and, of course, this is not possible in such a situation.

DOCUMENT COLLECTIONS AND SERVICE

The public document area is an important element of most large libraries, both academic and public, and should be located as close as possible to the reference department. Nearly any large library will be a depository library for United States government publications, and therefore will receive a substantial portion of its document output. Such a library will also have available many United Nations, state, and other governmental and quasi-governmental agency publications. While the collections of documents in depository libraries are of much the same size, the service areas will vary greatly, depending on whether the collection's use is encouraged and skilled interpreters of the collection are on hand. Very active document departments in large libraries may need staff space for 8 or 10 persons and seating space for as many as 50. Other libraries with less active use will need much less space and staff. Indeed, some libraries service documents through the reference department, though a person would have to be an absolute paragon to be a competent reference librarian and have a thorough working knowledge of the complexities of documents. There is, however, a considerable value in having some staff interchange between the documents and reference departments, in the view of some librarians. The common use of bibliographic tools by staffs of both reference and documents departments also argues strongly for a close physical relationship.

The physical appearance of a public document division will not differ greatly from that of a reference department except in comparative size. Document divisions generally have a service desk with nearby shelves and index tables for heavily used tools, seating at tables and carrels, and sizable shelf space, both in the immediate area and in nearby stack space, as well as sufficient work and office space for the staff and the considerable body of material in process. Steel-bracket-type shelving with dividers is particularly appropriate for this collection with its high proportion of thin pamphlet-type materials. In the last few years, many document series (e.g., ERIC) have begun coming in microform and at some institutions it has been necessary to set up a satellite microforms area in the documents department so that these series may be stored and serviced by this trained staff.

MAPS COLLECTIONS AND SERVICE

Some large libraries have comprehensive and spacious maps divisions and nearly all libraries have at least a few maps and atlases. The only practical way to store any quantity of maps so that they remain flat and useable is in flat cases large enough so that large maps can be stored unfolded (Fig. 2). These cases, available from many manufacturers, are commonly 4 or 5 drawers high and measure approximately 48 × 28 in. (1200 × 700 mm), a

FIG. 2 Map cases. The top of five-drawer units stacked two-high is a good height for using maps.

size that will accommodate nearly all commonly issued maps. When these cases are stacked two high, the top remains at a good height for standing users to use maps. In large collections, these cases are placed back to back with wide aisles between them. So that excessive floor space is not utilized, many collections will intersperse cabinets piled two high with others piled three high, thus providing occasional work surfaces without sacrificing effective floor utilization too greatly. Some libraries have had to pile all map cabinets three and four high because of space shortages, using conventional library tables for reference. This is never satisfactory because the top drawers in a four-high arrangement are very difficult to see into when retrieving or returning maps.

These cabinets along with large tables, chairs, and necessary shelving for atlases and other geographical material are the primary furnishings for map divisions. At least one light table is almost a necessity as are one or more lighted image-enlargers, such as Gaylord's Master Lens. Small collections will have one or more atlas cases with roller shelves for easy storage and a sloped top with lip for easy reference to the most heavily used atlas volumes. Map collections of any size require some shelving for

FIG. 3 Flat shelves, 18 in. deep with inverted brackets, are useful for storing very large atlases.

the large-sized volumes that are part of such collections. Smaller atlases will require shelving at least 12 in. (300 mm) deep while some flat newspaper shelving 16 to 18 in. (400 to 450 mm) deep with inverted brackets will be required for some of the largest volumes. When the latter is used double-faced, very large volumes up to 36 in. (900 mm) high can be shelved, lying on their sides from one face to the other (Fig. 3).

Maps make very attractive displays and some display space on walls or display panels will be well utilized. Wall-hung bookstyle display panels like those used in art galleries can be used effectively to display large maps that are of general interest but should not be freely handled.

A service desk and some office and work space will be needed in a map division of any size. It is not possible to integrate maps into the library's classification scheme, and their format requires a separate area. Thus it is essential that only specially trained staff be responsible for processing and public service of maps. The space used for processing will differ little from other processing areas except in the requirements for very large work-

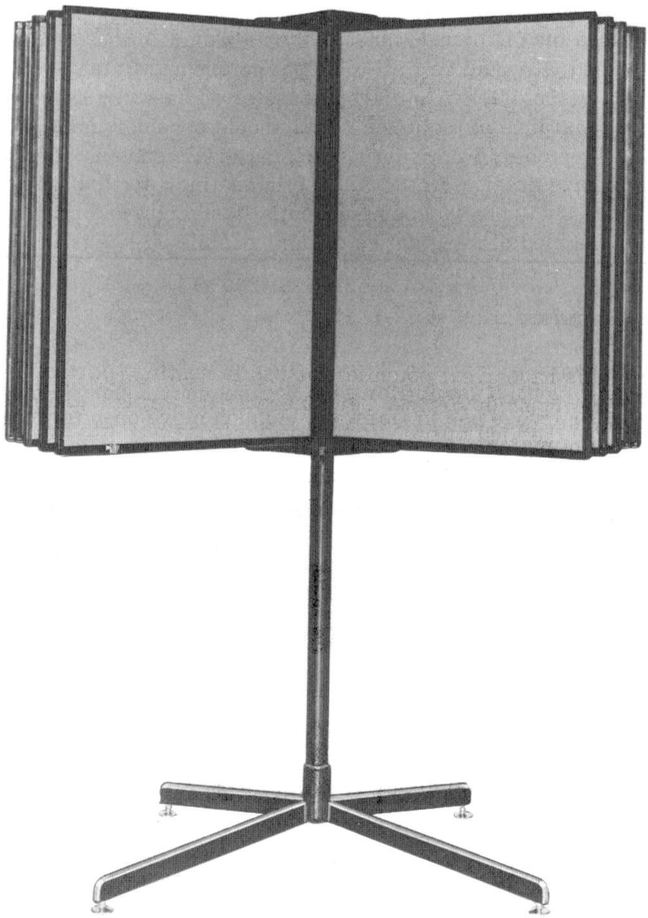

FIG. 4 These book-style display panels, free-standing or wall-mounted are useful in some libraries. (Multiplex Display Fixture Company, Fenton, Missouri.)

ing surfaces. This work area need not necessarily be physically separated from the maps service area if space is at a premium, for maps divisions are almost never crowded with users. This in no way denegrates the importance of maps but simply recognizes that the space demands of a sizable maps collection are extraordinary and use of some of this space for both service and processing will make these large demands easier to justify.

SUBJECT OR DIVISIONAL LIBRARIES

Most large libraries, both public and academic, have one or more rooms, areas, or separate buildings where are housed the collections and services appropriatc to distinct subject fields. Among the most common are music and art divisions, literature, history and social science areas, and business and science divisions. The composition and organization of these differ greatly; the discussion of this entire question would require a volume by itself and is not the province of this book. Briefly, however, these divisions generally will be miniature versions of the central library with separate collections, service areas, seating space, offices, and work space for processing.

For most of these subject collections, the furniture is similar to that already discussed for reading areas, work and staff areas, periodicals areas, and other functional areas. In any of these, there may be occasional specialized items of furniture and equipment for particular service or collection situations, i.e., Penn State's Life Sciences Library has a special large flat file for its collection of Audubon prints. Nonetheless, though there will be great differences in philosophy and concepts of service and in methods of operation among these branches and subject divisions, the actual furniture items and equipment will generally be similar to those used in the central library spaces already mentioned (Fig. 5). There are, however, two kinds of subject libraries that are conspicuous exceptions to the previous statement: music and art libraries are quite common both in academic and public libraries, and their furnishings and equipment are noticeably different from those in other libraries because of the special kinds of aural and visual material that form an essential part of these disciplines.

Music Libraries

Music libraries store and service several kinds of material that are not common to other libraries. These include musical scores, sheet music, phonorecords, and audio tapes and cassettes. These materials may occupy as much space as the music library's book collection, but all will require special kinds of storage space, and the phonorecords, tapes, and cassettes

FIG. 5 Smaller card catalog units will be found in service and staff areas of subject divisions throughout the library.

require special performance equipment so that they may be used. In addition, all of these special materials are expensive, desirable, easily damaged, and in most cases, quite portable; thus they present special security and control problems. Most music libraries operate their own lending systems for much of this material and in a great many cases, this special material is kept in locked-off areas or in special lockable cabinets.

Music scores and sheet music are often larger than most books and, if shelved, require shelves of 12 in. (300 mm) depth. Because scores are often thin and paperbound, divider shelves are a good way to store them. Sheet music is housed in pamphlet boxes on shelves or in file cabinets. Phonorecords, tapes, and cassettes are stored in a variety of specially designed shelves and cabinets, about which there will be more dicussion in Chapter 6. This same chapter on nonprint materials also discusses at some length the players used for these media.

Few music libraries today provide special listening rooms or booths. The use of earphones and cassette players have made it possible for listening to take place anywhere within a music library rather than at fixed locations. It is desirable, however, to have at least one seminar room or small classroom where group listening can take place and where small classes or groups can meet occasionally. The room should be equipped with a high-quality sound system with output from a "Dolby-ized" cassette player, turntable, reel-to-reel tape player, and AM/FM tuner. It should also have a chalkboard, projection equipment and screen, tablet armchairs and, often, a good upright piano.

When phonorecords and reel-to-reel tape are used in music libraries, players mounted in tables, carrels, or attended service through wired systems are generally the methods employed. Such table-mounted players are often abused and their maintenance is a constant problem and expense. Wired systems are very expensive to purchase and operate. But many libraries are avoiding these problems and costs by utilizing cassette players. The fidelity of Dolby-ized cassette players is so satisfactory that very high-quality reproduction is routine and the ease of dubbing from phonorecords or reel-to-reel tapes makes any recording available on cassettes in high-quality reproductions. Cassettes and cassette players can be kept under tight control behind lending desks so that users of hardware and software are identifiable and equipment or cassette damage is nearly eliminated.

Art Libraries

Art libraries have housing problems similar to those of music libraries; that is, a sizable portion of their collections are not in printed books and must be housed in special storage units of several kinds. Furthermore, many of the books that are in the collection are much larger than normal and require 12-in.- (300 mm) deep shelving for much of the collection and special shelving for even larger volumes. Divider shelving 12 in. (300 mm) deep will provide the best housing for the majority of the collection and inverted-bracket flat folio shelving will accommodate the largest volumes, shelved flat on their sides. Art libraries must also have storage capabilities for reproductions of works of art in the form of slides, both 2 × 2 in. (50 × 50 mm) and larger, roll film, and large prints if an institution has a significant art program. The faculty in art departments must have available a comprehensive collection of art reproductions in different forms. While it may be necessary or appropriate to maintain small collections of such material in the department or in classrooms, the comprehensive permanent collection of art reproductions should be in the library where it can be properly maintained and controlled. The library's longer hours of operation mean that these reproductions are available to those needing them at almost any time.

Closed storage facilities are needed for all art reproductions, whether slides, other films, or prints. A variety of slide cabinets, of different types are available; of particular interest are systems that provide for storage and easy review of slides. With such systems, slides can be backlit for easy identification and review. The AV Equipment Directory, published annually, provides up-to-date information about available slide files and systems. Prints are frequently stored flat in map cases although some libraries use custom-designed cases in which prints are hung or stored vertically. It would appear that map cases would be less likely to damage prints and they are certainly relatively inexpensive.

Art libraries should have at least one seminar or small classroom where classes or other groups can view slides, films, and other visual media. This room should be equipped with tablet armchairs (preferably those with folding tablet arms), a pull-down screen, chalkboard, and movable projector stand. The room light should be dimmable and windows should be covered by lightfast, sound-muffling draperies on tracks so that they can be opened or closed. An easel or two will be welcome for showing graphic works.

Many art libraries will find it helpful to have available a few carrels, with rear-mounted screens and power available, in which users can operate slide projectors and other small projection equipment. Art libraries will need to have available slide projectors for both 2 × 2 (50 × 50 mm) and large-format slides, film strip projectors, and opaque projectors, along with appropriate screens, projection stands, and cabinets in which to store them. Information about selection, evaluation, and purchase of this equipment is found in Chapter 6 on nonprint media.

Art librarians will need to be certain that equipment is kept secure. All of it is expensive, desirable, and portable, so it should be kept in locked cabinets and/or locked rooms with closely controlled keys. The maintenance of this equipment is critical to its continued satisfactory operation. Skilled service must be readily available or even the best equipment will prove less than satisfactory. When considering the products of various

FIG. 6 Specially designed exhibit cases for the Madison Building, Library of Congress, Washington, D.C.

vendors for possible purchase, the first consideration must be the proximity of trained service personnel. Also, when evaluating competing audiovisual equipment for purchase, consider the total cost of each product; that is, not only the initial price, but also the cost of maintenance and repair, along with the cost of operation. If slide projector "A" costs $20 less than projector "B," both being of the same quality and having similar features, but projector "A" charges $10 more annually for a maintenance agreement or must charge $10 more for each service call because of the greater distance a service man must travel, projector "A" is no bargain.

Art libraries will make particularly good use of exhibit and display space and exhibit cases; both vertical (Fig. 6) and horizontal should be available, as should be modular exhibit panels for two-dimensional display and bases for three-dimensional display.

There are a number of other special articles of furniture and equipment that art libraries employ usefully. They include dry-mounting kits to mount prints for hanging; light tables, which assist in examining slides; and slide previewers to enlarge and light slides for easy identification and evaluation.

OTHER SPECIAL COLLECTIONS AND SERVICE AREAS

The next library service/staff areas we consider bear some resemblance to the aforementioned subject areas, but are separated from the remainder of the library because of their material format, need for special security protection, or unusual service patterns. These areas—rare books areas, local history areas, and manuscripts and archives areas—bear a close resemblance to each other in facilities requirements, patterns of service, and the need for special security, so we treat them here in one section. Indeed, in many libraries they are combined in one or two areas.

These areas are likely to receive less patron traffic than other portions of the library, so they can reasonably be located far from the keys areas in more remote sections of the library. On the other hand, some feel that because of prestige and interest to alumni, potential donors, and others, these areas should be located in a prominent place near the building entrance. In many instances they will benefit from some common staffing, and administrative relationships are often found when one or more of the areas are not actually combined.

Rare books areas are repositories for all kinds of rare, expensive, and highly desirable print material that needs to be stored with special security precautions. Local history areas are relatively common in both academic and public libraries. Here are found local and institutional history in books and memorabilia, works of local authors, and often some archival material. Manuscript collections are found primarily in larger academic libraries, occasionally as separate facilities, but often are included in rare books areas. Archives, which are collections of official records, are occasionally kept in college or university libraries. This is not generally a good solution, for archives management is not the same as library management and archives often get short shrift from librarians.

RARE BOOKS LIBRARIES

Rare books facilities of some kind are found in nearly all academic libraries of any size and in larger public libraries. The unique research value of such materials, along with their aesthetic appeal, help to justify their high cost and the cost of providing expensive facilities and service for them. While the traffic generated within the library to this area is minimal, its

FIG. 7 Glass doors on shelves protect books while keeping them visible.

value for good public relations and encouragement of new gifts from donors is considerable. The rare books area will generally be the most sumptuously furnished area in the library.

Generally the rare books area is in a reasonably remote section of the library where casual traffic is at a minimum. Since security is so essential here, the rare books area is generally self-contained with its own service point, stack area, work room, and other staff quarters, which make up a suite with one easily controllable public entrance. Often patrons must use a bell push to gain entrance. Generally the reading room has no accessible books and required materials are brought to the reader at a table on request. Often an attendant is in the reading room at all times to oversee use of these rare materials. Frequently, the reading area has wood book shelves behind locked glass doors where some of the rare material is displayed (Fig. 7). Often there are display cases in the reading area or nearby where topical exhibits of this area's materials may be displayed.

Some rare books libraries have other facilities for readers, such as individual studies that may be assigned to readers pursuing continuing research projects and special reading rooms dedicated to the works or research of a single author or memorabilia of a single donor. Emory

University has quite a large reading room containing many of the effects of Robert Woodruff (of Coca Cola fame). Penn State has a restoration of John O'Hara's study, complete with the original furnishings, to accompany its collection of his manuscripts and papers. Occasionally, special collections within the rare books area will have rooms to themselves, sometimes with special funding for their continuing operation.

There should be a staffed service desk either in the rare books reading room or just adjacent to it, perhaps separated by a glass wall. A view of the entrance from this desk is almost essential. This kind of arrangement permits the staff member at the desk to see who is leaving or wishes to use the area, to watch the actions of users of rare material, and at the same time, to type or answer telephone inquiries without disturbing users in the reading room. If entrance to or exit from the area is controlled remotely, this is the appropriate place for the control mechanism.

The work area and staff offices in the rare books area will not differ much from those in technical processing. Extra care should be taken with lighting the area, for many of the materials to be used will be hard to read. One or more microform readers may be needed here because some rare materials and bibliographic sources are available on film. One or more very large tables for sorting will be useful, particularly if manuscripts and archival material are included in the collection.

The stacks area for rare books will employ regulation bracket-type steel shelving for the most part. If manuscripts and archival material are included in the area, some shelving of 12 in. (300 mm) depth will be required. Standard archival containers fit satisfactorily on these shelves. If relatively slender materials are to be shelved upright, divider shelves will be useful. A large amount of filing space in vertical or lateral files will be helpful in storing some kinds of local history or archival material. One or more map cases will be helpful for flat housing of very large material.

Because of the rarity, value, and impossibility of replacing the material housed in rare books areas, optimum environmental conditions are particularly important. Variations in temperature and humidity and the presence of unfiltered daylight are particularly destructive to book papers. An air-conditioning system that dependably controls temperature and humidity is essential; this is not particularly easy to achieve. In visiting more than 200 new libraries in recent years, the writer has heard more complaints about unsatisfactory heating, ventilating, and air-conditioning systems than any other single aspect of library system performance.

One way to increase the chances of having a dependable air supply of proper temperature and humidity is to get for the rare books area a system that has a conditioned air supply that is separate from the one serving the remainder of the building. The distribution system can then be arranged so that the air supply from the building's main system can be redirected into the rare books distribution system if the latter system's production of conditioned air breaks down. Conditioned air should be filtered to remove grit and dust that harms books. Unfiltered sunlight produces ultraviolet rays that can have a very destructive effect on book paper. To counteract this, glass that filters these rays is necessary for rare materials sections. If windows without filtration are already present, there is more than one transparent chemical film available that can be added to block out significantly these deleterious rays.

Since the materials in these rooms have special value, provisions for special treatment are essential. In view of the fact that some rare and archival records arrive at the library infested with pests, a small fumigator may be helpful. A walk-in safe should be available for the most valuable and irreplaceable items. Finally, fire protection is particularly important here. Sprinklers can be accepted only very reluctantly in other parts of the library, but in this area, their use is out of the question. Fire protection utilizing halon gas, too expensive for an entire library building, should be seriously considered for rare books complexes. The gas assures extinguishment of fires without endangering the lives or health of persons in the area where it is released.

CHILDREN'S LIBRARIES

Children's rooms or boys' and girls' rooms are found in nearly all public libraries and are considered essential in promoting lifelong habits of reading and library patronage. Academic libraries almost never have them although the University of New Hampshire operates a beautiful children's library as part of its added responsibility to provide public library service to Durham, New Hampshire. Some state colleges or state colleges turned universities operate laboratory schools and have children's rooms.

These rooms are essentially reading rooms with book shelving, service desks, and perhaps small adjoining work rooms. The reader accommodations are scaled down in size for the comfortable use of the area's clientele, and the seating is generally bright colored, often upholstered, and frequently informal in style (Fig. 8). Tables, either flat or sloped-top, are the usual reading surfaces. Sloped-top tables are particularly welcome here for many children's books are large picture books and difficult for children to hold while reading. In children's rooms of any size it is well to provide tables at both 25- and $27\frac{1}{2}$-in. (625- and 688-mm) height to accommodate both young and older children. Card catalogs and dictionary stands of proper height for children's use are available from library suppliers.

The service desk should be a conventional 29-in. (725 mm) high desk with charging desk inserts if circulation is taken care of here, rather than a stand-up circulation desk 39 in. (975 mm) high. Small children find a high lending desk intimidating. For children's libraries with heavy circulation loads, modular charging desks 32 in. (800 mm) high are available. Adults

FIG. 8 Informal seating in children's room. ("Bubble" chair by Stendig.)

can work behind them comfortably and children will find them much less formidable than with the higher desk. A children's library busy enough to need a large lending desk should have a separate desk for a professional providing reader advisory service. Although the professional will be on his or her feet most of the time, the desk provides a reference point for both librarian and children.

Wood shelving is preferred for children's libraries, though steel is occasionally used. Medium-height shelving (approximately 60 in. or 1500 mm high) with four adjustable shelves and a base shelf is the highest shelving that is acceptable and counter-height shelving with two shelves and a base shelf (approximately 42 in. or 1050 mm high) is preferred for some purposes. Some shelves 12 in. (300 mm) deep should be provided on counter-height shelves for the large picture books used by younger children. New book racks and display racks are commonly used in children's libraries to highlight special groups of books for a variety of purposes.

FIG. 9 Children are happy on the floor if it is carpeted. Kansas City Public Library, Kansas City, Missouri.

Children's libraries are so important an element in most public libraries that a special effort must be made to provide a truly exceptional environment for these young readers. All floors must be carpeted and some libraries will add area rugs for added accents and to create sit-down areas for group activities (Fig. 9). Carpet on walls or other soft covering will assist greatly in absorbing much of the noise generated by this area's users. Low soft seating and oversize cushions will be used enthusiastically. Several spaces where groups can assemble for storytelling sessions, watching films, or working together on projects will be welcome. At least one space should be a detached separate room; the others can be open areas between shelves or in corner spaces.

Nonprint materials, once pretty much confined to schools, are now finding their way into children's rooms in public libraries. "Wet" carrels are probably not appropriate for children's rooms, but cassette players built into tops of individual study tables may become stock additions to children's rooms. In any case, AV materials will probably be much more a part of children's libraries in the future.

MEETING FACILITIES

Meeting rooms and auditoriums are often provided in public and college/university libraries. Nearly all public libraries and some academic libraries need an auditorium that provides space for library-sponsored programs of all sorts or that can be available to community or academic groups for their programs. Lectures, public meetings, concerts, film showings, public affairs forums, and theatrical presentations are among the kinds of events that take place in such facilities. It will be a rare library that can afford to provide the needed space or equip a sloped-floor auditorium with proscenium stage, fly space, and full backstage facilities. Such a facility is probably available near most libraries and need not be duplicated. An auditorium with a flat floor and raised, curtained stage at one end without permanent seats will provide a useful, multipurpose facility. Stacking chairs will provide functional, flexible seating that can be arranged in different patterns or may be used in other parts of the library as needed. These can be stored compactly when not in use. There should be an enclosed projection booth and electrically operated projection screen. The auditorium should be wired for audiovisual use with at least one TV monitor, jacks to connect a podium or control desk with the projection booth, and a high-quality public address system with adequate speakers. Some stage lighting will be useful for speakers, performers, and simple theater productions. A separate outside entrance to the auditorium is necessary.

Smaller meeting rooms where 5 to 30 people can meet in committees, small classes, and other group meetings are needed in both public and academic libraries. They can be of any size from 150 to 600 sq ft; the first will seat about 6 or 8 comfortably while the larger will seat about 40 in row seating. A room of about 350 sq ft will seat 15 or 20 at tables, a good way to furnish such a room. If small folding tables 3 × 5 ft (900 × 1500 mm) are used, they can be arranged in many different ways, depending on the situation. A pull-down projection screen and a chalkboard-tackboard combination will be useful in this room.

NONPUBLIC AREAS

In this chapter we have discussed public service areas and their accompanying staff spaces in libraries of all types. There remain several staff areas less directly related to public service areas that should be discussed here. Among them are administrative areas, receiving/mailrooms, staff lounges, copying facilities and computer/data-processing areas.

Administrative Areas

Administrative areas provide office and work space for the chief operating officers of the library and others who have library-wide responsibilities contrasted to those staffers whose responsibilities relate to limited areas within the library. In the largest libraries there may be a principal administrative area with one or more subsidiary locations where administrative staff other than chief operating officers may be housed. In the smaller libraries a single office for the head librarian with an anteroom for a secretary will suffice, though there are libraries where not even this type of space is available and the head librarian must make do with a desk in a general staff office or in the library's public area. Of course, such arrangements make it impossible for an administrator to function effectively.

The administrative area can often be located in the more remote reaches of the building, since the number of patrons who need access to it are small. On the other hand, in smaller libraries where the chief librarian needs to "keep an eye on things" or may even man a service desk, the administrative area must be close to the center of operations.

The administrative area should provide offices for the administrators who need them, a conference room seating as many as 20 people, a secretarial/clerical area and, hopefully, a separate room where production-type tasks such as duplicating, collating, and mail preparation can take place. Smaller libraries will often manage nicely with an anteroom for one or more clerical staff members and a librarian's office large enough to house a table suitable for small conferences. Larger libraries with several clerical personnel often station one clerk near the entrance to the administrative area to act as receptionist and often as telephone operator. Nearby should be two or more comfortable side chairs where visitors can sit while awaiting appointments. The clerical area will contain at work stations other secretarial/clerical staff along with their files.

This area should be bright, neat and attractive with noisy and dirty activities relegated elsewhere. The attitude toward the library of many library users will be influenced by the appearance of the administrative area and the attitude of the staff manning it. The furniture should be of good quality and the atmosphere of the area should be warm, colorful, and welcoming. These things promote staff satisfaction, which is further communicated to visitors.

Administrative offices should be attractive, well-furnished, and sufficiently large—at least 250 sq ft for the chief librarian and at least 150 sq ft for other administrators. In too many instances, librarians feel defensive or insecure about their jobs and this is reflected in their requesting offices that are too modest in size. On the other hand, a few offices are much too large. Some chief librarians will want a small conference capability in their office along with a larger conference room in the administrative area. Most chief librarian's offices will have a wood desk, perhaps with either a return or separate credenza for additional work or "stacking" space, an upholstered desk chair, with two or more side chairs set at right angles to the librarian's seated position. Many library directors will add an informal seating group for conversation or casual meetings. Care should be taken to see that the appointments of this office are attractive, durable, and of good quality without being pretentious or overly expensive looking.

Receiving/Mail Areas

Receiving/mail rooms provide space for functions that are essential to any library's operation. Libraries of any size will need a space at least 250 sq ft adjacent to a loading dock where trucks of various sizes can load or unload shipments of equipment and supplies or library materials. The loading dock should be covered for weather protection and have a lift platform to provide for unloading of trucks with beds of differing heights.

A bell push should be located outside double doors connecting the dock to the receiving room. It is desirable to have an elevator connection between the receiving area and the technical processing areas so that library materials being brought in or taken out of the library have as short a path as possible and do not traverse public areas.

Reception and sorting of incoming mail, both letters and parcels, as well as wrapping or preparation of outgoing mail, will take place in this area. Mail-sorting racks and a mail-distribution truck will be useful for these tasks. Dollies and hand trucks will be needed for handling large packages or items of furniture or equipment. Shelves, preferably of the storage type 12 in. (300 mm) or more deep, should be placed around the perimeter of the room to hold incoming collections and inactive items. A separate small room or cabinets may be located here to store supplies securely. Some libraries will use this area to house duplicating equipment, sign-making equipment, and other noisy or dirt-producing operations. One large table should have wrapping and strapping equipment to help prepare packages for shipping.

Staff Lounges

Staff lounges are found in nearly all libraries of any size. Important for staff morale, they serve as places where staff can go during breaks or to have meals without leaving the library. They also provide a useful place for social functions and, when necessary, meetings. A few academic libraries enlarge these and call them faculty/staff lounges on the theory that improved social contact between library staff and teaching faculty will be mutually beneficial. Usually provided is a kitchenette or small unit kitchen which includes a refrigerator for storing bag lunches. Vending machines are often provided in staff lounges of larger libraries. Both casual seating or lounge furniture and table seating will be welcome. This room may be located almost anywhere in the library; certainly it need not be the center of activity, for staff using it generally want to get far away from their work stations while they are using it. Toilet rooms for staff use are often located in this area. Obviously the staff room should be bright and comfortable, with attractive furniture of good quality. Since use is light, furniture of less than institutional quality can be used here, inasmuch as durability is not usually a problem.

Photocopy Services

Copy facilities are important features in nearly all libraries today. The recent trend has been toward self-service copy service with coin-operated machines located in more than one part of the library. Many large libraries have both coin-operated self-service copiers and a copy center where staff will provide copies of material for patrons who bring material to be copied or where mail and phone requests for copies can be filled. Often in academic libraries, the copy center must provide copy service for academic departments and others for whom self-service copies would not be feasible. Copy centers often provide copies from microforms as well as from print material.

A copy center should be fairly close to the library's center of activity for it will receive considerable traffic. It will need, besides the necessary copiers, a counter where the public is met, shelves to hold materials to be copied, a desk or two, and at least one large table for sorting and collating copies. One or more cupboards for supplies, and a typewriter and adding machine for billing will be needed. The area must be air-conditioned because the considerable amount of heat generated by the machines makes the room unpleasantly warm for the staff and has a deleterious effect on copy paper and supplies.

Self-Service Copying

Self-service copy machines are purchased outright in some cases and operated by libraries. Other libraries have made arrangements with outside vendors who bring in machines, place them in operation where the library requests, keep them stocked with paper and other supplies, maintain them, read their meters, collect coins, and pay royalties to the library. This latter kind of arrangement usually is possible only in very large libraries where the volume of self-service copying is large enough to warrant it. Some smaller libraries may find a vendor willing to provide service for the library at a minimal rental which may be covered, or nearly so, by copy income.

Selection of copiers is not an easy matter. The "hard sell" generally prevails in this industry and those selling the machines often seem more interested in "knocking" the competition and promoting the gimmicks of their own machine than in providing real information to assist in their evaluation. A visit to an office machine convention of the kind held regionally throughout the nation will provide an opportunity to comparison-shop. Other libraries will have been through the evaluation process and can share their experiences. Hawken's book, Photocopying from Bound Volumes (with supplements) is most helpful in carrying out an evaluation. Library Technology Reports provides occasional testing and evaluation of copiers. One additional word—frequently small libraries with low-volume copier use, particularly in the realm of microform reader-printers, have chronic problems with their machines because, with low-volume use, supplies get stale before they are used and maintenance is not adequate. Libraries with low-volume operations should buy supplies in small quantities, even if they cost more per page; better that than bad copies.

Computer Terminals and Facilities

Finally, more and more libraries are acquiring systems utilizing computers and data-processing centers. This subject is much too complex to discuss here. Still, a few words based on some experience may be helpful. If only terminals are acquired, most of them will work almost anywhere, particularly if the building is air-conditioned. If it can be assured that locations are reasonably permanent, data transmission lines to the terminal should be "hard wired"; that is, permanent wires are installed between terminal and computer. Otherwise, telephone transmission lines (there is a monthly charge for their use) should be used when flexibility is necessary in order to accommodate the shifting of terminals from one location to another.

Computer environments will be specified by the manufacturer of the equipment. However, a raised floor and a separate, very high-capacity air-conditioning system are essential for any area housing computers. Distribution of conditioned air through the raised floor, using it as a plenum, seems to be the preferred method at the time of this writing. Incidentally, hard experience tells that having the manufacturer's systems maintenance and installation manuals available for study as early as possible can save service headaches later.

Library selection of computer systems is beyond the scope of this book. A few points, however are in order. First, keep it simple. Buy "off the shelf" rather than custom-designed computers. The mortality rate in the industry is high and the firm from which a special system is bought one year may be nonexistent the next. Cost estimates must frequently be regarded as fictional, and getting the whole truth about anything in this industry is not always easy. Ask all the questions. Finally, peripheral equipment for computers often is sold at wildly inflated prices; files and work stations are two examples. Disc packs can often be obtained from a number of sources. It will pay to shop around.

5
HOUSING THE COLLECTION

INTRODUCTION

Reader accommodations and public service, the subjects of the two previous chapters, are more important in libraries today than they once were. Only in recent times have libraries made any significant attempt to cater to the needs of their users. The universal requirement throughout the history of libraries has been the housing of the collection, whether it were one of clay tablets, papyrii, books, or video cassettes. This chapter discusses furniture and equipment for housing the collections.

Medieval libraries, some of which are still in evidence, housed books on wood book shelves stacked high around the perimeter of vaulted rooms. Ladders were needed to reach most books. As collections grew larger, galleries and balconies were added to provide additional shelf space. As collections continued to grow, albeit slowly, some freestanding ranges of shelves were placed in the center of the large reading room. Through the years, more shelves were added until large reading rooms and their balconies were inadequate to house collections. Separate stack rooms were added and eventually it became necessary to build multitier stacks (Fig. 1). These stacks, made first of cast iron and later steel, are of the sort where the stack uprights support not only the book-laden shelves, but also the higher stack floors and building structure itself. Most large academic and public libraries built before World War II used multitier stacks; they were, and still are, a very efficient way of housing large collections in a limited space. In these libraries, the ceiling height just above the top of a book on the highest shelf, at around 8 ft (240 mm), permitted two stack floors for each building floor; therefore they made effective use of volume. With 28- to 30-in. (700- to 750-mm) aisles, use of long ranges and narrow cross-aisles permitted storage of 18 to 20 volumes per square foot. However, multitier stacks, efficient as they were, were practically

FIG. 1 Multitier bookstack under construction. University of Kansas, Lawrence, Kansas.

abandoned after 1950. There were a number of reasons, among them the difficulty of making them fire-safe and their unsuitability for the subject-divisional libraries that became more popular about this time.

ORGANIZATION OF THE COLLECTION

Libraries of the last 25 years have generally housed book collections in one of two ways, either by segregating most shelving into one part of the building, separate from the center of public service activity and much of the patron seating, or by thoroughly mixing collections and readers throughout most of the building. The latter arrangement is characteristic of small and medium-sized public and college libraries and in some larger libraries organized by subject divisions. The first type is characteristic of large research libraries, both public and academic. It lends itself nicely to a closed stack arrangement where access to the collection is limited to certain groups or to staff only, who retrieve books requested by the library's patrons. On the other hand, some academic libraries with completely open stacks utilize the concentrated stack approach and group a variety of reader accommodations on the perimeter of the stacks.

Stack Towers

As we pointed out in Chapter 1, the last few years saw the construction of a number of research libraries with multistoried towers, containing mostly stacks, sitting atop much larger two- or three-storey areas, containing public service spaces and the larger part of reader accommodations. Examples of these are the University of Indiana (with its attached undergraduate facility), the University of Massachusetts, the University of North Carolina at Charlotte, and the biggest of them all, the University of Toronto. Indiana and Toronto do provide more than stacks and carrels in their towers; Toronto has seminar rooms and a number of subject service areas on the different floors, and Indiana has bibliographers and staff on each storey of its tower.

There are difficulties with stack towers. They do not utilize floor area so efficiently as the same space on one or two floors because of the necessity to use floor area on each stack floor for utilities, stairs, elevators and book lifts, lobbies, bathrooms, and, of course, work stations for lending department staff who maintain and service the collection. If floors are too small, as at the University of Massachusetts, so much space is taken by these supportive or nonassignable functions that little is left for housing books. Also, housing collections in stack towers always results in an awkward separation of some segments of the collection; that is, segments from the same subject classification must be housed on different floors. If the stacks in the tower are closed, the more floors there are, the more difficult they are to page. Personnel costs for manning stacks are higher, for staff either must be stationed on each floor or must serve two or more floors simultaneously, and thus spend too much time traveling between floors. If stacks are open, the segmented collection is more difficult to follow or browse. Finally, stack towers provide essentially inflexible housing for the collection. When collections are shelved in large open areas, it is easy, although not pleasant, to annex neighboring seating areas, install shelving, and expand the collection. With stack towers, there is generally no large contiguous space into which to expand.

TYPES OF LIBRARY SHELVING

Several types of shelving are used in today's libraries, though standard wood shelving and steel shelving of the bracket type are those most commonly used. Other types occasionally used are steel storage or warehouse shelving, standard or slotted steel shelving and built-in wood shelving.

All of these types of shelving (except built-in wood shelving) are available to use against walls or to stand in areas away from walls. The latter type, often called freestanding, is nearly always double-faced; that is, books may be housed on both sides. Occasionally single-faced shelving is used in room interiors, often with a back to serve as a space divider or to delimit an aisle. Wall-type shelving is single-faced and should be fastened to the wall. Double-faced shelving ranges are often tied together and fastened to columns or walls or are fastened to the floor.

Wood Shelving

Wood shelving is almost never used <u>throughout</u> libraries of any size because of its cost and relative inefficiency. Quite small public or special libraries are occasional exceptions. However, many libraries of all sizes use <u>some</u> wood shelving, particularly in prestige areas such as rare books rooms, children's rooms, director's offices, reference areas, keys areas, and behind lending desks for small reserve collections or for keeping books to be picked up or otherwise specially handled. Wood shelving can also be used for special-purpose or custom-designed shelving which is more easily produced in wood than in metal (Fig. 2).

Standard wood shelving is constructed by firmly fastening upright wood members to a base and top to form a box frame with a vertical opening 3 ft (900 mm) wide. Wood shelves are then hung between these uprights. Backs of wood or hardboard may be added to single-faced units or between the shelves of double-faced units; these provide some additional rigidity as well as a more finished appearance. Available shelf depths are customarily

FIG. 2 Wood periodical display shelving. Hazleton Campus, The Pennsylvania State University, Hazleton, Pennsylvania. (Sjostrom.)

8, 10, or 12 in. (200, 250, or 300 mm) for book shelving. Overall depths of wall units with backs are approximately $8\frac{3}{4}$, $10\frac{3}{4}$, and $12\frac{3}{4}$ in. (219, 269, and 319 mm) and for double-faced units approximately $16\frac{1}{2}$, $20\frac{1}{2}$, and $24\frac{1}{2}$ in. (425, 525, and 625 mm).

Shelf heights are generally adjustable by inch-long increments. Customarily, wood shelving is available in three heights: 82 in. (2050 mm), with base shelf and six adjustable shelves; 60 in. (1500 mm), with base shelf and four adjustable shelves; and 42 in. (1050 mm), with base and two adjustable shelves. These units will hold these numbers of shelves only if relatively short books are housed on them, as the openings provided are too small for tall books. The 60-in. (1500 mm) units are the highest shelves practical in children's rooms.

Units 42 in. (1050 mm) in height are especially useful in children's rooms and reference areas. Their tops serve nicely for patrons to stand at while reading large volumes and will hold swivel stands for unabridged dictionaries. They are also used to post notices or directories or to display new books, among other things. In short, they are very useful in public service areas.

While wood shelving is not nearly so popular as steel-bracket shelving, the ease of fabricating it without dies means that shelving for many special classes of material is offered as a standard item in the lines of several library furniture manufacturers. Among these special kinds of wood shelving available are storage and display shelving of both stationary and lift-up types for periodicals and newspapers; phonograph-record shelving, 16 in. (400 mm) deep; atlas shelving, with rollers; and shelving with special inserts for bulletin boards and newspaper racks. Another variety of specialized wood bookshelving used for special collections frequently is glass-fronted bookshelving. In this type, tracks on the base and top hold sliding glass panels which can be locked to preserve materials from damage or loss.

When considering purchasing wood shelving for libraries, these factors must be considered: wood shelving is more expensive than the steel-bracket type and houses books less efficiently. Although price differentials vary because of steel and wood prices, wood shelving generally costs about 30 percent more than bracket-type steel shelving. The lessened efficiency of wood shelving is due to lack of vertical storage space. Wood shelving is customarily limited to 82-in. (2050-mm) height for structural reasons and must have a top (cornice) to complete its structure. Often, the result is that sections cannot be more than six shelves high, contrasted with steel-bracket shelf sections, which will easily hold seven loaded shelves. This additional shelf per section makes a great difference and pretty much precludes the possibility of furnishing a library of any size with wood shelving, even if the price of the shelving is not a constraining factor.

The technology of wood shelving is not particularly complex and any of the library manufacturers are capable of producing shelving of satisfactory quality if they (a) use raw materials of good quality and (b) assemble and finish them correctly. This contrasts with card catalog cases housing wood catalog drawers, which only two or three library manufacturers seem to be able to produce to consistently high standards. Wood shelves are bolted together through bushings, and cutting the components so that they can be satisfactorily joined is not difficult. Finishing components satisfactorily should be no great problem to any manufacturer. The greatest opportunity for cutting corners in quality is in the wood used in construction of the shelving. The end panels and intermediate uprights must be made of solid wood or lumber-core plywood, not of particle board or any of its relatives. The shelves themselves must be of solid wood, not chip-core nor particle board; these materials, while useful in some applications, are unacceptable for shelves because they can sag or deflect under load.

Built-in wood shelves are occasionally designed for special locations, such as office walls or special collections areas. They usually are not expected to carry any significant load. Another attractive, low-density shelving method for offices utilizes wall-attached uprights with wood shelves resting on brackets hung from these uprights. Built-in glass-fronted book shelves are often used on the perimeter of special collections areas; the shelves within should be of solid wood and adjustable. Wood-framed glass doors are superior to sliding glass doors if there is room for the door to swing. Metal mesh is sometimes used in these doors instead of glass.

Metal Shelving

Metal shelves used in libraries are of three kinds, storage or warehouse shelves, slotted or standard shelves, and bracket-type shelves. The first of these is relatively inexpensive, but is inflexible and not suitable for housing library collections. It is useful for storage of bulk materials and for housing boxed or stored materials in library receiving rooms and storage areas. It is customarily available in 36- or 48-in. (900- and 1200-mm) wide sections with an overall height of 75 to 85 in. (1875 to 2350 mm). Shelf depth is commonly 12, 18, or 24 in. (300, 450, or 600 mm), and from five to eight shelves may be fitted into the opening. These can be adjusted, but only when unloaded. They can be completely open or have closed backs and are available in different configurations with functional inserts, such as parts bins, but libraries will generally use only the flat-shelf type. Industrial equipment firms sell this shelving, as do office equipment firms.

Standard or slotted-type shelving (Fig. 3), also occasionally called case-type shelving, is preferred by some librarians and is sold by most library shelving manufacturers. Standard shelving has a neat appearance and a closed top. It is very sound structurally and has superior stability; however, there are a number of disadvantages and this type of shelf is not much used in any but special libraries such as law libraries where variations in book heights are few. Among the problems with standard shelving are lack of capacity, greater cost, unavailability of special-purpose inserts and accessories, interference with light and ventilation, and the difficulty of moving loaded shelves up or down within the section.

The construction of case-type shelving is similar to wood shelving with a finished top and bottom fastened to flat metal uprights which are slotted so that shelves may hang from them. The finished top limits the height of book storage and interferes with light distribution in the same way wood shelves do. The comparatively low volume of sales are certainly responsible for the higher cost and lack of accessories and special application units in this type of shelving. The basic design, of course, reduces ventilation and prevents easy relocation of loaded shelves. It is probable that there will be no substantial increase in the popularity of this type of shelving and that it will continue to be used primarily for special situations.

FIG. 3 Standard (case-type) shelving, common in law libraries. (Library Bureau.)

Bracket Shelving

Bracket-type steel shelving is the most popular shelving in all kinds of libraries, for it is the most universally satisfactory for all kinds of situations. Of the three types of shelving suitable for general library use (wood shelving, standard steel shelving (Fig. 4), and bracket-type shelving), the latter is the least expensive, most versatile, and has the largest capacity. It has a relatively light, airy appearance and can be given as finished a look as is desired. It is available in a variety of sizes and heights and there are many accessories available. A large number of special applications can be carried out by using special inserts of various kinds within the upright forming each section.

Bracket-type shelving consists of slotted steel uprights in hollow squares or half squares (bolted together) which are bolted or welded to top stretchers and bases to form a closed frame. The base may be a narrow stretcher fastened between the uprights (open base) or a full base (closed base) that functions as the bottom shelf of the section. The closed base will be comprised of two base brackets bolted to the upright with a stretcher and shelf

FIG. 4 Bracket-type shelves. Colgate University, Hamilton, New York. (Phoenix Photography.)

or shelves between them. The top stretcher is generally a hollow square and may be covered by a canopy top for aesthetic reasons. Steel brackets hook into the slots in the uprights, supporting the shelves themselves. In some designs, the brackets and shelf are a single unit with the brackets folding flat against the shelf for easy storage. More commonly the brackets and shelves are separate pieces with shelves hooking into openings in the brackets. The shelves themselves are generally flat smooth surfaces with exceptions to be detailed later.

Stability

Bracket-type shelves are not as inherently rigid nor as stable as wood and standard steel shelving, and different devices are used to increase their soundness. Longitudinal stability can be a problem with bolted-together frames; sway braces, with turnbuckles for adjustment, can alleviate this problem. Sway braces need not be used on each section; one in every four or five will do. Welded frames are free from this problem, but can be a bit more expensive and are more difficult to store.

Freestanding shelves lacking lateral stability can cause serious accidents. Lateral stability is improved by such devices as using end panels or closed bases that are wider than the width of the shelves, tying shelf ranges together with strut channels, and fastening ranges to the floor. When ranges are tied together with strut channels, added stability is assured if the assembly is attached to a wall or column. Double-faced shelves with closed bases, especially if base brackets are continuous, tied along with other ranges to some part of the building structure will provide a high degree of stability and there should be no possibility of an accident. Some prefer to bolt shelf bases to the floor but this is not desirable in today's carpeted libraries and not really superior to the "fasten-to-the-wall" method. Strut channels should be tied between every third or fourth section. Occasionally strut channels are used to mount fluorescent light fixtures parallel to stack ranges.

Use on Carpeted Floors

With most of today's libraries placing bookstacks on carpeted floors, planners face some new problems. Since many libraries and planners feel that it is not wise to assume permanent location of bookstacks in particular locations on carpeted floors, it is wise to lay carpet everywhere rather than between stacks. Then, if proper precautions are taken, it will be possible to dismantle and move stacks, leaving undamaged carpet behind.

The solution that the author feels most confident about is to specify carpet pins on shelf bases. These are small steel pins (really screws) with sharp points (Fig. 5) that penetrate the carpet and rest on the concrete subfloor. These pins raise the weight of the loaded stack enough so that it does not depress the carpet pile so much. When shelving is equipped with these pins and properly installed, it is possible to relocate loaded stacks and, in a short time, not see any depressions in the carpet to show where the stacks had been previously.

Variant Sizes

Bracket-type book shelving, being the most popular type in today's libraries, is available in different sizes and shapes and with a great variety of specialized units and accessories. Today 36-in. (900-mm) units are the norm for American use. At least one manufacturer lists 30-in. (750-mm) wide units as standard items, with prices slightly under those of the 36-in. (900 mm) wide units. While the technology would undoubtedly permit wider shelving units, there seems to be little call for them currently. Building modules currently call for stacks of 36 in. (900 mm) width. Manufacturers would undoubtedly prefer to stick with a familiar technology and continue to use

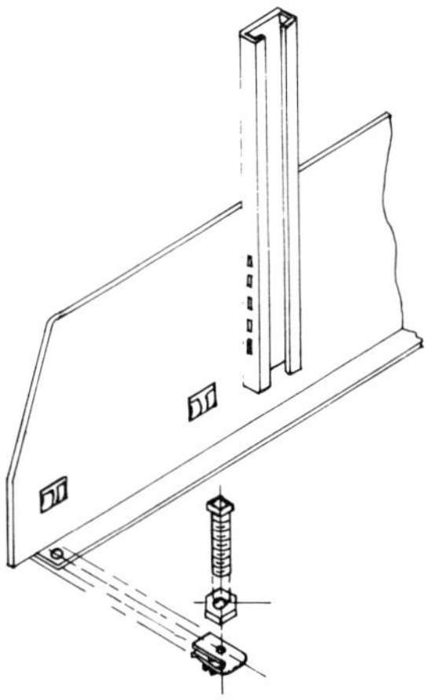

FIG. 5 Carpet pins help distribute shelf weight and protect carpet from permanent damage. (Library Bureau.)

dies and fixtures already in use. While it is true that a few more books would fit in a 24-ft range of six 4-ft (1200-mm) units, rather than eight 3-ft (900-mm) units, there is some evidence that 4-ft (1200-mm) wide shelf sections are a bit too wide for the eyes to encompass comfortably. The 30-in. (750-mm) wide unit, mentioned above is especially useful when trying to create a shelf layout in an area with columns, while leaving uniform aisles. The author has seen lesser widths used to fit into tight or leftover spaces, but they are generally not worth the great additional cost, since they are custom pieces and therefore quite expensive.

Steel-bracket-type bookstacks are customarily produced in high, medium, and counter-height versions with the high unit standard at 90 in. ($7\frac{1}{2}$ ft or 2250 mm). The high units are standard in library stack areas and for free-standing shelves in open areas. This height represents a compromise between maximum book capacity and ease of accessibility for most users and staff. These shelf sections contain six adjustable shelves and one base shelf per face. A person of average height can see and reach materials on the top shelf. If upright and shelf go higher than 90 in. (2250 mm), few persons can reach the top shelf, a condition which immediately necessitates the cluttering up of aisles with step stools and ladders. As a result, aisles must be wide enough to allow room for both these "reaching aids" and normal traffic; therefore, space gained by additional high shelves is lost. One approach used in some places (Mars Hill College, North Carolina, for instance) involves using high shelves above 90 in. (2250 mm) for little-used materials. In this way, a storage collection is reasonably accessible.

At least one manufacturer, Andrew Wilson, Inc., makes available shelving sections as standard catalog items in several intermediate heights, such as 54, 66, and 78 in. (1350, 1650, and 1950 mm), and these will fit some special situations. Other more generally available standard heights are 60 in. (1500 mm) with four adjustable shelves above the base and 42 in. (1050 mm), or counter-height with base plus two adjustable shelves. The 60 in. (1500 mm) is occasionally used in open areas where lower shelves are more attractive and storage density is not essential, while counter-height shelving is useful as room dividers to house some reference materials and in children's libraries. Shelf tops (canopies) are almost always used with these counter-height units and serve a variety of purposes, among them being display space and a location for dictionary stands or unit record files. These tops may be of the same metal surface color as the shelves themselves or tops of either wood or high-pressure laminate may be provided.

Shelf depths for books are generally 8, 10, or 12 in. (200, 250, or 300 mm). These are nominal depths, with actual depths being generally an inch less, that is 7, 9, or 11 in. (175, 225, or 275 mm). Metcalf (1965) and others point out that well over 90 percent of all books in general libraries are 9 in. (225 mm) deep or less. Nearly all of the remainder will be adequately housed on 12-in. (300 mm) shelves. Since it makes no sense to purchase shelves of three different sizes and since 10-in. (250 mm) shelves will hold such a high percentage of the collection, this writer advocates the general purchase of 10-in. (250 mm) shelves, with a few 12-in. (300 mm) shelves for reference areas, art and music sections, and perhaps general areas where oversized materials are housed. In a $22\frac{1}{2}$-ft (6750 mm) bay, the use of 10-in. (250 mm) shelving generally will provide five ranges of 10-in. double-faced shelving and 34-in. (850 mm) aisles between ranges. Not only will this allow for shelves deep enough to handle nearly all the collection, but it also provides aisles wide enough for comfortable patron use and easy passage for book trucks.

Shelf Capacity

A great deal has been written about shelf capacity, nearly all of it helpful, although this information is somewhat confusing in the aggregate. For many years, some planners have projected housing 100 volumes per shelf section 36 in. (900 mm) wide, 7 shelves high (including base). This is based on 21 linear feet of shelving (7 shelves of 36 in. or 900 mm), each housing 7 volumes per linear foot about two-thirds full ($7 \times 21 = 147$, or almost 150, 2/3 of which is 100). If 7 volumes per linear foot is valid for the library, this rule of thumb will be reasonable, though perhaps slightly conservative. Recently when the research collection at Penn State was measured, it was found that nearly 10 volumes per linear foot was the utilization rate. Actual full capacity is therefore about 200 volumes per single-faced section and two-thirds capacity is 134. This figure is corroborated in other research libraries, it has since been discovered. The increase of paperbacks and pamphlet-sized volumes is probably responsible for the difference between 7 volumes per linear foot generally quoted as "gospel" and the nearly 10 volumes measured in the collection. It was also determined that Penn State's shelves are at practical capacity when they are 80 percent full. When shelves are full beyond that point, so much money must be spent on shelf maintenance with constant shifting to accommodate new acquisitions that most libraries will consider 80 percent a practical maximum.

Each library must work out its own formula for housing the collection. The first step is to develop an accurate shelf count of the collection and to measure the linear feet the collection occupies. Most libraries do not have these figures, although some may think they have the shelf count. Dividing number of volumes by linear feet gives a figure for volumes per linear foot. This will vary from 7 to 10 or more for different libraries. The number arrived at will probably be reasonably accurate for the future since most collections retain their essential character. Once this volume-per-linear-foot figure is determined, some considerable thought must be given to the projected growth pattern of the collection. If dynamic collection growth is expected without anticipation of additional facilities beyond those being currently planned, some planners may want to plan to fill their shelves to no more than 50 to 55 percent of capacity. Others anticipating less collection growth, having less space to work with, visualizing the need to separate and compress portions of the collection via compact storage or transfer to microform, will be content to use the more usual two-thirds capacity projection.

Once the planner has determined the volumes per linear feet and decided how nearly full the shelves will be on move-in day, the calculations are easy. For example, if the planner finds that a library is shelving an average of 10 volumes per linear foot, to house 100,000 volumes will require 10,000 linear ft of shelf space. If the shelving is two-thirds full, 15,000 linear ft will be needed. Fifteen thousand divided by 21 linear ft per section of shelving (90 × 36 in. or 2250 × 900 mm) with six adjustable shelves and one base shelf) means 714 sections of shelving. On the other hand, if shelves are only 50 percent full, 20,000 linear ft of shelving divided by 21 ft per section, or 952 sections will be needed. If the top and base shelves are left empty and the five middle shelves are two-thirds full, the sections will not look too empty.

Obviously, a good deal more could be said here about this important problem. However, Metcalf (1965), Thompson (1974), and others have discussed it thoroughly and there seems little point in repeating their presentations. Further, each library's available spaces are different and require a new analysis. A competent library interior consultant or an experienced representative of one of the shelving manufacturers can be most helpful in analyzing this matter for an individual library.

FLOOR LOADING

The question of floor loading should be mentioned here. It is fairly common knowledge that most planners use 150 lbs/ft^2 live load as the factor for floor loading where fully loaded bookstacks are placed. Although a building structure of greater than average strength and cost is required to accomplish this, it is, of course, essential. Furthermore, wise planners will insist on this floor load capacity throughout the building on the premise that future funding problems and lack of new facilities may result in bookstacks being placed in portions of the building not originally planned to house books. In fact, all assignable areas in the building, with the possible exception of offices and rooms too small to "stack," should have the 150-lb/ft^2 floor load capability. Obviously, the load will not be even; intermediate stack uprights may have an impact load of 900 lb. Floor structure will equalize these punch-type loads so that they are not a problem; the casualty may be the carpet if this weight is not partially absorbed by carpet pins.

VARIANT DESIGNS AND FEATURES

Since steel-bracket-type shelving is the most popular in library use, there are a great number of variations in design as well as a large number of special function units and accessories available. We mentioned earlier that frames for individual sections are either bolted or welded. Bolted frames consist of stack uprights (approximately square) bolted to top and base spreaders. The first section in a range (starter) has two uprights and each additional section has only one, since the spreaders are fastened from the one new upright to one in the section already erected. Bolted frames need to be strengthened for longitudinal stability, so sway braces are added each four or five sections. Welded frames are half-uprights welded to top and base stretchers to make a rigid frame. To form ranges, the half-uprights are bolted together. No reinforcement for longitudinal stability is necessary and the lack of sway braces means that books can extend behind the back of the shelf anywhere in the range. Bookstacks with welded frames are not as widely available as those bolted together and, when disassembled, are harder to store.

Bracket-type shelves may be purchased with open or closed bases. Open bases are really suitable only for stack floors where uprights are fastened to the ceiling. Otherwise, closed bases are superior because they add to the stability of the range and they have a more finished appearance. Canopy tops are sometimes used to improve appearance but they do have at least two serious disadvantages: (a) they cut down on light spill onto book spines; and (b) they limit the height to which books can be shelved. When they are not used, tall books on a top shelf will occasionally reach above the top of the upright; if canopy tops are used, this is not possible. Also, they can show dirt if there is a vantage point above their level and, of course, they add to the cost of the installation.

End panels are another commonly used option available with bracket-type shelving. In wood shelving and standard steel shelving the uprights function as end panels at the ends of a range, but with the polelike upright used in bracket shelving, the ends can be left open and book covers will be visible from the end of the range. Actually, with occasional exceptions, end panels nearly always are used in public areas; stacks in separate stack areas often do not have end panels. Although there are those who like the openness afforded when end panels are not used, the finished appearance they provide influences many librarians to favor them. From a functional point of view, they improve lateral stability and provide a highly visible location for information about the contents of the range behind them. They are available in steel, wood, or laminate and in a great variety of colors and textures.

Most bracket bookstacks look pretty much alike except for the presence or absence of some of the options just mentioned, such as closed or open bases, end panels, and canopies. However, there are notable exceptions. In recent years, a variation sometimes called the T-base has become popular and is available from several manufacturers. In this design, the upright is attached at right angles to a horizontal member which lies flat on the floor and prevents lateral sway by the upright. Thus, base brackets may be eliminated with the base member assuming its normal function, that of providing lateral stability. Shelving in this T-base design is attractive and an interesting variant to the conventional bracket stack. In many libraries it is used for special groups of materials or displays near the library entrance; or in a few libraries it is used throughout the premises. In most designs, the T-base does not hold quite as many volumes as conventional designs because the bottom shelf must be higher. Nonetheless, this style of shelving offers an interesting contrast to bracket shelving of conventional design and bears consideration for limited use. It is probably not wise to use this type of shelving throughout an entire library because of the added cost and the slightly lessened capacity.

SPECIAL PURPOSE SHELVING

Because there are many specialized materials in library collections and because special reader facilities are needed in stack areas, manufacturers of steel library bookstacks offer a number of special inserts that hang from the uprights of bracket-type shelving sections.

Periodicals

Unbound issues of periodicals and newspapers are often housed in steel bracket shelving. Frequently, lift-up or fixed storage and display shelving, similar to that available in wood shelving is used. In this type, a slanted shelf, either fixed or movable, displays the current issue while the other unbound issues are housed on a flat shelf underneath the slanted shelf. In the lift-up type, the display shelf lifts up to reveal the flat shelf containing the back issues. This type of shelf permits attractive display and easy retrieval of current and back issues. Since each single-faced section displays and stores only 15 or so periodical titles, it is not as effective in utilizing space as other ways of housing periodicals on bracket shelves.

Another possible shelving method is housing unbound issues on flat shelves with the current issue on top. If inverted-bracket shelves are used, 45 to 60 titles can be housed in a single-faced range. With legible labels on the front edge of the shelf and with the periodical's spine showing, it is easy to retrieve individual issues. Periodicals are also housed upright on regular book shelves in pamphlet boxes or erect on divider-type shelves. If the latter are used, no pamphlet boxes are necessary. In "pam boxes" it should be possible to house slightly more than 40 titles per section and divider-type shelves will probably house 80 or more. Of course, neither of these shelving types permits display of current issues, but if necessary, the most-used current issues can be displayed in other locations on magazine racks.

Some libraries prefer to combine bound and unbound periodicals in one location, and the use of pamphlet boxes or divider shelves permits this. Of course, mixing bound and unbound journals does make browsing difficult for those who are interested in seeing late issues of a number of periodicals. Problems with classification and arrangement are exaggerated by combining bound and unbound issues. Many libraries feel strongly that bound journals should be classified and shelved with monographs on the same subject. When this is done, it is hardly reasonable to shelve current issues with bound ones because those wishing to find current periodicals will have to find their way through the entire collection. Even if monographs and periodicals are separated, with the latter in alphabetical order, there still will be a large area for a periodical user to search through if current and bound volumes are combined. Based on what seems to be the prevalent practice, most libraries of any size have apparently decided that the advantages of shelving current and bound periodicals together do not outweigh the handicaps to public and staff, although in smaller libraries the unwieldiness of the combined collection is not such a problem. Currently, common practice in libraries of any size is to classify periodicals and shelve bound volumes with monographs, leaving current issues to be housed separately in periodicals rooms, either on storage/display shelves, divider shelves, flat periodical shelves, or in pamphlet boxes on book shelving. To be sure, there are other practices, such as housing issues flat on divider shelves with the divider set according to the width of each magazine. This does display the top issue of those magazines effectively, but it is not efficient in space utilization.

Newspapers

Newspapers are housed in several ways and, like periodicals, the current issue is often housed separately from other recent issues. Current issues of papers are often placed on newspaper sticks which are hung on freestanding tables or racks, or on special inserts in stack sections (Fig. 6).

FIG. 6 Current newspapers on sticks in shelf sections. (Library Bureau.)

FIG. 7 Current issues of newspapers can be displayed in slanted display shelves with acrylic flaps holding them upright. Berks Campus, The Pennsylvania State University, Reading, Pennsylvania.

Remaining current issues are often placed on flat shelves 16 in. (400 mm) deep hung on inverted brackets, often called newspaper shelves. Some libraries stack them on regular book shelving although these really are not deep enough to hold them satisfactorily. Other libraries use a sort of storage and display insert in shelf sections to hold newspapers with the current issue on a slanted shelf and previous issues stacked on a flat shelf below the display shelf. Because of the larger size of folded newspapers and their thickness, a clear acrylic panel is often flapped over the displayed newspaper to keep it flat and visible on the display shelf (Fig. 7). All these methods are popular in libraries, and while there are other approaches, none is satisfactory enough to have received wide adoption. The special inserts and shelves needed for these different approaches to housing periodicals and newspapers are available from firms manufacturing steel bracket-type shelving.

The inserts for hanging newspaper sticks and the storage/display units for periodicals and newspapers serve those purposes admirably but are

FIG. 8 Divider shelves are particularly well suited to house documents, phonorecords, and periodicals. (Library Bureau.)

not used generally for other purposes. Flat newspaper shelves and divider shelves, on the other hand, are useful for a number of other tasks in the library. Flat newspaper shelves with inverted brackets are well-suited for shelving large oversize volumes on their sides. Penn State uses them in its maps division where very large atlases can be laid on their sides in a space up to 36 in. (900 mm) from shelf face to shelf face. Divider-type shelves (Fig. 8) are wonderfully versatile and useful for many things beside periodicals. They are used for housing phonorecords and are useful in art and music libraries for housing the tall, sometimes thin, art books, portfolios, scores, and similar materials found in those areas. Libraries having collections of public documents will find divider shelves ideal for housing the mixture of all kinds and sizes of material found here.

Other Specialized Shelf Inserts

There are other library materials that are sometimes housed in special inserts on steel bracket-type shelves. Among them are 16-mm film, filmstrips, and microfilm. The growth of microfilm use in libraries and the quantities involved have induced many librarians to look seriously at

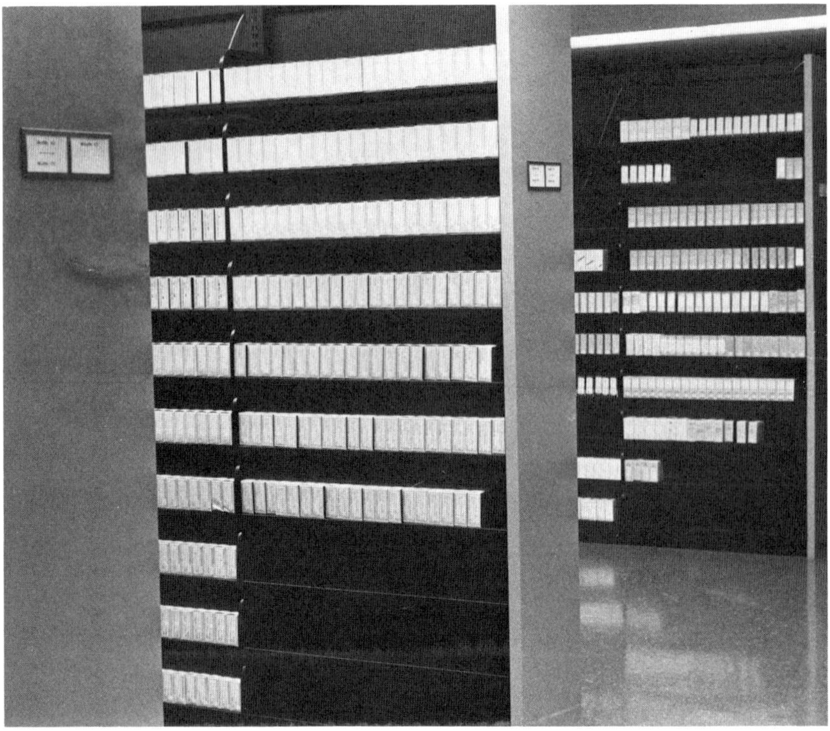

FIG. 9 Microfilm housed on steel shelves.

the possibility of using book shelves to house them. They can be placed either on special shelves that hold them securely side by side (Fig. 9) or in special inserts such as those made by Princeton Microfilm Corporation that sit on regular book shelving. In neither case can shelving provide the storage capacity for microfilm afforded by the over- and under-cabinets available from several sources. To compare, the cabinets hold about 254 boxes of 35-mm film per square foot while boxes on microfilm shelving hold 140 boxes per square foot, and boxes on inserts on book shelving hold 93 boxes per square foot. The shelves do fit close to the wall and this is useful in some constricted microforms areas.

Finally, there are several kinds of reader stations and conveniences housed in steel bracket-type bookshelf units. Coatrack inserts are occasionally used in shelf sections, though these take valuable shelf space when coat hooks and costumers can be placed in other, less valuable places around the library. If coatrack inserts are used, they sometimes house umbrella racks and drip pans. Some libraries use sections of shelving for

FIG. 10 Pull-out reference shelves provide convenient consultation space within stack area. (Wagner International Photos.)

lockers that are available for assignment to library users. With lockers, nearby carrels can be left unassigned and can have much greater utilization than assigned carrels with built-in lockers. Pull-out reference shelves (Fig. 10) make possible easy reference to heavily used materials right at the shelves where they are located. They are also helpful to members of the library staff when they instruct patrons in library use. They are simply shelves that can be pulled out from another stationary shelf so that books can be examined on them. Carrels are sometimes used in stack sections but can be used only in limited locations because stack aisles are too narrow for a reader to be seated comfortably, and they restrict traffic through aisles. Also, if aisles are left wide enough for carrels to be hung in them, valuable space for stacks will be lost. Finally, bibliographic centers or index areas are often created in bracket-type stacks by hanging work tops 36 in. (900 mm) wide by 24 in. (600 mm) deep at the 29- to 30-in. (725- to 750-mm) level in wall-hung uprights with book shelves above the work surface. In this way indexes and bibliographical materials not so heavily used as those on index tables can still have a working space immediately available.

Shelving Accessories

A number of accessories are available and are often necessary to assist the library in getting maximum value from the book shelving. Some libraries use label holders on the front edge of some shelves with printed labels which list, by name or call number, the material on the shelf. As the collection moves, the labels are changed. These are certainly helpful to some users and they are particularly used in public libraries. They do get lost, broken or moved and maintaining the proper notation on them can be a nuisance. Labels or cards are also used at the ends of ranges to indicate what material is located on the entire range. These can be flat against the end panel or end upright, or may stick out so that they may be seen easily by a person coming down an aisle at right angles to the end of the range. The latter are often called range finders. Both use 3 × 5 in. cards to carry the needed information. If these are to be viewed across a large room, letters larger than those that can fit on a 3 × 5 in. card will be essential. Some libraries are using supergraphics or very large letters or numbers on end panels to call readers' attention to collection location. More discussion of this will follow in Chapter 8.

Supporting books upright on shelves may not seem like an important concern to the unenlightened reader, but librarians familiar with managing stack collections know the problem to be serious, with book damage often the result of the wrong book support. Book supports are either freestanding or in some way attached to the shelf. The freestanding ones which slide freely or may be easily removed from the shelf are of metal or plastic and many have cork or composition bases so that they do not slide too easily. Now available is a magnetic-style support which has the same effect as the cork in preventing freestanding supports from sliding easily. Some sharp-edged supports can knife into books when books are shelved carelessly, so "nonlosable" supports are available with surfaces facing out so that they cannot knife into books.

There are also several kinds of book supports that are physically attached to the shelves themselves. Among them are the wire- or butterfly-type, which attaches to the front and back edge of the shelf above the one where the books to be held erect are shelved, and the lock-on type, which hooks under the bends at the front of the shelf and slides along the shelf. Another is the type that is used with the slotted or two-bar shelf, such as Library Bureau's "Loc Tite." (See Fig. 11.) In this latter type, a slot is made in each shelf into which a specially designed book support is placed that holds books firmly in place, yet slides easily in the slot as required. This type does not knife into books as does the butterfly type, nor scratch shelves

FIG. 11 Slotted shelves with sliding book supports. (Library Bureau.)

as does the lock-on type. The shelves are actually slightly strengthened by the metal treatment that produces the slot and the supports do not fall off or hang loose from the shelves as do other types. In most cases there is a trick to removing them, so mischievous users cannot easily walk off with them. In short, the slotted shelf with book support has much to recommend itself and has been used in a number of libraries with success.

Color

Steel bracket bookstacks were once available only in gray and green. Beige became popular a few years ago, then black had its period in vogue; today paint used on steel shelving comes in many colors. Most manufacturers will offer 10 to 12 colors to select from and, if the job is big enough, they will supply any color requested. The reflectance value of the lighter colors should be taken into consideration, as well as the consequent improvement in light level on the lower shelves. End panels offer a fine

FIG. 12 End panels are often made of metal or wood but unusual materials are sometimes used. St. Louis Junior College District. (Mae Mizuki Photography.)

opportunity to provide color, texture or material in contrast to the painted metal stacks. Real wood or high-pressure laminates in wood finish are popular. Wood slats and butcher block have been used. End panels of metal painted in colors contrasting to the shelf color are used (Fig. 12). The author would not be surprised to see end panels of wall carpet in some library with a particularly acute noise problem.

EVALUATION OF SHELVES

When evaluating steel bookstacks for purchase, several considerations should be uppermost in mind. The first, obviously, is that the shelves should be strong enough to do the job and should be able to be installed so that their stability is not in question. Although one generally need not be concerned with moving parts, some stacks will hold up much better under hard use than others. When paint is not well applied or permanent, the possibility of corrosion and ultimate failure must be expected. Several installations of each different manufacturer whose products are under consideration should be visited. Among the defects to be concerned with are chipped and worn paint, rough metal edges on brackets or under the bend at the shelf front, and deflection of shelves under load. Any of these conditions should raise questions about the overall quality of the manufacturer's workmanship. Incidentally, apparent wear on the top front edge of the shelf may be worn paint or may be pigment from book bindings; check carefully before deciding that paint is worn away here. Check also for stability of the completed installation by pulling and pushing the loaded shelves. Since manufacturers of shelving are generally responsible for installation, they should be concerned that shelf ranges are straight, plumb, and stable. For detailed information about desirable characteristics of steel bracket-type shelving, see Appendix A, where a sample specification for steel shelving is given, along with discussion of some of the points in their specification.

COMPACT SHELVING

Metcalf's book, written in the prosperous 1960s when new buildings were being erected all over the world, discussed at some length the means by which libraries could house more books per square foot than is possible with the collection housed in classified order on shelves that are not too full and which patrons and staff can use easily and comfortably. He suggested such collection-compressing measures as shelving by order of accession, not leaving as much expansion space as projected growth indicates, shelving by size, shelving books behind others on shelves (two deep), shelving books higher, using less deep shelving and narrower aisles, using longer ranges and narrower cross aisles, and using compact shelving. All of these, except the last, are generally considered desperate measures because of their adverse effects on service of the collection and public access to it. Housing the collection by size, two deep, or by date of receipt, implies closed stacks, with the expense and adverse public reaction that accompanies this policy. Additional bibliographic records to locate materials on shelves is another complicating factor. Using shelves that are higher, closer together, or surrounded by less traffic space make public access or staff servicing more difficult. Use of compact shelving does, however, have arguments in its favor without some of the disadvantages of these other solutions.

Today, when large new buildings are not so plentiful, many libraries are looking for more space to house their growing collections or ways to house a rapidly increasing amount of information in a fixed physical space. Libraries are achieving these aims to some extent by the substitution of microforms for some lesser-used materials and by entering into cooperative arrangements with other libraries, with the aim of reducing individual acquisitions by agreement and by storing lesser-used materials in commonly held warehouses. Other libraries are maintaining remote

FIG. 13 Storage shelving, moving-aisle type, with manual operation. (Library Bureau. Mark Schaeffer Photographs.)

storage warehouses of their own for housing less commonly demanded materials. All these are solutions that deserve serious study by many libraries; they are not in the province of this book since they involve equipment only peripherally. We have already talked about microform equipment in Chapter 3 and shelving used in storage warehouses can be one of the conventional shelving types or compact shelving, which is the subject we are going to consider now.

The most reasonable large-scale method of compacting the book collection is the use of this so-called compact shelving. Libraries running out of shelf space will, of course, investigate all the possibilities of adding shelf sections wherever possible—in corners, at the end of ranges with extra-wide end aisles and, if necessary, in seating areas. Some libraries will make wholesale rearrangements to gain a few thousand linear feet of shelf capacity. These measures need to be taken but gains will usually not be large enough to solve the problem permanently. Compact shelving is one way a relatively small area can be used to house a large quantity of books.

Compact shelving has been with us for a number of years and has been devised in a variety of types and concepts. Metcalf (1965), Gawrecki (1968), and others have written about the various developments and products in some detail. As a matter of fact, this is one aspect of library equipment that is well covered in the literature. We will not go into this subject in any depth but will try to bring the reader up to date and add a few other observations.

There has always been great interest in this subject by the innovators in the library profession. For years the hinged-type shelf devised by Angus McDonald and the drawer-type were those most in vogue. Then, more recently, the movable range or moving aisle developed as "Compactus" has come to the fore and the earlier types are, as of this writing, no longer available. In this form, slightly modified ranges of bracket shelves are mounted on carts with wheels which roll on tracks set in the floor. Double-faced stack ranges (Fig. 13) are set in almost against each other with one aisle for each five ranges. When a book is needed from a shelf where there is no aisle, entire ranges are moved, either manually or with the aid of motors, and an aisle is left where it is needed to reach the required book. The installation is designed so that the ranges roll freely and so that they will not move when a person is in the aisle. Obviously, these are not well suited to open stacks, though at least one public library exists that has this compact shelving in a public access area. If books are shelved by size, it is possible to shelve twice as many books in an area on these shelves as in conventional shelves. Compact shelves are expensive and because of their heavy load-bearing equipment (at least 300 lb/ft^2), they should be installed on a slab-on-grade (i.e., ground floor) area. Nonetheless, if space is available where the floor load is not a problem and compact stacks are within budget, an enormous amount of material can be stored in a relatively small area.

6
HOUSING NONPRINT MEDIA

INTRODUCTION

For many years the demise of the book-oriented library has been confidently predicted by prophets of advanced technology, who claim that information in nonprint form or in computer storage would supplant the book. On the other hand, the defenders of the book point to the high cost of nonbook information and the vast number of formats and machines involved, and decry the facile promises and gimmickry that characterize the arguments of some of the nonprint proponents, suggesting that the chief beneficiaries of nonprint material are the intellectually underprivileged. Both sides tend to overstate their cases, but there certainly is truth in both their claims: the book-oriented library is changing greatly and building up collections of library materials in all media, some of which have special value for users with less than adequate intellectual capacity. Some librarians indulge in snobbery here, by suggesting that only community colleges and teachers colleges make much use of nonprint media. Actually, some of our more respected and prestigious institutions, realizing their great value for enrichment, make significant use of nonprint materials in their libraries. More and more libraries of all sorts will need to make available some of the hardware and software for their patrons. In this chapter, we will try to provide information for the librarian who needs an introduction to the subject and wants to know something of the kind of hardware that is needed and how to select and evaluate it. We are not concerned with the complete learning resource center nor the instructional materials center found in some colleges and universities. These often have campus-wide production and distribution facilities which are manned by instructional materials specialists rather than librarians. Here we are interested in helping the librarian who is responsible for integrating nonprint materials into the library and who has little or no training in the subject.

INSTRUCTIONAL MATERIALS CENTERS AND LEARNING RESOURCES CENTERS

The instructional materials center (IMC) generally operates on the premise that all the instructional resources of an institution are centered there, and that teaching faculty will develop course work around student use of instructional materials found at the center and throughout the campus. IMCs have instruction and learning resources in all forms, both print (books and periodicals) and nonprint (slides, filmstrips, audio and video tapes and cassettes, graphic materials of all sorts, motion pictures, etc.). In these institutions, most often community colleges, new universities, and experimental colleges (e.g., Hampshire College), the instructional program is focused on the IMC, and print materials are de-emphasized in favor of other instructional and learning resources. In other institutions, instruction continues to be centered in the classroom, where instructional materials are used. Some faculty encourage the use of learning resources in all media and the library houses all learning resources emphasizing books, but generally not instructional resources. The distinction made here between learning and instructional resources and materials is this: learning resources and materials are those used by individuals outside the classroom away from direct instructor contact, while instructional resources and materials are those used by groups in the teaching situation.

Obviously, a clear-cut distinction is not possible; most materials can be used as both instructional and learning resources. Transparencies and opaque projectors are rarely used outside the classroom, while cassette players with earphones and self-contained sound/slide units like Singer's Caramate are seldom used in classrooms. For those media common to classroom and library, some duplication of equipment is necessary and desirable (e.g., video cassette players and receivers). In other cases, the same software, say a sound/slide presentation, will require a slide projector with synchronized cassette player in the classroom, while a self-contained sound/slide viewer with rear-screen projection and sound will be used in a carrel in the library. In any case, software is obviously easier to duplicate than hardware and a complete file of the institution's collection of software should be housed in the library.

LIBRARIES AND NONPRINT MEDIA

Today there are only a very few libraries that do not house nonprint media; there are also a mere handful that almost ignore classroom lectures altogether and concentrate instruction in the instructional materials center. Between these two extremes is a wide spectrum of libraries that have varying degrees of concern for the use of nonprint media. Most librarians are becoming more aware of the value of media in libraries and are willing, even eager, to add to their collections those nonprint materials that will be helpful to their clientele. Public librarians have used audiovisual materials heavily for many years, presenting music, art, and public affairs programs that make use of films, records and tapes, art prints, slides, and a variety of audiovisual materials and programs. Academic libraries have not utilized nonprint materials heavily until the last 20 years. However, in the 1950s three phenomena stimulated a sudden spurt of interest toward developing programs in nonprint media in college and university libraries. These factors were: (a) the availability of federal funds for all sorts of academic needs, both real and perceived; (b) the enrollment in institutions of higher education of high school graduates who were accustomed to using these techniques; and (c) the emergence of new institutions of all kinds, many of which eschewed traditional educational methods and welcomed media-centered instructional programs with open arms. These factors deserve some further discussion, for their presence in the 50s and 60s directly affect the situation today.

THE GROWTH OF HIGHER EDUCATION AND THE NONPRINT REVOLUTION

The availability of federal funding made possible the magnificent growth that all of higher education has experienced over the past 20 years. Established institutions, both public and private, were able to expand programs and enrollments, build new buildings, produce significant new research, and improve the quality of all their efforts. Many small, struggling private institutions were kept alive and enabled to grow in size and quality. The changes in the public sector were much more dramatic because the infusion of federal funds helped bring about massive increases in funding by state governments and the results of this combination were indeed impressive. Junior colleges became four-year institutions, teachers colleges became state universities, and community and junior colleges sprang up everywhere.

The opportunity for some kind of higher education became available to nearly all potential students nationwide. As a result, students of the kind who had not considered themselves or been considered "college material" were now matriculating at these new or upgraded institutions. Federally funded grants or loans available to them made it financially feasible for these students to attend college. Because many, for varying reasons, had not been strong students in secondary school, programs offering remedial or "catch-up" work in writing, reading, and mathematics were essential in order that these students would be capable of gaining some benefit from postsecondary education. Some students could barely read or write, and techniques like "programmed instruction" were necessary to develop literacy. The nonprint media previously used sparingly as "enrichment" or supplementary material for conventional college students became an essential learning device for the new kind of student colleges were now accepting.

The High School

Of course, secondary schools bore a larger part of the responsibility for the accelerated interest of colleges in nonprint materials. The availability of federal funding enabled them to expand vastly their programs utilizing audiovisual materials. Secondary schools were accustomed to making considerable use of these materials, which fit well into most secondary school programs and are often essential in public schools, whose students range from the best to the poorest. The acceleration in use of these nonprint materials by secondary school students had the result, in many cases, of producing students who were ready to go to college, but "literate" only in media, i.e., they had not had to learn to read or write well, but had absorbed enough material and concepts through nonprint material to enable them to graduate from high school. Because of the increased opportunity to attend college, many of them were academically ready to enter college but were not sufficiently literate to do conventional college work. The results were an increase of remedial programs to enable these students to make the transition to college and the introduction of new postsecondary and vocational programs on an academic level which many of these students could achieve. These new programs made heavy use of media.

Thus, nonprint media have become essential elements of the educational program of many of our newer institutions as well as those of existing institutions that have dramatically changed their size or status. At many or most of these colleges and universities, students who are less well prepared for higher education than many students attending more traditional institutions do much of their learning through media, which often fits well into the vocation-oriented programs they like. If their basic skills are too weak for college work on this level, remedial assistance is available through nonprint materials. At more traditional institutions, on the other hand, classroom instruction and library resources are at the center of the educational program for good students, with nonprint media being very useful as enrichment and illustrative material to assist all students in learning.

The Fuel of Federal Funding

In the early years of the media explosion, federal funds were available in such quantities that many large commercial firms were attracted into the business of providing hardware, software, and complete systems of nonprint learning materials. These firms were large enough and so technically competent that they were able to develop very sophisticated systems that promised excellent educational results for those institutions acquiring them. They also brought to the marketplace superb marketing skills, in many cases overmatching the buyers and specifiers with whom they contended. Many educational administrators found themselves unable to resist the blandishments of salesmen offering highly impressive, elaborate, and expensive media systems.

Since so much "soft" money was available from federal and state governments to pay for these exotic systems, their acquisition was easy and painless. Funds were also available for the hiring of personnel to develop and operate the systems, and even for facilities to house them. Unfortunately, these elaborate systems were often acquired by institutions that had developed neither a solid rationale nor philosophy for their use. Because of the rapid development of funding programs and the necessity for proposal preparation under great time pressure, many programs were inadequately thought through and systems were evaluated too quickly. The results in some cases were "white elephants"—custom-designed systems that were poorly designed or executed. In other cases, operable systems were delivered with software that was incompatible with any other system or with interconnected or interfaced hardware, but no available software.

Even when such systems were valid and operational, they often foundered because of faculty indifference or hostility. In those days, administrators were generally the proposers of such systems and there often was not enough time to "sell" teaching faculty on the program and secure their cooperation if, indeed, the administration concerned was so inclined. Less-enlightened administrators frequently bought systems, had them installed, and then told the faculty to use them. The result, of course, was halfhearted faculty utilization of the systems. Since enthusiastic acceptance of such systems by the faculty is essential to their success, many early operations were seriously underutilized. In order to insure successful utilization of these systems, it is essential that faculty be firmly involved in their conceptualization and that they reprogram their courses to utilize the nonprint material in the system. Many systems have failed to be effectively utilized because faculty have been unwilling and incapable of successfully integrating nonprint materials with their courses; to do so requires more planning and investigation than some faculty care to do. Preparing lectures is easier than reorganizing a course to include media, which is an activity that involves restructuring and outlining the course anew, evaluation of available media for possible inclusion, and often development or even production of media not currently available. Even at institutions that have been developed to be media-centered, where faculty are hired with the understanding that media development is part of their job, the production and use of media have often fallen far short of expectations. Many faculty find the creative use and development of nonprint materials difficult.

THE INCOMPLETELY REALIZED REVOLUTION

The result of all these factors is that the media revolution has not developed in the way its proponents dreamed it would. Many systems have been purchased, some of them have become fully operational, and a few have met all the expectations of their planners. Unfortunately, many have not come close to achieving their potential or today are gathering dust in some closet or storage room. Nonetheless, nonprint materials have made a significant impact in the world of higher education and, while some of the more grandiose systems developed in the last decades are dead or dying, many of the techniques, machines, and media have clearly demonstrated their lasting value.

One lesson clear to many observers of the media scene during the last 10 to 15 years is that elaborate wired systems with centralized programming (Fig. 1) have often been less than successful, while libraries and media centers utilizing portable and flexible single-purpose machines have had greater success at less cost. One reason, of course, is that software for single-purpose machines sold in volume is more available than that needed for some of the systems and multipurpose machines. Another reason is that users often prefer to study and use media in places other than the fixed locations characteristic of wired systems.

FIG. 1 Media carrels grouped together.

LIBRARIES AND MEDIA

How have college and university libraries responded to this new world of media? Public libraries have long made use of some nonprint materials. Many of them have music and art rooms with audio recordings found in the former and slides and prints in the latter. Some public libraries have collections of 16-mm films, filmstrips, and nonmusical recordings, although smaller public libraries often serve as sources of information about these media and borrow them for use from larger libraries or media centers. Some innovative public libraries do provide nonprint programs for self-instruction and lend all sorts of nonbook items (even pet animals) to readers. Most special and governmental libraries do not make significant use of nonprint materials, though of course, there are exceptions.

However, today the libraries most concerned with beginning to utilize nonprint materials are academic libraries and it is to them we particularly direct the material in this chapter, although planners of other libraries may find helpful information here. Also, to repeat what we said earlier in the chapter, we are not trying to provide information for planners or buyers equipping resource centers that are essentially programming or production centers for nonprint materials. Rather, we are providing information that may be helpful to librarians and those planning libraries, by whatever name they are called, where materials of all media to help students learn are collected and made available.

THE ENVIRONMENT FOR NONPRINT SYSTEMS

Notwithstanding the desirability of flexible systems with portable components, the special preparation of areas to house media service is essential. Since all machines need electrical power, they are limited as to location. Further, some machines require a reduction in ambient light to avoid glare on viewing screens and because of this and noise generated by other machines, locations with special preparations are necessary. It is essential that planning for the newer, simpler media systems be carefully done, though it is nowhere nearly so complicated as some of the earlier wired distribution systems. TV systems which do use wired distribution systems require particular care in design.

AC Power

Some smaller audio devices, cassette players for example, can operate on battery power, but the continuing cost of batteries and recharging make this a less than satisfying arrangement for most libraries. Many libraries, when planning to provide power for audiovisual hardware, want to avoid permanent installations that deface carpet or limit options for future space rearrangement. One way of doing this relatively inexpensively is use of plug mold around the perimeter of a room or area. This provides more machine locations than conventionally spaced convenience outlets at lower cost per outlet, but of course, only provides for the perimeter. Outlets at building columns should always be available and carrels can often be located advantageously near such columns. In many libraries carrels, ganged (fastened together) near columns and around the perimeter at those widely provided power outlets, will make up all the media stations.

If stations need to be positioned away from columns and walls, power can be provided in the center of library areas in several ways. Many older libraries, built before the use of carpet on floors was common, had outlets set into the floor at regular intervals, using some of them for nearby equipment and covering unused ones with metal plates that could be lifted for later use. These were unsightly and hazardous.

The use of carpeted floors caused new problems. One answer is the under-floor duct system where conduits crisscross an area beneath the subfloor and carpet, making outlets available at very close intervals, perhaps every 2 ft. Holes are then drilled through the carpet into conduits wherever an outlet is needed. When outlets are no longer needed, the hole can be filled and the carpet patched or restored. This is an expensive solution, but one often used in technical processing areas and media production centers; libraries needing large numbers of carrels with electric power or "wet" carrels not near walls or columns may find this to be a good solution.

Another way of providing electric power in the middle of open areas is the "power column," a pole that extends from carpeted floor to ceiling where power is available. These can be placed wherever needed and are not expensive. They are unattractive and a traffic hazard; however, they are flexible, inexpensive, and have much to recommend them.

Other Environmental Needs

While all viewing and listening machines require AC power, there are other wire connections necessary for some kinds of equipment. Dial-access systems require a cable to each station, as do TV receivers. Computer terminals require either a telephone line or "hard wire" connection to the computer along with AC power. Incidentally, while telephone computer connections give more flexibility than hard wire connections, the monthly charges add up rapidly. When relatively permanent locations can be established, hard wire connections that are owned, instead of rented, should be used.

Other environmental conditions for areas where media stations are located are not particularly strenuous. As a matter of fact, the library reading room atmosphere, with carrels dedicated to certain media, provides the best sort of atmosphere for media use. General reading areas are customarily designed to provide comfortable, quiet, adequately illuminated study conditions, ideal for the use of nonprint media. Most media hardware operates relatively quietly and use of carrels with carpeted walls will absorb any motor noise generated. Any media used in such areas should, of course, provide sound through earphones and these should be good enough to prevent the sound from "leaking" into surrounding spaces. Machines using response mode or "answer back" should be relegated to closed rooms or separate areas. Viewing hardware today is generally designed to be operated successfully in fully lit rooms with no loss in viewing quality. Also, there is usually no difficulty caused by heat generated by hardware of the kind used for individual study/learning.

Media Storage and Distribution

Earlier we alluded to the desirability of providing media stations in general library reading areas. This reinforces the idea that the library provides the ideal center for the acquisition, storage, distribution, and use of learning resources in all forms. Although many libraries will not wish to get involved in the instructional use of media, with its component functions of hardware scheduling and maintenance, presentation scheduling, and media development and production, few libraries will fail to provide some material in other media for those users who need them. If used in general library seating areas, there is less of a feeling of separation between print and nonprint material users. Also, the high cost of nonprint hardware and software dictates that it be used largely in nonprivate areas where a measure of security is present. Media software and smaller hardware are frequently stored behind circulation desks at which users can be identified and condition of materials and machines can be checked upon return. Many libraries hold student identification cards or money deposits against the safe return of players, viewers, and software. Since the smaller items of equipment, like audio cassette players and slide and filmstrip viewers and projectors, as well as the media themselves, are not particularly bulky, they can be stored in cabinets and cases behind the desk.

Location of Hardware

Large equipment will often be placed permanently in carrels because of its weight and the wear and tear it suffers when it is constantly transported. When carrels must house equipment, they should be oriented so that the equipment they contain is easily visible to staff as well as library patrons in order to discourage vandalism. Smaller equipment, such as audio cassettes, will last much longer and need repair much less often if charged out from lending desks rather than built into tables or carrel tops. The author has visited libraries where record and tape players, both reel-to-reel and cassette, were built into table tops and was told that half of the units were out of operation at any given time. Cassette players are slightly more "idiotproof" than record players and reel-to-reel tape players, so they hold up somewhat better when built into carrel tops. On the other hand, storing reel-to-reel and record players behind lending desks is not really advisable because of damage to electric components when they are carried about freely. If it is necessary to hand these out across the desk, be certain that the models purchased are solidly built and will absorb considerable use and abuse. Some of the damages to players built into carrel and table tops can be prevented by the use of lockable covers over the players. Keys to the covers can be charged out to users upon presentation of identification. The condition of units so housed should be checked frequently, after each use, if possible.

Media in Carrels

Larger units such as sound/slide viewers need to be installed in carrels. They are too large to be housed under lockable covers and they cannot be built into work tops because of their size and shape. Fortunately, such equipment is designed specifically for this type of use and is really quite sturdy and easily operated. While vandalism causes some equipment damage, difficulty of operation due to inadequate instructions or ignorance on the part of users is a more common cause of damage.

When media hardware are to be placed in open library areas, carrels are the preferred housing although tables are occasionally utilized, particularly for built-in equipment. Carrels are in many ways ideal for the location of media hardware: they provide a good degree of privacy; the inside rear walls are fine locations for projection screens; the walls muffle noise, particularly when covered with carpet or other acoustic material; they can easily be constructed to house built-in units of various shapes and sizes; and they are easily supplied with electric power and other electric connections. Unfortunately, during the early years of the media explosion, many carrels of very poor quality were used to house media hardware in libraries. Sometimes manufacturers of media systems had subcontractors produce cheap carrels to house their equipment. In other instances, libraries bought low priced carrels from unfamiliar sources because the usual sources of library furniture were slow to offer carrels to meet the special requirements of media systems. Many of the inferior carrels purchased in these early days did not prove satisfactory under heavy use. To house media today, many wise specifiers order carrels that are identical to others in the library. All manufacturers of library technical furniture now offer in the same quality as their other carrels some with special provision for media use. These are not inexpensive but their continued good appearance and utility long after purchase will justify their added initial cost.

The trend to smaller individual media players and viewers is lessening the demand for elaborate, specially designed carrels with built-in machinery. The trend is to carrels which look similar to conventional carrels except for the addition of electric power sources, usually at the back of the carrel, utilizing double convenience outlets or plugmold and small projection screens applied to the back wall. If there is a wired distribution system, there will often be a telephone-type dial or touch-tone panel to address the system and an earphone jack. Carrels will frequently be fastened (ganged) together for convenient power or program distribution. It is often advisable to order carrels with work surfaces larger than the standard 24 × 36 in. (600 × 900 mm) because of the large size of some hardware and the desirability of providing space for writing. In some designs, either a pull-out writing surface or tablet-arm arrangement provides space for writing. To cut down glare and eliminate the distraction of those viewing projected images, the inside surfaces should be subdued and not reflective.

Group Use of Media

Although libraries, particularly academic libraries, will be most concerned with providing access to media for individuals using them as personal learning resources, in some instances it will be necessary to provide facilities for group viewing and listening. Small group studies, or even individual study rooms, in libraries can serve quite well as preview rooms or places where two or more persons can listen or view together audio or visual media presentations. A small table with chairs and, when appropriate, a portable projection screen, along with a source of electric power, will provide all the support needed for small group media use. Larger groups may be accommodated in large group studies or seminar rooms. Seating can be at tables or on side chairs arranged auditorium-style. Some libraries will wish to have at least one room equipped with built-in speakers where group listening to music can take place. At the University of Maryland's undergraduate library, a large comfortable room furnished with lounge furniture, has a quadraphonic speaker system and scheduled "quad" programming is provided for part of the day with "on request" programming at other times.

WIRED DISTRIBUTION SYSTEMS VERSUS INDIVIDUAL VIEWERS/PLAYERS

Earlier we described the trend away from programming centers with elaborate packaged systems that used wired distribution of media in favor of more standardized, portable single-purpose machines that utilize easily available, often commercially produced, software. Such centers house walls full of reel-to-reel players and turntables which are in constant operation, playing programmed material piped to dial-access stations in the library and other campus locations. Here a large number of programs can be run simultaneously, many of them tied into current course requirements. If enough channels are available (often there are 80 to 100 or more), many can repeat much-needed material endlessly so that all who need it can "catch" the program. In other cases, programming of needed material is provided on a scheduled basis, with printed schedules notifying users of program availability. In such systems, the needs of those wanting material other than the scheduled or repeated material on dedicated channels can be met for performance on certain free channels if they call the programming center and request what they need.

Many such systems have been purchased and installed in colleges and universities throughout the country. Some have worked well; others lie dormant. All were expensive, both to purchase and to operate. Personnel costs in programming centers can be heavy. The systems are difficult to expand and maintain, and in many ways are inflexible. Today, with funding sources dwindling, there are only one or two companies that still produce these systems.

Today all the benefits of wired systems, plus a few more, can be realized with portable cassette players and easily duplicated cassettes. Instead of going to a carrel wired to the distribution system and requesting a program or tuning to a channel, a student can come to the library circulation desk, request a cassette player, earphones, and a copy of any cassette in the collection and use them anywhere he wishes. Those needing a particularly high level of reproduction can use Dolbyized cassette players which approach the fidelity of the best reel-to-reel tapes and phonodiscs. Cassettes are easily duplicated by untrained personnel, and operation of reproduction and performance equipment is nearly "idiotproof."

Other types of equipment beside audio equipment are available in flexible, relatively portable versions. However, TV continues to be used frequently in campus-wide systems with centralized programming. TV receivers are placed throughout the campus and in library carrels, with scheduled programming on channels available in each location. However, individualized programming is relatively easy to provide by using video cassette players coupled with TV receivers, and it is becoming quite popular, although the software is costly to duplicate. The anticipated advent of videodiscs will make inexpensive, individual programming of TV a reality. When this happens, wired systems may become extinct.

THE SPECTRUM OF NONPRINT HARDWARE

There is an enormous variety of nonprint media hardware available today. Thirty years ago, visual software in libraries consisted mainly of 16-mm motion pictures, glass-mounted slides ($3\frac{1}{4} \times 4$ in. or 9×10 mm) and filmstrips, the last two being silent media. Audio materials were limited to phonodiscs (records), with reel-to-reel tapes used largely in radio stations. Television, audio cassettes, and the popular use of 2 × 2 in. (5 × 5 mm) slides were still only in the future. Today most of these media, such as 16-mm motion pictures, phonodiscs, and filmstrips, are still popular, while glass-mounted $3\frac{1}{4}$ × 4 in. slides have been largely supplanted by 2 × 2 in. slides. But for this one exception, all these ancient and honored media have been improved and updated.

Projected Images

The 16-mm film, sound and silent, is still extremely popular. Nothing has supplanted it for group viewing of dramatic productions. But today the film has acquired new dimensions. Films in 8 mm and "Super-8" have achieved great popularity and 35-mm has given many institutions the professional quality of film presentation desirable in some situations. The use of 8-mm and Super-8 has encouraged the development of self-contained viewers which contain both projector and screen. Such viewers lend themselves to use by individuals and they fit conveniently into library carrels. Super-8 and 8-mm also can be projected for small- to medium-size group viewing. Film for these formats is available on closed-loop cartridges as well as in conventional reels. Film on the closed cartridges requires no threading or rewinding and can be played continuously in unattended operation. Super-8 and 8-mm software and hardware are small in size and store easily. Sound (magnetic) is supplied on some films and can be added on some projector models. Other systems synchronize films with audio cassettes to achieve sound. One popular application of 8-mm has been in the so-called "single concept" cartridge where specially produced short films in Super-8 concentrating on one idea or concept in some academic subject can easily be reviewed by students until the concept is completely understood. These are often used in laboratories for subjects so oriented, e.g., physics, chemistry, and biology.

Many educational purposes require single photographic images rather than the continuous action of motion pictures. The slide, once $3\frac{1}{4}$ × 4 in. and clad in glass, but now mostly 2 × 2 in. and mounted in cardboard, has met this need for many years. Indeed, today color slides and filmstrips, with the addition of sound, form a very important element in the array of nonprint media. Not only is it easy to linger over an important point during a presentation, but slides and filmstrips are inexpensive, easily stored, and produced quite easily. The hardware is simple, easily repaired and maintained, and technically near perfect for its purpose. Sound is now generally provided by a synchronized cassette player and there are available well-proven combination units in which slides and filmstrips are projected on rear screens with synchronized cassette players providing sound, all in the same "box" (Fig. 2). Filmstrips are inexpensive and easily produced,

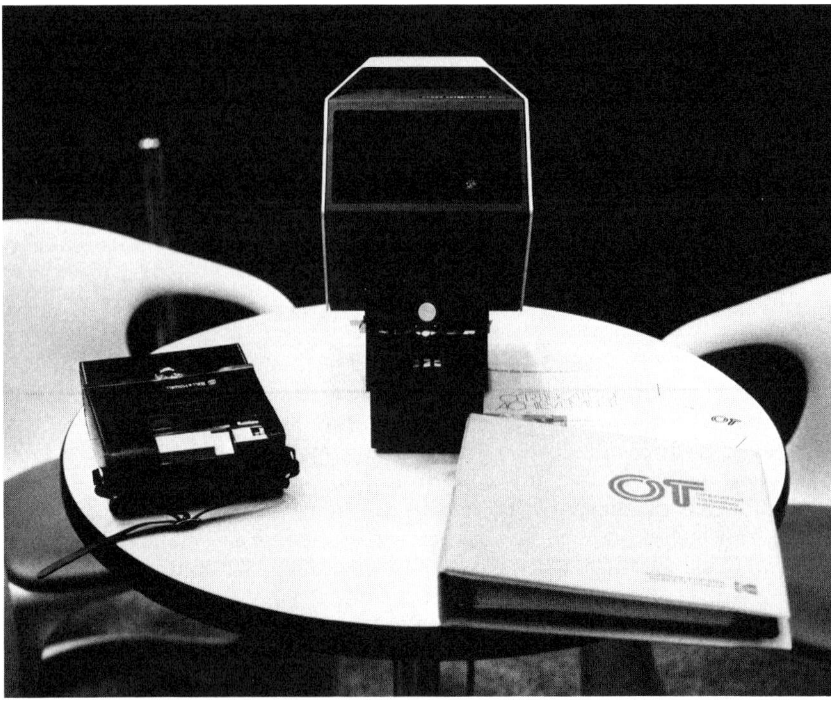

FIG. 2 Cassette player and microfiche reader can supplant slides or filmstrips synchronized with tape.

while slides, although somewhat more expensive per image, are individual images which can be arranged in innumerable ways. The great flexibility of color slides gives them long life in many presentations. The development of similar systems utilizing color microfiche used with cassette players may ultimately supplant the sound/slide and sound/filmstrip machines.

Two other kinds of screen images, those of the overhead and opaque projectors, are extremely popular for classroom use, but their utility in libraries is limited. The overhead projector projects transparencies—clear, acetate film with black or color line images that can be prepared in advance or drawn during a lecture by an instructor. These are excellent for illustrating points in lectures and for outlining material. Although of comparatively recent origin, the popularity of transparencies is great and their use in classes almost universal. The opaque projector, on the other hand, is a means of visual projection that has been used for many years. The large, cumbersome projectors are used to project printed material for group viewing. Since they must use reflected images rather than transparent material, the optics take up more space and the projectors, therefore, are large and the projected image not of high quality. However, for some teaching situations when it is necessary to show print material to a group, the opaque projector is essential.

Sound Recordings

Since the early days of sound reproduction, the phonograph record, or phonodisc, has been the most common means of recording and reproducing sound. It continues to be the most universal format for sound storage and has achieved a high degree of technological development during its more than 70-year history. Today the most common formats of phonodiscs are the LP, a 12-in. plastic disc with playing time of 15 to 30 min or more per side at $33\frac{1}{3}$ rpm and the 45, a small record 7 in. in diameter which plays for about 3 min per side at 45 rpm. The latter format is used primarily for popular hits and is of little interest to most libraries. The LP, with high-quality monaural, stereophonic, or quadraphonic reproduction available, and its relatively long playing time is the phonodisc most suitable for libraries.

The last 20 years have seen the introduction and increasing popularity of two serious rivals to the LP record. Actually one, the tape cassette, is a more convenient version of the other, the magnetic reel-to-reel tape. Reel-to-reel tape was first used in commercial application, where the utmost in fidelity of sound reproduction was required, then became popular as a consumer product. Tapes are relatively expensive and somewhat difficult to handle. Music lovers needing the highest-quality recording capability generally use reel-to-reel tape. Tape can be used to record almost anywhere for very reasonable cost; whereas phonodiscs can only be recorded commercially. Tapes are easily reproduced or duplicated, but phonodiscs can only be duplicated in quantity at considerable expense. Tape players are quite expensive, but most libraries with a requirement for good-quality music reproduction should have at least one high-quality reel-to-reel tape player; they record and reproduce in monaural and stereo, two- and four-track.

The past decade has seen the phenomenal development of the cassette tape player. Begun as a novelty for those who wanted convenient tape recordings of popular music, it has become a very important element in all segments of audio reproduction. Its convenient size and simple, drop-in operation make it ideal for many applications. Cassette players can be quite small, can operate almost anywhere, and are capable of sound reproduction of good quality. Most users find controls almost foolproof on a cassette player, and consider dropping in a cassette to be played simplicity itself, compared to the "gyrations" involved when some users try to thread tape onto a reel-to-reel tape player, or the care with which one must place the tone arm of some record players on a phonodisc to avoid damage to the record. Small cassette players require little power and are often designed to use AC power or batteries. Thus, recorded sound equipment can be lent freely without concern for damage. The cassette duplicators which provide such copies are not cheap but their usefulness is great. A limited stock of relatively inexpensive blank cassettes can be used for duplicates many times by being erased and rerecorded on demand. In order to make the full inventory of sound recordings freely available for users, many libraries purchase dubbing equipment (Fig. 3) which makes possible conversion of recordings on phonodiscs and tapes into cassettes. These dubbed cassettes can then be available for routine use and circulation with the original copy on disc or tape reserved for dubbing additional copies and as the archival copy. Dubbing is not difficult—a competent technician can manage it easily using readily available equipment, and several companies produce mobile dubbing and performance units which provide several recording and conversion capabilities; however, dubbing and duplicating any audio material may violate copyright.

FIG. 3 Performance/dubbing unit can house record player, tape deck, cassette player/recorder and AM-FM tuner/amplifier.

Television

The aural and visual records we have been considering have been strongly supplemented in libraries first by radio, then television. The early days of both media offered the spontaneity and immediacy of live broadcasting. Soon, however, recordings were used for broadcasting and telecasting, thereby sacrificing some immediacy but eliminating human errors and generally improving technical quality. It did not take long for educational institutions to discover the magnificent potential of television, not only as an adjunct to and sometime substitute for classroom instruction, but also as a source of well-produced, up-to-date program material on nearly every conceivable subject. Eventually many educational institutions acquired TV production facilities of their own and began producing programs, acquiring multichannel distribution systems, and in some cases, establishing educational television (ETV) stations. It now is imperative for many libraries to have TV receivers readily available for many purposes. Students view televised lectures they missed when given "live." Interest groups want to see broadcast or recorded programs concerning their fields of interest. Users want to see educational programming on ETV channels. Indeed also, TV receivers are essential components of some library security systems and TV receivers (monitors) must be watched to catch violators. It is unusual to find a library of any size today that does not own at least one TV receiver.

Many libraries have felt the need to retain TV programs of particular value for their permanent collections. Until recently the equipment and tapes for this purpose were expensive and difficult to use. Lately, the availability of videocassette, in many ways analogous to the audio cassette, has made recording TV programming more convenient and somewhat less expensive. New technology utilizing $\frac{1}{2}$-in. video cassettes will further improve this capability. Now the videodisc promises to make recording video programming so inexpensive and convenient that video recordings will become almost universally available. Many libraries will amass substantial collections of video performances of all kinds: speeches, historic events, concerts, dramatic performances, political campaigns and conventions, and discussions of current issues. These should be of great value to future users of libraries. Once the necessary video recording equipment is obtained, the cost of videodiscs should become an inconsequential burden on most budgets. Again, copyright regulations must be considered.

Other Media

Other forms of media will be found in libraries, although the ones already discussed are the ones most commonly used. Among these are the various self-instructional devices which utilize various combinations of print and nonprint media to assist users to study some concept or subject, e.g., "How to Program Fortran IV." These provide brief instructional sequences, followed by questions which are answered by the respondent, the correctness of whose answers indicates the level of understanding. The library is certainly the preferred location for these devices. Tachistoscopes and other reading devices assist groups and individuals in improving reading skills. Where such programs exist, their inclusion in libraries where private self-study is encouraged, is certainly appropriate.

Accessory Equipment

A great variety of accessory production, presentation, and storage equipment is necessary to operate nonprint media effectively. Film programs of any size require the presence of devices for editing, inspecting, splicing, and winding, along with storage racks and cabinets, reels, cases, and projection tables. Slide collections need portable previewers, light tables, and mounting devices along with their own distinctive storage cabinets. All the visual media need storage cabinets, projection tables and, of course, the all-important projection screen.

Screens are frequently taken for granted, but are essential to any viewed media. Some devices used by individuals have self-contained screens. Small projection screens are frequently mounted within carrels for individual viewing. Much larger screens are needed for larger group viewing when such is part of library operation. These vary from very small screens which roll up and fold into easily handled and carried packages to those permanently hung above chalk boards or concealed in ceiling and unrolled for use by remote control. Screens are marketed with several kinds of surfaces, depending on the kind of media to be projected on them. Beaded screens are better for overall use, lenticular screens are preferred for wide-angle, and matte-finished screens are especially suited for use with overhead projectors. Screens must also be selected to suit the size of room in which projected images are to be viewed. The Audio-Visual Equipment Directory and other media handbooks give charts which match screen size to room size.

Software Storage

While much of the specialized equipment used for elaborate motion picture and television production and operation will not generally be found in libraries, nearly all will need equipment for storage of software and hardware, projection stands, and other aids for media presentation. Several firms make rather complete lines of this support equipment and the major library

FIG. 4 Media can be housed on library shelving in special inserts.

supply houses market some of these lines. Much of this equipment is of lightweight metal with plastic inserts. At this writing, at least one of the major manufacturers of media storage equipment produces cabinets of superior construction and finish. When evaluating for possible purchase, it is particularly important to examine each of the four or five major lines. There are some specialized media storage units offered by library furniture manufacturers, mostly special inserts for library shelving (Fig. 4). These are often somewhat more expensive, and without locking doors, can be a security problem, but are ideal for some applications. Recently Gaylord and Demco began offering wood-clad versions of media storage cabinets at reasonable prices (Fig. 5). These may be more compatible with the decor of some libraries than metal cabinets.

FIG. 5 Attractive, moderately priced wood media storage units. (Gaylord.)

EVALUATION OF MEDIA

The selection of media hardware and software, along with storage and other peripheral equipment needed for a library media program is made somewhat difficult by the librarian's unfamiliarity with the field. Some segments of the industry have not regarded libraries as important potential customers and have made little effort to reach the market. As more and more libraries have media collections and programs, this situation is changing. Further, the industry itself is changing. As those developing and operating programs in nonprint media change their emphases from elaborate systems employing custom components to simpler systems employing proven "off the shelf" viewing and listening devices, so the industry has changed drastically. Many of the giants of industry as well as the "fly by nights" have gotten out and most of the firms remaining are reasonably solid and competent. Earlier in Chapter 3, we pointed out that the library market was such an insignificant one to manufacturers of microform equipment that this equipment was never designed to meet library needs, but rather those of business, which was their prime marketing target. When we consider the hardware (and software) of nonprint media, this is not true, for libraries need the same hardware and software that is required by the entire educational market and this market is the prime one for the industry.

How does one select and evaluate audiovisual equipment for purchase? First, most libraries will have one or more experts in their own or related institutions who will be competent to assist with equipment selection. The advantages and shortcomings of the various machines are very apparent to those who work with them regularly. Other institutions whose libraries operate media programs will have expertise they will gladly share. A visit of some duration to such a library will provide an opportunity for acquaintance with the equipment and its operation in some detail, which should greatly assist evaluation.

Library conventions, state and national, present some exhibits of media. However, manufacturers of media hardware and software are more likely to show their products at conventions of media specialists. Most states have such groups and the AECT (Association for Educational Communication

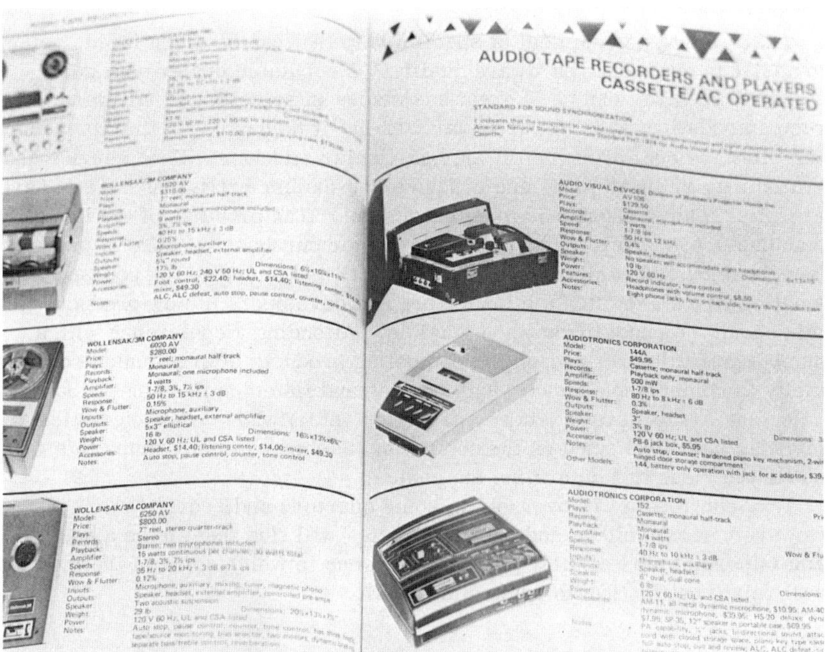

FIG. 6 The Audio-Visual Equipment Directory, published annually, provides comprehensive information on audio visual hardware.

Technology) is the most important national group. Attendance at these shows will permit one to see the lines and new products of the most important hardware manufacturers and publishers of software.

The Audio-Visual Equipment Directory, published by the National Audio-Visual Association, Inc., is the single most useful source of information available about the whole range of nonprint hardware. Arranged by type of machine, i.e., 16-mm motion picture, slide projector, sound or silent, etc., it provides a separate entry for each major model of equipment available. Each entry gives a rather complete specification, lists available accessories and the price for each item (Fig. 6). There is also a list of AV dealers and manufacturers keyed to their entries in the handbook. Also included is a valuable table of projection screen/room ratios and other reference charts. Altogether, this is a most useful publication that most libraries should acquire annually. For evaluation and rating of hardware, Library Technology Reports occasionally rates entire categories, e.g., sound slide projectors and also occasionally tests individual models. The ratings in Consumer Reports magazine will occasionally be helpful, particularly their discussions on what to look for in products such as stereo components.

There is not a great deal of specific help that can be given in this volume to assist in evaluating hardware quality. A reputable dealer with good service capability can be of great assistance in selection of hardware. His recommendations will be particularly useful if he has competing lines and can offer the best of these for your particular situation. Good service and availability of spare parts and consumables (bulbs, extra lenses, etc.) are essential if any program is to be successful. The products of the larger manufacturers will often be better "bets" for purchase because of proven performance and easier availability of parts and service. Of course, smaller firms are often the innovators and developers of new products and this should be encouraged when feasible. Attending a conference with a number of exhibitors presenting competing products offers a unique opportunity to comparison-test various viewing and listening machines. Software belonging to the library (slides, cassettes, etc.) whose characteristics are familiar should be tried on the competing machines. Many times this will settle the issue and determine the choice.

Nonprint media are oversold in some quarters and scorned in others. However, most college and public libraries will find them to be a useful and important part of their programs and one to which some of their users will relate better than to printed material.

7

SELECTION, EVALUATION, AND PURCHASE OF LIBRARY FURNITURE AND EQUIPMENT

INTRODUCTION

In Chapters 2 through 5, we discussed the functions of the various parts of a library and the furniture needed in these areas. We talked about how these items of furniture should be designed and constructed in order to function properly and maintain their appearance through years of use. Discussed and compared were variants such as carrels with different configurations, in different sizes, and with a variety of accessories. In this chapter, information is presented to assist the reader in selecting, evaluating, and procuring specific pieces of furniture and equipment.

When librarians are involved in new library buildings and spaces or renovated ones, a great deal of help in selecting and evaluation of furniture and equipment is commonly available, although much of it is misleading or oriented to particular products. Librarians interested in obtaining furniture and equipment for an ongoing program, on the other hand, will generally be dependent on their own resources. The material in this chapter presents objective information of some help in both cases.

CREATING THE SELECTION TEAM

The first matter of importance is to determine who is to select the furniture and equipment for the library. If it is a new building, many people will probably want, or indeed be required, to become involved in the process. They will represent a number of areas of concern or interests that need to be met or satisfied.

The chief officer of the institution, whether college president, public library board president, school superintendent, or law or medical school dean will be concerned primarily with cost and public impact. He will have probably been responsible for making available the budget to furnish the library and will be concerned that the allocated amount is not exceeded. This person will also be greatly concerned about the library's effect on the public and particularly any special constituency of the institution. For instance, the president of a small church-related college will be desirous of creating a favorable impact on the entire community with a new library and its furnishings, but he will be particularly concerned if the members of the church, who have contributed to the building and equipment funds, feel that the furniture is too luxurious or, conversely, too poor to last any length of time. The character of furniture provided will need to answer these important concerns adequately.

IMPORTANCE OF THE LIBRARIAN

The librarian is the most essential member of the team, for he or she must assure that the library's furniture is functional and that the furniture and equipment that specifically meets the library needs is actually ordered. This point seems obvious, but the author has seen dozens of libraries throughout the country where the librarian and the staff were not permitted to determine what furniture was ordered for the library. In these cases, either the chief officer, architect, or purchasing agent ignored the librarian's suggestions and decided what furniture was to be ordered; the results of this sort of situation are always disastrous. While not all librarians are equally competent in the area of furniture selection, they certainly understand the functional needs of libraries better than a layman. Any wise librarian furnishing a new building will not trust solely in his own information or competence but will seek information and advice from consultants or at least other librarians who have recently furnished a library.

The author does not mean to suggest that the librarian must do all the research involved in trying to find the most suitable items of furniture for use throughout the library. Architects and designers can and should bring their knowledge and experience to this search and present a choice of apparently suitable furniture items from which the librarian and others responsible for the final selection can make choices. The point that is essential here is this: when the librarian does not make the final decision, he or she must have the right to veto any item that does not meet the functional needs of the library or one that investigation shows to be unlikely to bear up under library use for any length of time. Further, the librarian will nearly always have to be the one person who manages the whole selection process. Of course, in large libraries the chief librarian will often deputize someone to be responsible for a new library facility and its furnishing. However, if there is not some librarian who takes responsibility for seeing that the furniture and equipment are suitable for the library's needs, a designer or a purchasing agent will do so and the results will generally be unfortunate. Designers tend to overemphasize aesthetics, while purchasing agents are frequently most impressed by low cost; neither characteristic is as important as suitability and durability to a librarian. Thus it is essential that librarians be the pivotal figures in the process of selecting, evaluating, and acquiring the furniture and equipment for any library facility. They must make it their business to become familiar with the range of library furniture with the assistance of consultants, designers, purchasing agents, and vendors. The ultimate success of the furniture and equipment, its suitability for the functions it must perform, as well as its long-term retention of function and attractiveness, can only be assured by informed, intelligent librarians. The other team members—the architect and/or designer, the consultant, and business and purchasing personnel—should all be allowed to contribute to the selection and procurement processes, but only the librarian can assure the functional success of the planned solution.

There will, of course, be more than one librarian involved in these deliberations in all but the smallest libraries. Any chief librarian today who fails to give his or her staff an opportunity to consider and discuss the choice of furniture and equipment for the library is not only overlooking a most important source of information and help, but is also creating a severe morale problem. It is particularly essential that a staff's specialized knowledge of their own work areas be fully utilized in furnishing these areas. Here it will be useful if staff members are familiar with similar operations in libraries other than their own. A series of visits to other libraries will be of great assistance, not only for the librarian/selector, but also for other members of the staff. Such visits are particularly useful because of the tendency of staff to accept the current arrangement in their own library uncritically without the stimulus of seeing how other libraries do things.

While it is essential that staff input and preference be given careful consideration, this author is not convinced that a committee or committees can provide the efficient coordination necessary in such projects. An advisory or reactive group will certainly be helpful to the coordinating librarian, but when it comes to the day-to-day effort and the necessity for quick decision making, a committee is not an appropriate mechanism.

ROLE OF THE CONSULTANT

Most librarians will find a librarian/consultant particularly helpful in finding and evaluating appropriate furniture and equipment. In some cases the building consultant will be knowledgeable enough to be of assistance; in many cases, however, this may not be true. There are many librarians who list themselves as library building consultants on the basis of limited experience. Very few have any significant acquaintance with library furniture and equipment. Experience in furnishing one library is enlightening, but hardly provides a broad enough range of experience to make one a competent consultant in this area. The ideal consultant has had experience both in furnishing his own buildings and consulting on others. Further, many competent library building consultants have had significant experience only with arranging furnishings in library interiors, but not with selecting and evaluating library furnishings. The two processes are quite different. Arrangement can generally be changed if not satisfactory; furniture selection and procurement had better be right the first time.

The library furniture consultant should be able to perform a number of services to earn his fee. If he is good and knows the furniture market, he can easily save several times his fee. Here are some of the ways in which he can be helpful:

1. He should start by examining and critiquing the furniture layouts created by architects and designers as part of the building planning process. If the furniture consultant and building consultant are the same person, this person will have been involved in the process from the start. If, however, the library furniture consultant comes onto the scene late in the planning process, his intimate knowledge of furniture capabilities can prevent mistakes in design and arrangement.

2. The consultant should have a comprehensive and up-to-date knowledge of library furniture and equipment and must be thoroughly conversant with the different ways of manufacturing various kinds of furniture and know which ones are superior. He should have visited furniture factories to see how different companies produce their products. He will have visited libraries where different brands and lines of furniture have been installed to observe how well different items of furniture have held up under use. The consultant should have attended conferences where furniture useful in libraries is exhibited. Attendance at conference exhibits for librarians is not enough. Some manufacturers of furniture that the consultant may consider appropriate for library use show their wares at conventions outside the library world and ignore national, state, and regional library conferences. We could ignore companies who are not wise enough to display their wares at library meetings. However, these companies do show their products at conferences attended by architects, designers, and purchasing agents, often preferring to try to sell to them rather than to librarians. A consultant had better be knowledgeable about these companies or another member of the planning team may propose a line of furniture about which nothing is known. Even a knowledgeable consultant will get an occasional surprise here, for companies go in and out of the library business so rapidly that it is nearly impossible to keep track of them.

3. A good consultant will be well acquainted with the world of library furniture manufacturing and its individual firms. He will know such things about these firms as their financial resources, apparent commitment to the library market, pricing strategy (if any), general reputation for overall quality, marketing methods, concern for customer satisfaction, engineering

and design capability, as well as a host of other matters important to clients concerned with purchasing library furniture and equipment. He will certainly be acquainted with the key personnel of these companies and will be aware of new lines and other developments.

4. The consultant will be conversant in other items of furniture and equipment, not specifically library-oriented, which are often needed in furnishing libraries. Among these are such diverse objects as blackboards, sound-retardant partitions, costumers, planters, duplicating machines, collaters, lecterns, tablet armchairs, pianos, floodlights—the list goes on.

ROLE OF THE DESIGNER

An architect will have been responsible for the design of the library space whether it is a new building, addition, or renovation of existing space. Any competent architect will be concerned about all aspects of the space in question, including the furniture and equipment to be placed in it. It may be that its selection is part of the architect's contractual obligation. If this is true, a designer within his organization or from an outside design concern will generally do this work under the architect's direction. In some cases, the architect is not responsible for furniture selection, and the client institution itself will hire a designer. In a few cases, an institution will have a designer on its staff who can provide necessary design services.

The Necessity of Design Service

It is true that when considering the purchase of furniture and equipment for existing facilities, a small addition, or new building, a competent librarian, with the benefit of advice from a consultant, should be able to make the necessary selections. However, in larger projects where new or renovated facilities are involved, the services of a trained and experienced designer are almost necessary. A trained designer can provide invaluable assistance in selecting, matching, and mixing colors and textures; in suggesting new materials and techniques; in suggesting styles and forms of furniture that complement the architecture and spirit of the building; and in designing sign and graphics systems for the building.

A qualified designer should not have the last word on the suitability of furniture for library use. Even those designers whose experience and training lies in commercial or institutional applications generally have little understanding of the functional requirements for library furniture and the extraordinary need for durability. Many commercial customers expect to redecorate or refurnish a space each 7 to 10 years; therefore durability is not an important factor in furniture selection in such applications. Even most institutional applications do not require furniture of the durability that libraries do. Furniture in libraries is frequently exposed to heavy use 12 to 16 hours or more a day, nearly every day in the year. And the useful life of this furniture must be thought of in decades rather than just years. Extraordinary requirements like these are found in few other places. Even the infamous airline terminal receives renovation every few years. The other kinds of installations where such extraordinary requirements for durability prevail (bus terminals, government offices, etc.) generally use hard-wearing, unappetizing-looking furniture that is expected to be merely functional and not attractive. Libraries, on the other hand, are expected to convey an atmosphere that will entice those entering into using their resources and services, and they are expected to retain their good looks for more years than any one has the right to expect. Obviously, the component parts of this inviting atmosphere must be selected with great care to assure their attractiveness (enter the designer) as well as their durability and suitability (which is the responsibility of the librarian).

A few librarians, by virtue of their training, experience, or superb taste, will themselves be capable of creating the interior design, perhaps with some help in color coordination, and some designers who have previously done good library designs will fully understand the importance of function and durability in library furniture. Both are very rare types of people. Very few librarians would claim that they are capable of doing the designer's job. Unfortunately, many designers believe they can select and specify any kind of furniture, including library furniture, without any meaningful input from anyone. Hundreds of libraries all over the country bear testimony to this misplaced confidence. The most frequently committed error in furnishing libraries is the use of designer-selected furniture that is not suitable for library use. In his travels around the country, the author has seen scores of libraries affected by furnishing misjudgments by designers. Typical of this problem is use of fabric upholstery on side chairs that have, of course, become dirty, worn through, or have had to be replaced. Another frequently observed problem is the use of lounge chairs and other furniture of household quality which is simply inadequate to hold up under heavy library use; this furniture generally falls apart or looks terrible in a few years.

Among the most essential and hard-used items in any library are the reader chairs, that is, the chairs used throughout most libraries for seating readers at carrels and tables. These must be most carefully selected, for their longevity is vital to the successful operation of the library. It is difficult to convince designers of this, but failure to do so causes great problems, as many recently furnished libraries attest. If upholstered (and this alone will detract from a chair's useful life), the padding and suspension must be as durable as possible and the upholstery cover must be of a material that resists wear and dirt equally well. Although designers frequently want to use fabric seats and backs on reader chairs in order to add color to the decor, they should not be permitted to do so. No fabric can resist wear and dirt for the required useful life of library reader seating. The author has visited many libraries throughout the country, including some highly acclaimed ones, with fabric-covered upholstered chairs. The chairs were uniformly faded, dirty, or worn through, and there was usually no hope of their replacement or reupholstery. If upholstery is used on reader chairs, it should be of vinyl or leather. Leather is more expensive, but the extra cost will be repaid by longer-lived beauty and utility.

On the positive side, designers will have superior sources of information about possible lines and items of furniture that might be suitable for the library. As mentioned earlier, they will also almost certainly bring to the development of the interior aesthetic judgments which will greatly enhance all aspects of its appearance. If the librarian and librarian/consultant are equally knowledgeable about the functional and construction requirements of the furniture, the furniture specified will be beautiful and durable and the interior arrangement pleasing and functional.

THE PURCHASING AGENT

Furniture and equipment for most library projects will be processed through some kind of purchasing agency. Colleges and universities generally work through a department of purchase or, in some smaller institutions, through a college business office. Public library systems sometimes have their own procurement departments, otherwise they generally must buy through a municipal or other official purchasing agency. Sometimes the library administration will have the entire responsibility for the procurement process. Later we will talk about these agencies in greater depth, but here we mention them because they can often be helpful in pointing out possible sources of furniture and equipment, and their experience and acquaintance with the furniture industry and with many vendors can be of great assistance.

Such agencies, however, should not be depended upon to do the whole job, though the agency will often be willing, even eager to select, specify, evaluate, and procure the furniture and equipment. This is almost always a mistake and should be resisted firmly. Purchasing agents tend to place a premium on buying at the lowest price and from vendors with whom they have had previous dealings. It is sometimes difficult to convince them of the functional specialization of some kinds of library furniture. Also, some purchasing agents operate as procurement bodies only, performing only the actual purchasing function and are not able to be very helpful with advice and information on vendors and products. Other purchasing departments more adequately staffed, are most knowledgeable and helpful and can be of great assistance in helping to select and specify furniture for libraries. Whatever its capabilities, the library will probably have to buy through such an agency, so an early, carefully nurtured relationship is essential. One should not wait to establish relations until the time when orders must be placed; rather, library planners should become acquainted with the agency early in the design stage. Most purchasing departments have considerable libraries of catalogs and other information on vendors, including prices, specifications, swatches, and color chips. Gaining access to this material can be most helpful.

OTHER SOURCES OF INFORMATION

Any or all of the parties just mentioned can provide information about the furniture and equipment to be considered for purchase, but there are many other sources of information a wise librarian will become familiar with so that his information about available furniture and equipment is complete.

Journals

Manufacturers of furniture and equipment appropriate for library use often advertise in library journals and periodicals. Library Journal, American Libraries (formerly the American Library Association Bulletin), and the Wilson Library Bulletin are library magazines with national coverage, and all three carry advertising by manufacturers of library furniture and equipment. Library Journal has two pertinent issues each year, one reviewing new library buildings, and the other being a buying guide issue that attracts many advertisers of library furniture and equipment. In the buying guide issue, along with many ads are (a) a classified listing of library products and services with a brief listing of companies producing them; and (b) a separate alphabetical listing of the companies with addresses.

Journals covering other aspects of the furniture business are often helpful in acquainting librarians with products they might consider for library use. Contract covers the field of institutional or contract furniture thoroughly, has a large number of ads, and publishes an annual buying guide issue that is particularly helpful. General architectural and design magazines such as Architectural Record, Architectural Forum, Progressive Architecture, and Interiors, provide helpful advertisements and useful articles. College and University Business and American School and University report on the educational market and have some ads and editorial material helpful to library interior planners, as do some of the magazines aimed at the office equipment market, such as Office, Modern Office Procedures, and Administrative Management. The latter group is particularly useful for presenting products and techniques for materials handling and storage and work simplification that often do not come to the attention of librarians. The above should in no way be considered a complete list of journals useful to library interior planners, rather the ones listed are those that the author is familiar with. There are other journals covering more specialized areas of library interest, such as nonprint materials, microforms, music, and art. These journals, some of which are mentioned elsewhere in this book, should be familiar to specialists on library staffs and contain advertisements and editorial matter dealing with furniture and equipment appropriate for these specialized areas.

Importance of Exhibits

Shows or exhibits at professional meetings are very helpful to librarians responsible for selecting furniture and equipment for libraries. The annual conference of the American Library Association draws a large representation of the firms manufacturing furniture and equipment for the library market, while state and regional conventions, although they draw smaller numbers of exhibitors, generally attract many of the important ones. Librarians who are attending these conventions and who are responsible for selecting and evaluating furniture and equipment, should plan on devoting considerable time to walking through these exhibits, examining furniture carefully and comparing construction methods.

Librarians should be sure to talk with the firm's representative in the booth, ask all the questions they can think of, and listen to the representative's presentation. The presentation some representatives give is brilliant, but it will not necessarily answer individual questions. Librarians should be sure he tells them what they need to know. When claims are made, listening librarians should ask for proof, preferably documented. If a librarian finds a line or product of interest, he should ask for a list of present installations and check with the librarians at some of them. He should be a little chary of brand-new products. Although somebody has to be the first purchaser, the role of the unhappy "guinea pig" is not a pleasant one. When considering some kinds of microform and AV equipment, it is helpful to have samples of software, i.e., microfiche, color slides, and cassettes, which are familiar so that these floor samples can be roughly compared with each other and with equipment at home. Obviously, a manufacturer exhibiting such "performance" equipment would be foolish to demonstrate his product with software that failed to show his equipment to the best advantage. Using a library's own software will provide a much better base for comparison.

When considering furniture displayed at shows, one cannot assume that floor samples are especially manufactured to be superior in quality to production models. While this is occasionally so, it is more often true, in the writer's experience, for floor samples to be of poorer quality than the identical items delivered as part of a contract. While one would expect a manufacturer always to make his best showing in an exhibit, in practice this is often not possible. Floor samples are often made up hurriedly or are used at several shows and become worn and battered from too much travel, packing/unpacking, and assembly/disassembly. Few manufacturers have the ability to produce samples as needed without interrupting production or incursion of extraordinary expense. As a result, floor samples are sometimes wobbly, battered, or just plain tired. In addition, samples of brand-new products or lines are particularly likely to be less than perfect. Firms producing such new items generally do so under the pressure of having them ready to show at the exhibit. Engineering and design problems often remain unsolved and the handmade sample examined may resemble the production model only superficially. Be sure the final evaluation is made on the basis of a production model rather than a prototype.

Exhibits offer two great advantages to librarians wanting to acquaint themselves with furniture: the opportunity to know what is available and the chance to compare similar products. No one show will give planners the opportunity to see all that is available in any category, but attendance at several shows, along with other approaches to be detailed later, will provide a broad acquaintance with products in any category. The other advantage, that of permitting easy comparison between competing products is only possible at shows or showrooms where similar products are displayed within the same area. In such a setting, it is possible to compare appearance and construction methods as well as to listen to salesman's claims. Some salesmen will confine their presentation to claims about their own products; others will downgrade the competition and its product. Even the latter can be useful, for, while one appraisal of the competition is useless, the aggregate opinion of a number of sales representatives can be helpful in assessing the overall situation within a particular product category.

While nearly all salesmen will claim that their product is the best available, careful questioning of a number of representatives will reveal a consensus about the relative position of firms in their industry. Further, gossip about the industry often reveals information most useful in considering products for purchase; for instance, word that a certain company has drastically changed its construction methods. Be doubting the first time you hear something detrimental to a competitor (you seldom hear anything complimentary), but hearing it several times should cause you to check further and can sometimes prevent embarrassing errors in judgment.

How to Utilize the Show

It is important to get the best value for the time and money invested in the show. Here are a few hints. First, walk through quickly and assess the exhibits. This gives an opportunity to estimate the time needed to devote to the show, based on the number of likely looking exhibits in view. The tendency here is to underestimate, so a time cushion should be provided, so that one does not have to rush through exhibits of interest. Have business cards available to hand out so that vendors can send additional information and representatives to visit if so desired. If exhibitors have in their booths literature that is especially interesting, one should take it along rather than having it sent. It is hard to understand when one considers the expense of convention exhibiting, but manufacturers often fail to follow up on conference prospects who visit their booths and leave their names and addresses. So if literature about an item really interests the librarian, to be safe, he should take the literature with him, or he may lose the contact with the item of interest. Finally, along with a flexible folder to hold the literature picked up, a miniature camera with fast film can be most useful. After seeing a number of products, interspersed with conversation with exhibitors (and old friends passing by), what has been seen often remains a mental blur. Pictures will provide a reminder of the products seen and furnish a reference point when talking about them with others.

Library shows are the best place to see furniture specifically directed at the library market. However, every library uses furniture and equipment that is not specifically library oriented. For librarians responsible for procuring substantial amounts of nonlibrary furniture, visits to other furniture shows can be most helpful. Those concerned with selecting seating, lounge furniture, office furniture, special lighting fixtures, carpet, and draperies will find a visit to NEOCON, the national contract furniture show, most informative. The show is held in Chicago each June at the Merchandise Mart. The format is different from most, in that the show takes place in the dozens of manufacturers' showrooms within this mammoth building. Some seminars and educational programs are part of this show, but visits to the myriad of showrooms, with their thousands of square feet filled with furniture and furnishings, form the chief attraction of NEOCON. Another show that contains many items of interest to libraries is the annual conference of the American Association of School Administrators (AASA), generally held in February. Most of the vendors who want to sell to the school market appear at this show, for this is where the decision makers in elementary and secondary education assemble. Although most of the merchandise displayed is not library oriented, enough of it is to make the show worthwhile to the library planner. Furthermore, many of the library lines shown will be new to librarians familiar with those manufacturers who regularly appear at the library shows. At the 1976 AASA show, of 42 manufacturers listed in the program under "Library Furniture and Equipment," only 6 were regular exhibitors at library conventions. The others concentrate on the school market, but will occasionally bid on another kind of library job. As a result, library interior planners will find it useful to attend this rather expensive show in order to become acquainted with library manufacturers who are not likely to be familiar to them.

Several other shows that cover special fields often have items of interest to librarian planners. Among them are the National Micrographic Association (NMA) for microforms, the Association for Educational Communication Technology (AECT) for nonprint media, and the National Office Products Association (NOPA) for office equipment.

Showrooms

Less informative than trade shows and conventions, but still of some value to those interested in seeing furniture from which to select, are manufacturers' showrooms. Only a few of these show library furniture, but a number show seating as well as lounge and office furniture of interest to library interior planners. These are found in New York and Chicago, with lesser numbers in Dallas, Los Angeles, and San Francisco. The Merchandise Mart in Chicago is the one single location with more showrooms of contract furniture than any place else in the world. Showrooms exist primarily for the wholesale trade, but firms dealing in contract or institutional furniture will generally welcome persons specifying contract furniture.

THE SALES REPRESENTATIVE

The ubiquitous sales representative can be most helpful in bringing new or unfamiliar products or lines to the attention of potential buyers. Some of them know their products very well; others of them even have some understanding of library operations and needs. The best of them, whether salesmen, sales representatives, or sales engineers, can be very helpful. Often they have a broad acquaintance with other libraries and their problems, and they may have assisted in solving some of these problems. Some are so knowledgeable and effective that their sales presentations are educational experiences; that is, they explain how a product should perform or be constructed, rather than simply claiming that their products are the best and telling how bad all the competitors' products are. The best salesman should know his product thoroughly, although some product lines are so extensive that comprehensive knowledge of them is difficult. Salesmen for a single manufacturer should be most knowledgeable while manufacturers' representatives (individuals or firms who have exclusive sales rights to several lines for a geographical area) will often deal in too many lines to know any of them intimately. Salesmen who work for dealers will generally have still more product lines to sell and will be less knowledgeable about particular products than either of the other two kinds of representatives. On the other hand, the dealer representative will often have several choices of products available for consideration, while representatives for a single manufacturer and manufacturers' representatives will have fewer choices to offer.

Sales representatives can be helpful in other ways; for instance, they will often discuss new products offered by competitors or will talk of new products they have seen or heard about that do not compete with their offerings. Finally, they often know more about the library world than most librarians. In short, many of them are a marvelous source of information about all sorts of things of interest to the librarian. Properly interpreted, this information can be most useful. Only a very busy or very foolish librarian/planner will fail to find time for at least some salesmen. A few, of course, are so bad or so partisan that they waste your time.

VISITS TO OTHER LIBRARIES

Visits to other libraries are one of the most important sources of information in furniture selection. New and newly furnished library buildings are often publicized in the library press and a sufficient number are located in most sections of the country to "exhibit" a reasonable selection of furniture lines by different manufacturers. The architectural issues of Library Journal showcase some of the most interesting new libraries, and the lists of new libraries with statistical data compiled by Jerrold Orne (academic libraries) and Hoyt Galvin (public libraries) are the most comprehensive listings of new and recently renovated libraries.

Some sections of the country have more new libraries than others. In this writer's experience, the single best area where a number of the newer interesting libraries can be seen conveniently, is the Boston metropolitan area, where are found such new or relatively new buildings as Boston University; Tufts University; the addition to the Boston Public Library; Radcliffe College; the University of Massachusetts at Boston (unheralded, but very interesting); the Episcopal Theological School Library (a gem); Wellesley College; and various libraries at Harvard, including the Gutman (education), Loeb (design), the new Science Library, and the Pusey Library. Within easy driving distance are the Brown University Libraries in Providence, Rhode Island; Clark University at Worchester; Southeastern Massachusetts University at North Dartmouth (a horror, in this writer's opinion); and Philips-Exeter Academy in Exeter, New Hampshire. A little further away in Amherst, are found the recently built libraries at the University of Massachusetts, Amherst and Hampshire Colleges, all of considerable interest. Neighboring Connecticut is also rich in noteworthy buildings, so that a librarian/planner wanting to see outstanding new libraries with a variety of furniture and equipment can find a great number of interesting examples rather close together.

North and South Carolina also boast a goodly number of recent libraries in a relatively compact area, including the University of North Carolina at both Greensboro and Charlotte, the addition at Duke University, both Salem and Davidson Colleges (all in North Carolina), and the University of South

Carolina, Clemson University, Wofford, Winthrop, Voorhees, and Francis Marion Colleges and the College of Charleston (all in South Carolina).

Both Ohio and New York also have relatively large concentrations of interesting newer buildings. During visits to libraries, adequate notes and photographs will help to recall the furniture and equipment examined. A questionnaire or checklist can help organize written notes; color slides in 35-mm organize easily and show colors and textures accurately.

DESCRIPTIVE LITERATURE

Finally, printed brochures and promotional literature are other ways in which information about furniture and equipment can be gathered. Some of this literature will be unsolicited; other information will come from contacts with sales representatives, responses to periodical advertisements, or from visits to exhibits or showrooms. The literature will vary in size and format from single-page flyers to multivolume binders, swatch boxes, wood or laminate sample wheels, specifications, and carpet samples (Fig. 1). Some of this will file easily in ordinary file equipment and some of it will be difficult to house properly. Lateral files five shelves high with hanging folders will provide good storage for most of it. Each manufacturing company or vendor should have a folder, and each item filed should be dated and given one or more subject classification. A card system can then be kept by subject, providing cross references to the files which are arranged alphabetically by company. Information by company will be needed most frequently, but often information on the companies who produce various products will be required. The file should be kept up to date. Whenever a salesman appears, take a few minutes to see that he brings his catalog information up to date.

EVALUATION

Once potentially useful products have been found, the next part of the selection process is the evaluation or analysis of the adequacy of the product being considered. Many possible choices can be eliminated upon initial examination, being too expensive, poorly constructed, not aesthetically pleasing, of the wrong color, too old-fashioned in appearance, etc. These "early eliminations" can take place at exhibits or shows, in showrooms, when visiting other libraries, or when talking with salesmen, indeed anywhere selection is taking place. However, once the number of candidates for actual purchase have been whittled down to a manageable size, the remaining products deserving serious consideration must be measured against each other. How is this done?

FIG.1 Manufacturers' catalogs, upholstery swatches, and laminate and carpet samples are essential aids in furniture selection.

Some of the means already mentioned as useful in selection are obviously helpful in evaluation. Contacts with libraries using the items under consideration and actually seeing the products in use at other institutions provide useful information about the product's performance over a period of time. When information about specific products is not available, often libraries can relate experiences with other products or lines by the same manufacturers. Viewing competing products side-by-side in shows or showrooms can provide a basis for comparison.

The available literature can be useful. Library periodicals sometimes carry articles on furniture, equipment, and related subjects that report favorable or (very occasionally) unfavorable experience with individual products. General periodicals sometimes carry feature articles that contain evaluative information about more general furniture and equipment. Consumer Reports and Consumers' Research Bulletin are long-established publications and their evaluations occasionally cover equipment of library interest.

At least one agency, Buyers' Laboratory, Inc., publishes detailed product analyses of office equipment and systems, and this involves extensive testing and evaluation of individual products. This publication is sold as a service and is expensive, but may be helpful to some specifiers.

Library Technology Reports

The evaluative service best known to librarians is Library Technology Reports, which has since 1965 attempted to provide detailed evaluative information about equipment, furniture, systems, and supplies useful in libraries. The principal content of this bimonthly publication is detailed analysis of product groups, ranging from circulation systems to book trucks, with detailed analytical reviews of individual manufacturers' products, along with summary comparisons of physical characteristics and performance of product groups. There are also occasional evaluations of individual products, answers to subscriber inquiries, nonevaluative news articles, and abstracts of books and articles on furniture, equipment, and other library fittings. Until recently, it was published in a loose-leaf format, which was useful for updating purposes, but somewhat difficult to handle. Now there is a microfiche version of the first 10 years of publication, which should simplify the periodical's use and handling since the bound edition now comprises 6 full loose-leaf volumes. The current issues now come bimonthly in a more conventional magazine format.

Library Technology Reports was established by the American Library Association under the astute direction of Frazer Poole, a prominent consultant on library interiors who was chief preservation officer for the Library of Congress. Although its early years proved the desirability of and need for such a publication, the changing priorities of the association have strangled financial support for the Library Technology Reports so that it has never realized its early promise. Although it has done much useful work, lack of staff, space, and resources has limited the magazine's scope and effectiveness in recent years. Nonetheless, it is the only available publication of its kind and merits library utilization and support. Perhaps someday the climate in the association leadership will change and there will be the realization that the kind of information published can save for librarians money that can be put to other use. In any case, the result of the association's failure to support these programs adequately has been some lack of consistency in the magazine's overall quality and reliability. A forced dependence for testing on different outside firms has resulted in reports that are not always as sound as they might be. Overall, however, the reports have been of good quality and their value to librarians has been significant.

Value of Library Visits

Earlier, we pointed out that seeing furniture and equipment in operation at other libraries is of great value to the librarian/planner considering those items of furniture and equipment for purchase. Durability under use and effective continued performance particularly lend themselves to being evaluated by this method. When evaluating furniture and equipment in other libraries, it is essential to consider such factors as period of use, amount and pattern of use, special environmental circumstances, and the life expectancy of the materials used. All other things being equal, identical furniture in different libraries for differing lengths of service will wear according to length of use. However, use varies widely among libraries. Within the last few years, the author saw two installations of identical furniture that had been in place for about the same time. One installation was in a small, rather "sleepy," private denominational college in the Middle Atlantic region, and the furniture looked nearly new. The other installation was in the undergraduate library of a major southern university where the same furniture in use for about the same time had become badly worn and battered. It is well to photograph furniture when visiting other libraries in order to ensure the correctness of your impressions.

SAMPLES

Once, however, one has selected items of furniture and equipment for consideration, has checked written evaluations, and visited library installations, it is important to obtain samples of some of the items being considered for purchase. This is particularly true for seating and for items that operate or have moving parts. Manufacturers will often be willing to provide samples free of charge for larger projects in hopes of obtaining the contract. If several similar items (for instance, reader chairs) can be obtained and placed in use in one location or several locations with similar patterns of use, it is possible to obtain comparative evaluations of their performance or effectiveness. While such impressions will be somewhat subjective, they will certainly be of value. With items that operate or have moving parts, such as book trucks or microfilm cabinets, it will be possible to load them and put them into operation. Smoothness of operation and the incidence of problems can be evaluated in this way.

Having such sample pieces in the library provides an opportunity to check carefully their methods of construction and component quality (for instance, that of glides or hardware). When samples are not freely available, it is often advisable to purchase them. It is better to spend a few dollars at this stage, than to have inadequately evaluated items of furniture and equipment fail or prove to be otherwise unsatisfactory. It is occasionally desirable to "destruct-test" samples, that is to disassemble them in order to discover whether they indeed meet the library's or even the manufacturers' specifications. As will be seen in our analysis of specifications (Appendix A), small hidden details often greatly influence the durability of such objects of furniture as chairs, and there are manufacturers who will not meet specifications if they can get away with it. The author recalls tearing apart the same study chair presented as samples at three successive bid presentations before the manufacturer finally met the specifications he claimed to meet. Obviously this was an extreme example, but this sort of thing happens often enough that librarians selecting furniture should be aware of the problem. "Destructive" evaluation of a chair will answer such questions as whether enough glue of the right kind was used, whether the dowels were those specified, whether upholstery components were as specified, and whether metal fasteners were used where they should not have been.

If a furniture or equipment item being considered is of an experimental design or is a variant form of a common library item, it is particularly important to obtain a sample for evaluation. Take, for example, a specially designed carrel for microforms with some sort of tablet arm arrangement for writing. In such a case, it would be advisable to obtain a sample and try it out with different library users, having it house a variety of microviewing equipment. In this way one can ascertain whether the carrel is well engineered for use by persons of different sizes or assuming different postures, and whether different microreaders function equally well within the carrel's confines.

The item in question would not even need to be as specialized as the aforementioned carrel for microviewing. The author has seen fairly ordinary carrels or tables used with armchairs where the reader could not be comfortably seated near enough to the work surface. Obtaining and trying out sample items of furniture and equipment will help to prevent the occurrence of such problems.

Evaluation by testing is not possible, except for the largest or most wealthy libraries. Some states have test facilities and programs that can be helpful to state and state-related institutions. Others requiring testing will probably need to acquire the services of private testing laboratories, which is an expensive proposition. Large testing firms should have available standards and test procedures appropriate for the product being tested. Only the rare library will be able to take advantage of professional library testing, but it can be helpful when available. If a high-volume item such as a side chair is of special concern, a few hundred dollars spent on testing could result in a considerable saving if it helped avoid a disastrous selection.

PURCHASING

In a few cases, once selection and evaluation are complete, the librarian has only to prepare a simple list of the desired furniture and equipment, including a brief description, noting additional information, such as quantity, manufacturer, model number, and price, colors, finishes, or accessories desired. This list is handed to a purchasing agency and in due course the exact items requested arrive ready for use.

In exceptional cases, the library itself may place orders. There may be a few such paradises in the library world but few librarians/planners will ever experience them. Financial exigency and institutional regulations generally require that competitive bidding be conducted and often the product of a particular manufacturer may not be specified. Actually, competitive bidding is generally beneficial to those acquiring furniture and equipment for libraries. The institutional constituency, whether local taxpayers, college alumni and trustees, or state legislators will appreciate and usually demand adherence to the principle of competitive bidding. Even when it is not required, a wise librarian will utilize competitive bidding with rare exceptions. Lower prices will nearly always result from competitive bidding—for one thing, when the word gets around that more than one vendor is in the running, prices generally go down immediately. By contrast, a vendor who is assured of an order will sometimes take advantage of the situation by raising his price, sometimes on the rationale that this will make up for some of what he loses when there is competitive bidding. Also, competitive bidding will often bring to the librarian's attention vendors whose products, while lower in price, may be equal or superior to those that have already been selected.

SPECIFICATIONS

The crux of the matter here, of course, is to assure that all bidders are indeed bidding on products of equal quality and performance. In order to do this, it is necessary to establish written standards that spell out in detail the performance required of the product as well as describing its physical characteristics. These specifications, if well written and equitably enforced, will assure that vendors who are offering products that are truly comparable in quality and performance will have a fair chance at the business and that the lowest bidder among them will get a contract to supply the needed merchandise. Specifications are written to assure standards of performance (revolutions per minute, number of cycles before failure, etc.), physical characteristics (dimensions, colors offered, thickness of paint), or standards of construction (type of joinery used, glue required in assembly, requirement for air and kiln drying). Only a few items of library furniture and equipment can be adequately described by a performance specification, although many specifications will include some elements of performance, for instance, the specifications for a steel shelf might require a minimum deflection under load.

Most specifications for library furniture and equipment will contain a description of the purpose and function of the item concerned, a detailed physical description listing the dimensions of the whole and its components, and a complete description of all component parts and their assembly. Somewhere, either in this item specification or in a general specification covering an entire group of items, will be a section detailing standards for each kind of raw or finished material or assembly. For instance, in describing a chair or group of chairs, specified are the characteristics of the wood used, such as its species, the area it comes from, degree of dryness, and whether it should be air dried or kiln dried. Other components of a chair, as glue, dowels, glides, and each part of upholstery are described in detail. Appendix A provides sample specifications that mention these factors in respect to chairs, library technical furniture, and for steel bookstacks on the assumption that these form the three groups of furniture and equipment most commonly purchased for libraries.

Unless one is able personally to select and have purchased all the exact items of furniture and equipment wanted, a well-written specification, concise yet filled with adequate information, is essential for most kinds of purchases. However, on occasion, only one manufacturer may produce an item which exactly fills the stated requirements or, rarely, one vendor may provide a product so superior to that of his competition that bidding is inappropriate. In these cases, many purchasing agencies will permit a contract award on the basis of quotation from the preferred manufacturer without soliciting bids from competitors. Naturally, the agencies will not want to tell the preferred bidder that he has no competition so that there is no temptation to increase the price. It should be remembered, though, that the very process of public bidding in a competitive situation will bring to one's attention manufacturers and products that may have escaped the specifier's research. A good specification will bring one's requirements to the attention of many vendors who will attempt to provide material meeting the specification at prices lower than the competition. If the specification is precise enough to assure the desired quality and performance, yet not so strict that it unduly limits competition, the purchase of an economical but desirable product should be the result.

Buying from a single or sole source is, on the other hand, frought with peril; this point is important and deserves further discussion. The previous section pointed out that utilizing various means of furniture evaluation should enable a buyer to select from among a number of comparable products the one that best meets his needs. Such choices based on rational comparison are most desirable but, of course, they are not always possible. Often an astute or aggressive sales representative will manage to influence a librarian/planner or designer to believe that his product has qualities or features that are impossible for competitors to match, and that only his product can meet the library's needs. If competitive bidding is the norm for a library's purchasing, he may try to suggest that an exception to the rule be requested; failing that, he may ask you to submit his own "proprietary" specification, one so specific that only his product can qualify. Once in a while, aesthetic or design considerations may dictate the purchase of a particular item from a particular manufacturer. Rarely, however, is an item so distinctive that it cannot be duplicated exactly by other manufacturers at competitive prices. Designers will sometimes insist that a particular manufacturer's product is the only one that will "fit" the library. Designers have been known to maintain financial arrangements with selected manufacturers that are not to the benefit of the client library. With rare exceptions, librarians should insist on nonproprietary specifications and competitive bidding to assure that they are buying high-quality furniture fitting the library at a reasonable price. If the number of pieces to be ordered is large enough, it is reasonable to select a distinctive design and insist that all the manufacturers bid on it.

Often when a particular design in furniture is desired or when one item of equipment is clearly superior to its competition, or indeed, may set the standard in its industry, some specifiers use an "or equal" specification; that is, instead of describing carefully a product such as a microfilm cabinet, by listing materials used, method of construction, dimensions and performance, these specifications say only, for instance, "Microfilm cabinet, Watson MF-11 and MF-4 or approved equal." This method is used fairly frequently, certainly more often than it should be. It is convenient and does not take much time or research. It does set barriers to true competition, for some potential bidders will consider that it indicates that the specifier is prejudiced in favor of a particular product and that there is no point in his bidding. The product specified for comparison may not be good enough, or conversely, better than it needs to be, for the installation. The "or equal" specification may stifle competition so that a library does not get the best product for the least money and it may prevent the discovery of alternative products that might meet needs better than the one specified.

When dealing with "or equal" specifications, still another problem lies in evaluating bids and awarding contracts. Other manufacturers can and do say that their product is equal to the one specified and such claims, even if clearly untrue, are often very difficult to refute. Purchasing agents will sometimes require the librarian to accept their award to a manufacturer whose product is, in the librarian's opinion, clearly inferior to that specified because the manufacturer concerned complains vigorously or threatens legal action if his product is not considered to be "equal." Differences between similar products that seem clear to specifiers are not often readily apparent to purchasing agencies, and competing manufacturers often disagree vigorously on whose product in their industry is superior; indeed, they are not even in agreement about which qualities in their own and competing lines are most important in evaluating the products concerned. With all these areas for disagreement, it is clearly chancy to make excessive use of "or equal" specification. Occasionally, when design is important, it is useful to prepare a complete specification <u>and</u> to use manufacturers catalog numbers for each item, the latter serving to illustrate clearly to potential vendors the exact item they are to bid on. There should be clear indication that a number of bidders are encouraged to bid on the specifications but that they are required to provide material that also matches in appearance the product of the manufacturer whose catalog numbers are listed, although their product in other respects meets the printed specifications.

General Conditions

What is the source of specifications? There are a number of answers. First, the initial portion of a specification, containing the general conditions, will generally be provided by the purchasing authority, for it defines the legal relationship being proffered to potential vendors. The general conditions will discuss such things as the respective responsibilities of buyer and bidder, qualifications of bidders, including requirements for such things as experience, financial responsibility and relationship between dealers and manufacturers, and financial guarantees required. The qualifications of manufacturers who are not also bidders, will be stated here as well, including experience, financial responsibility, whether necessary raw materials and machinery are in their possession or readily available, and assurance of capability to fill orders for additional items in the future.

Also frequently specified within these general conditions are price guarantees (how long the quoted price will stand) and discussion of the specific bidding procedure that the buying agency will follow. The latter will specify the number of specifications supplied; how they are to be filled out; where, how, and when bids are to be submitted; whether and how bids may be amended <u>before</u> they are opened; when and where bids are to be opened; whether bidders may be present at bid openings and how bids will be awarded, that is, to the lowest qualified bidder or at the discretion of the agency.

General conditions will also say whether deviations or alternates will be permitted and will frequently require the submission of photographs, cuts, shop drawings, and other materials illustrating exactly what material the bidder proposes to supply. There may also be enumerated here various legal requirements that vendors must meet, such as adherence to Occupational Safety and Health Act (OSHA) standards, various nondiscrimination clauses, and prevailing wage clauses. There may also be clauses dealing with institutional liability, additions and cancellations, patentability, vendor bankruptcy, tax exemptions, limitations on foreign purchase, and the right to reject inferior merchandise.

Finally, the section will describe how price information is to be supplied, whether item by item, for all the items on the specification, or both. There is a benefit to the purchaser in requiring both, for if all items proposed can come from a single vendor, he will often offer a lump sum price lower than the total of the item prices. On the other hand, if one bidder offers significantly lower prices on one or more items, but not on the others, it is possible to accept his bids on the lower-priced items while purchasing other items from other vendors. This assumes that there is no need for the items in the specification to match each other or to be mechanically compatible.

The general conditions usually constitute a very nonspecific document used by purchasing departments to notify potential vendors of prevailing purchasing practices in the agency or institution. It will frequently be followed by a group specification which details more exactly the desired characteristics of the group of related material intended for purchase. This will also provide more specific requirements for bidders, including such matter as period for delivery, requirements for samples, warranties and guarantees required, requirements for servicing, including provision of maintenance contracts (if appropriate), specific shipping and delivery requirements, names and addresses of persons to contact on questions about bidding and delivery and information about partial payments and discounts.

The formats used in specification preparation will vary greatly among different institutions. Some forms will have lengthy general conditions, with the specification itself only describing the articles under discussion. Others will use forms that leave blanks for listing such things as names of contacts, delivery period, shipping method, etc. Whatever the format, there will always be general conditions of some kind, which will provide the standards that the institution sets forth for all its purchasing, while information more specifically dealing with the library furniture or material concerned will be listed further along in the specification. Appendix A gives examples of such specifications for wood library furniture and seating and steel book shelves.

THE PURCHASING AGENCY

The actual purchasing operation will not usually be the direct responsibility of the librarian/planner, except occasionally for small libraries. Generally, however, an official or department at the institution, government or firm concerned has the responsibility for purchasing for the library, as well as for other departments or agencies. Frequently these people are expert and often will cooperate enthusiastically to assure that the library's furniture and equipment is the best, most long lasting, and functional that is available. In other instances, such offices may be more concerned with price or with doing business with familiar suppliers than with quality, durability, or function. No matter what the attitude toward library requirements may be, it is essential that the librarian establish relationships with the purchasing agency early in the planning process so that they understand what the librarian is trying to achieve and so that the librarian understands how they function, the sort of information they want, and the kinds of constraints or controls under which they operate. The human factor is, of course, very important. A pleasant relationship with at least occasional discussion of problems in person will greatly assist mutual understanding. On the other hand, all relations with purchasing departments should be businesslike with written documentation of decisions, telephone conversations, and verbal discussions. It is much easier to throw away excess or obsolete copies of documents than not to have them when needed. Failure to document or confirm verbal communication may result in the denial of agreements thought to have been made, particularly when changes in personnel occur or details are not remembered.

It is essential that the librarian demonstrate to the purchase agency a thorough knowledge of library operations and the items of furniture and equipment that will best carry out these functions. He should have researched furniture and equipment needs and have documentary evidence to support his recommendations and evaluations. He should have readily available specifications for the needed furniture and equipment, which generally should not be proprietary or limited to the products of one manufacturer. He should have good reasons for any special requirements or special features, for instance, why reading tables should not have aprons or why is it desirable for some special carrels to have carpeted sides.

It is also essential to submit requests for purchases to purchasing departments in written form in multiple copies so that the librarian can receive automatic notification of action on his request, and retain one or more copies for the files. If the volume of requests is large, more than one file copy will provide for a master file and a "tickler" file, that is, a file of requests ordered by date placed, so that it is possible to check occasionally on requests that have not been acted on. It is useful to give requests a serial number so that requests for similar objects can be kept separate. The requests will be more easily accounted for in the files by using one request form for each different product. Of course, when assembling these item requests for transmission to the purchasing department, the librarian will gather these into appropriate groupings. From these groups the actual specifications can be prepared by either the library staff or the designer/architect.

Grouping Furniture for Purchasing

This matter of how furniture and equipment are grouped for purchase is very important. If the groups ordered are too small, the best prices will not be realized, for prices are often dependent on volume. Further, the desire to have some unity of style, design, and color will be much harder to achieve without grouping. Finally, a great deal more work will be made for both library and purchase department. Groups that are too large, on the other hand, can present problems. Very large groups of furniture or equipment that contain substantial quantities of nonspecialized items and carry a considerable dollar volume may arouse the interest of nonlibrary vendors who may want to assemble collections of miscellaneous commercial furniture and equipment with a minimum of library furniture and equipment from a variety of manufacturers. Or, if the library technical furniture request is combined with the one for seating, a vendor of good library technical furniture may offer a mediocre chair line. Also, the longer the list, the more vendors will want to bid on only part of the list, with "no bid" on the remainder, which can be a most unsatisfactory situation.

In nearly all situations, three or four groupings will cover most of the important furniture and equipment and will constitute the largest part of the cost of equipping the library. Here is a suggested list with some comments about each grouping:

1. Steel book stacks. The manufacturers of these form a distinct group and most will bid only on the stacks.

2. Seating. Although some planners are known to have bid this along with other library furniture, the author's own preference is to do this separately. Manufacturers of tables, carrels, and card catalogs do not customarily make their own chairs but buy them from others. Furthermore, some of the best chair manufacturers do not make their seating available through library manufacturers.

3. Library technical and general furniture. In order to procure furniture of consistent design and quality, it is most desirable to have tables, carrels, and such technical items as card catalogs, index tables, atlas cases, and dictionary stands produced by the same manufacturer all appear in the same bid request. However, occasionally there is a requirement to open up the bidding of some of the furniture to firms other than library manufacturers. If this ever does happen, it is possible to separate the tables and carrels from the more specialized furniture. With good, tight, and well-enforced specifications as guides, it is possible for good furniture firms unfamiliar with library furniture to make good tables and carrels. The more technical items (card catalogs, catalog reference tables, etc.) should never be awarded to nonlibrary manufacturers, for they will almost certainly make them badly. With the tables and carrels in a separate bid, other bidders will not be attracted by the relatively low-dollar-volume technical furniture. This is a rare problem and one the author hopes the reader never encounters.

Furniture not Limited to Libraries

Other furniture and equipment items for the library will form natural groupings. Audiovisual dealers often sell a full line of this equipment and many such items can be grouped together into fairly large groupings for purposes of competitive bidding. Office furniture dealers will handle not only a variety of desks, office chairs, and filing equipment, but also can often provide cabinets for microform storage. In preparing for bidding on those furniture and equipment items which are not so familiar to librarians, it is particularly important to prepare specifications carefully. For instance, microfilm cabinets come in a great variety of sizes and shapes with widely varying storage capacities. Cost per cabinet is much less important than cost per box stored. Also, the floor space occupied by such cabinets is important to consider. The specification should specify rolls stored in linear inches of storage capacity. Prepare the specification carefully, especially for this kind of equipment where dealers, whose good intentions or other reasons will sometimes cause them to try to supply office equipment that takes up too much space, lacks storage density, or otherwise fails to meet a library's needs. One must research these problems thoroughly and get competent, disinterested advice when preparing requirements. The adviser should have an understanding of library needs as well as those of the commercial world.

POTENTIAL VENDORS

Who should be invited (or permitted) to bid on the library's requirements? The purchasing department often has the final say. An absolutely first-class purchasing department, with knowledgeable personnel who have time to be thoroughly conversant with firms producing for specialized areas such as libraries, may have available a list of qualified bidders who are competent to meet requirements. Such purchasing departments are extremely rare, for hardly ever are there enough buyers in such departments that they become thoroughly knowledgeable about bidders of specialized equipment. As a result, the librarian, along with a buyer or purchasing agent, will have to go looking for competent vendors.

Many purchase departments will require that bids be selected from three bidders, and this is most desirable. It provides the values of competitive bidding, but avoids having to disqualify large numbers of bidders. Other departments will have fairly lengthy lists of vendors to whom they send bids, whether or not the companies are known to provide the equipment that the library seeks. Others must publicly advertise their requirements. When such open bidding is required, good specifications are even more important.

If bidders can be limited to those whose products are roughly comparable to each other and meet specification requirements, the information the librarian has assembled about various manufacturers' products over a period of time will help in the selection of potential vendors. This process of elimination will result in relatively short lists of vendors who are capable of adequately supplying needs for furniture and equipment groups, as well as for individual items. The librarian will probably want to update his information about the most likely suppliers of particularly vital furniture, for instance, library technical furniture, tables and carrels, seating (particularly side chairs), and steel book shelves.

If it has been some time since the librarian's previous evaluations of vendors, a recheck with other libraries possessing recent installations and other information sources will be advisable. There have been surprisingly large fluctuations in overall quality, durability, and time of delivery through the years among firms supplying the library market, including some of the best known. One very well-known leading firm, which markets a complete line of library furnishings, manufactured some steel shelving in a branch plant that was such a bad operation that, despite the fact that it was quickly closed down, some of the shelving produced there turns up to embarrass the firm years later. A manufacturer of steel shelving had such "start-up" problems at a new plant that for awhile its deliveries were measured in years instead of months. The librarian should seek out information on the current state of operation of potential vendors, and he should not believe without question the representative's statements about his own or a competitor's company. Information from a number of sources should give a consensus which will be close to the truth. While one can never be completely confident that even the latest reports will reflect the situation as it truly is at the time of the order, the latest information should be more accurate and may indicate whether a vendor's product or service seems to be getting better or worse.

Factory Visits

Now is the time to consider visiting the factories of a few of the manufacturers whose products are being considered. This is a valuable procedure for a number of reasons. First, visits to one of the leading factories will provide a standard by which to measure other firms, as well as an education about how wood furniture or steel bookstacks are produced. Then, if the librarian is interested in a firm but has doubts about its capabilities, a visit based on knowledge gained from other visits will greatly improve the ability to evaluate its manufacturing facility. Also, insights into factory operation will be much improved if the librarian has along with him a consultant who is knowledgeable about library furniture manufacture. In addition, the material in Chapter 8 on the manufacture and marketing of library furniture and equipment will help the librarian to know what to look for when visiting library furniture factories.

Such visits are only appropriate for items or groups of items where there is considerable dollar volume. Visits are also sometimes very desirable, indeed, sometimes essential, when bids are in the process of being evaluated. A low bid from an unfamiliar vendor or an unusually low bid by a well-known vendor often necessitates a quick visit to see if the firm concerned is actually capable of producing what the library wants. A firm should have no objection to a visit—if they do, there may be a reason for suspicion. For example, the firm may not have the production facilities needed to produce the furniture required. Others may be assemblers of subassemblies, rather than fabricators, and though perhaps it is possible to assemble good furniture from subassemblies, an assembler can hardly control the quality of subassemblies made by subcontractors as well as he can control operations in his own plant.

It is not a bad idea to include in the specification a statement that visits to facilities may be made either during bid evaluation, or after award when furniture is being manufactured. Visits during construction will provide an opportunity to see that the furniture is being manufactured to the agreed specifications. The author has been involved in more than one case where a factory visit during construction phase has exposed a manufacturer's intent to cut corners and not meet the specification.

TIMING OF FURNITURE ORDERS AND DELIVERY

The timing of order and delivery is a matter of great concern both to librarians/planners and to furniture manufacturers. From the librarian's point of view, the furniture order should be placed so that all of it is delivered right after the completion of the building, so that he can move in and begin operation immediately. He also would like it if the order arrives just when the manufacturer's factory becomes idle so that his order is not delayed and receives the manufacturer's undivided attention and, because the company would have at that time an empty space in the production schedule, the price would be rock bottom. The manufacturer, on the other hand, would like to have the order in hand years before delivery so he can plan his production schedule around it and save money by ordering raw materials early. He would be ecstatic if the order could be grouped together with other orders for identical items so that his cost of production would be significantly lowered. However, the long lead time is worrisome for the manufacturer because of the difficulty of predicting inflation. A price low enough to get a bid one year may not cover production costs a few years later due to inflation, which is not a happy situation for a vendor. He could make it early in the contract period, saving on cost inflation for raw materials and labor, but this saving could be eaten up by the cost of warehousing or storage, for it is a rare library that can accept furniture very soon before building completion. In point of fact, both parties will almost inevitably end up somewhat unhappy, although the manufacturer almost always comes off better than the library since he has more control of the situation.

Some libraries include a penalty clause in their specifications by which the manufacturer agrees to pay the library for each day delivery is delayed beyond an agreed-upon delivery date. These can be helpful but few libraries are willing to enter into legal action over such a clause. Besides, the receipt of the furniture is more important than any penalty money and initiation of legal action will bring the entire transaction to a halt. Further, the construction of libraries is often not completed on schedule, and if such is the case, it can be very embarrassing to insist on a manufacturer's being penalized for not meeting a delivery date. Most of the better manufacturers will try to meet a schedule as closely as possible, but both parties should be flexible and reasonable. Frequent communication will help to assure mutual satisfaction.

DOCUMENTING THE ORDER

There will necessarily be considerable correspondence between library or purchasing agency and various vendors during the process of equipping the library. There will be inquiries about colors, finishes, changes of all kind (caused by material shortage and other factors), and a host of other details. If such matters are handled by the purchasing agency, the library must be consulted and receive copies of all correspondence in order to avoid some very unpleasant surprises.

Librarians may find it convenient to keep a separate folder on each order with a cover sheet which summarizes information about each. In the folder one should keep all correspondence about the order, copies of bid requests and purchase orders, and ultimately, shipping notices and copies of invoices. One should also keep records of telephone conversations and interviews with salesmen and dealers about individual orders and place these in the folder. When the furniture or equipment concerned is received in satisfactory condition, the folder can be removed to a "dead" file, where it can be found if needed in the future.

RECEIPT AND INSTALLATION

The final steps in the process of procuring furniture and equipment, delivery and installation, are more important than many purchasers realize. In many cases (e.g., steel bookstacks and wood library furniture), ordering furniture installed is most desirable. In this way, the vendor is responsible not only for making available specified items, but also for seeing that they are properly assembled and installed. The user then can see all the final furniture set in place where it should be located and can more easily evaluate how well it meets his requirements before he approves payment for the material. Steel shelving should nearly always be purchased installed. It is not easy for nonexperienced workers to erect shelving correctly and economically, and a good installation crew will see that the shelving is set in place level, straight and securely.

If local labor must be used for the installation, the librarian should try to arrange with the vendor to send someone skilled in stack erection to supervise or instruct the workers. Large wood furniture is generally sent in "k.d.," that is, knocked down or in subassemblies, and must be assembled on or near the spot where it is to be located. If the vendor is responsible for installation, the librarian can be reasonably certain that the furniture will be assembled correctly. This is particularly important with circulation desks which must often be built into constricted areas. Generally, circulation desks are designed and laid out from plans before buildings are completed and there are often slight differences in dimension between plans and completed buildings. For most purposes, these differences are matters of inches, and not significant, but when trying to fit a circulation desk into a restricted space, inches become critical. To solve such problems, experienced installers can make modifications on the spot more easily than inexperienced personnel. Still another advantage of ordering furniture installed is that the vendor is responsible for each piece as it is set in place and therefore is responsible for the furniture during the critical unloading and unpacking phases. If dock delivery of large numbers of boxes containing steel shelving or parts of wood library furniture is accepted, the library will have to be concerned with such problems as damage in shipment (and consequent negotiations with shippers), missing items, and the possibility of damage or loss between delivery of the furniture and its installation. The arguments are very strong for ordering larger items, and others requiring assembly, installed.

On the other hand, chairs, filing cabinets, and other small stand-alone nonmechanical items should generally be ordered delivered only, for it is a waste of money to order these items installed. They usually come boxed or crated and their condition can be easily checked at the time of delivery when their packaging is removed.

Mechanical/electrical equipment of any great size and complexity will often be ordered installed so that factory personnel can make it operational. Indeed, such items as microfilm readers and electric typewriters often have written on the packing boxes prohibitions against unwrapping or installation by noncompany personnel. This is particularly true of larger companies with well-dispersed service organizations.

Service

Service is exceedingly important for some library furniture and equipment, especially that with mechanical or electrical components. Most such equipment will have warranties in effect for some time after delivery or installation. Warranties often require some act on the librarian's part, such as mailing a card to the company, in order to be validated. To secure service after warranties expire, it is often possible to purchase a service contract; these generally provide for routine maintenance at intervals and for repair service as needed. Sometimes there will be an additional charge for some or all parts. The alternative is to request and pay for repair services when needed. Service contracts are usually expensive, sometimes surprisingly so. They do, however, provide preventive maintenance which can help to avoid serious problems later, make equipment work more satisfactorily, and contribute to a longer useful life. On the other hand, some equipment requires only occasional service and it is more economical to purchase service as needed. Location of a service point in relation to the library is an important factor to examine when considering service contracts as compared to service on demand. A library with a remote location far from service facilities can result in large charges for travel time in addition to parts and labor for on-demand service.

Many libraries, when contemplating the acquisition of relatively complex mechanical or electrical equipment, will want to consider the desirability of leasing or renting, rather than purchasing it. Examples of such equipment include photocopying and duplicating equipment, microform cameras and duplicators, computer equipment, and some office equipment. With some lease plans, it is possible to acquire equity as time passes and to eventually own the machine. Such plans also solve the service problem. Of course, over a period of time more money will be paid than if the machine had been purchased outright, but sometimes this is worthwhile. Also, as new models come onto the market and improvements are made, the renting or leasing library can upgrade its equipment without concerning itself with utilizing or getting rid of older equipment. Also, rented or leased equipment will receive the best service a vendor can provide because of its continuing income to the manufacturer.

When considering any electrical or mechanical equipment, the service factor is an essential one in evaluating possible vendors. Savings in purchase price can quickly become deficits if the machine concerned cannot be serviced well enough to keep it operational. The manufacturing giants (Eastman Kodak Co., Xerox Corp., etc.) may charge more but one can be sure of their continued operation; some smaller firms produce at lower prices machinery equal or superior to the giants, but have no effective service organization. Sometimes if a machine is relatively simple in construction, if an independent repair capability exists, one can take a chance with a machine from a company with no service capability. Again, location near cities with many more facilities is a factor. In any case, when dealing with a purchase agent concerning such equipment, it is necessary that he understands the importance of service when considering potential vendors and their prices.

Thus far in this chapter we have tried to introduce readers to some of the factors involved in the selection, evaluation, and purchase of library furniture and equipment. The subject of purchasing has barely been touched, for it is a complex one. The following section on the manufacturing and marketing of library furniture and equipment contains additional helpful information and the section containing sample specifications (Appendix A) will further illuminate some aspects of purchasing. Of course, since local practice differs so greatly and some aspects of the process are outside the library's province, it is neither possible nor desirable to be too specific about purchasing policies and procedures.

8

THE MANUFACTURE AND MARKETING OF LIBRARY FURNITURE AND EQUIPMENT

THE INDUSTRY

The library furniture industry is not large, nor does it have a large dollar volume. It is not a wonderfully stable industry, and with the exception of a very few long-established companies, firms enter and leave the industry with some frequency. Library Bureau was the first firm to meet specifically the supply, equipment, and furniture needs of libraries. The company was established in 1876 by a group of librarians who were unable to purchase "library fittings," such as catalog cards and cabinets to hold them. Interestingly, one of the early products developed by Library Bureau was the vertical filing cabinet, which was quickly adapted by nonlibrary buyers. The firm has continued in business to this day, and is still known as Library Bureau. Estey, a manufacturer of steel bookstacks, also has a long history of manufacturing shelving for libraries.

The industry remained very small until the middle 1950s when the construction of new library buildings accelerated, and by the 1960s there was such a boom in library building that many new firms had begun manufacturing library furniture and equipment. Then, as the boom petered out in the 1970s, many of the newcomers to the industry dropped out, along with some of the longer-established firms. At this writing, the industry continues to be in a state of flux, with some respected and older firms having problems and even disappearing, and few new firms are replacing them. Corporate mergers, with the resulting conglomerates, have been an important factor in this attrition, for such firms are often looking for spectacular profits and generally are not content with the slow steady growth and modest profits characteristic of library manufacturing. Other library manufacturers have found it necessary to reduce the quality of their products in order to remain competitive. In still other cases, use of new facilities or corporate reorganization have caused firms to have severe problems, which have been reflected in the quality of their products. In short, the library furniture industry is anything but stable at this writing and does not seem likely to stabilize in the near future. More now than ever, it is essential for librarians/planners to (a) research the current state of the industry when they are ready to buy; (b) seek competent advice; and (c) draw up good furniture and equipment specifications which will be enforced.

There are a few firms whose products are entirely or nearly all intended for use in libraries, such as Library Bureau, Sjöstrom/Gunlocke, Gaylord, Bro-Dart, Worden, and Estey, while other firms, important in other markets, produce some library furniture and equipment. Examples of the latter are Republic Steel, Andrew Wilson, and Interroyal for steel shelving, and Risom and Buckstaff for wood furniture. Those firms whose entire business is directed to the library market do not, unhappily, all produce furniture of the highest quality, nor do those not dependent on the library market necessarily produce furniture of lesser quality, as might be expected. Each firm, therefore, must be individually evaluated on its current merits.

At this point, it might be well to make a distinction between the terms manufacturers and vendors. Vendors are those firms or individuals who try to sell (or lease or rent) furniture and equipment. Manufacturers are those who actually make or assemble the item of furniture or equipment. In a few cases the same firm both manufactures and sells its product. An example is Library Bureau, which manufactures and markets its wood library furniture and steel bookstacks. Estey Corporation manufactures steel bookstacks and markets them, at least in most parts of the country. Both of these firms use a few dealers but, for the most part, operate their own sales organizations. Most other manufacturers of library furniture and equipment market through dealers or manufacturers' representatives. More discussion about marketing will follow later in this section.

A relatively small percentage of firms manufacturing library furniture produce absolutely first-class products. This will be true as long as there remains the large and undiscriminating market found largely among schools and public libraries, whose buyers are only interested in price and apparently unfamiliar with quality. That is not to say that there are not many school and public library administrators who know the value of good furniture and actually buy it. (In fact, colleges and universities sometimes buy terrible stuff!) The standards of manufacturing quality of individual furniture items discussed in Chapters 2, 3, and 4, along with the detailed specification in Appendix A, should assist greatly in discriminating between furniture of good quality and more ordinary furniture. In this section we will consider some more general criteria for judging manufacturers of library furniture.

THE MANUFACTURE OF WOOD LIBRARY FURNITURE

The best wood library furniture is fabricated, not assembled; that is, the manufacturer controls the furniture making process from rough lumber to finished product. In at least one case, the manufacturer begins with logs and owns its sawmill. This type of operation makes good sense, for the manufacturer has greater control over the wood he has to work with, can cut it in the most advantageous way, and can use the sawdust to fire his kilns. Beginning with the rough lumber also gives the manufacturer the advantage of controlling wood quality. In addition, of course, he need not pay another firm to do the work he can do in his factory. Other firms purchase wood frames ready to assemble and finish. They therefore operate with two inherent handicaps: first, they cannot control a subcontractor the way they can control their own personnel; and second, such a subcontractor's price to the assembler/manufacturer must include a profit, which is added to the cost of the furniture. Thus, the manufacturer with a more vertical operation, that is, one who begins with logs or rough lumber and carries through the manufacturing process to the shipping of the finished product, is in a better position to produce high-quality furniture at the most reasonable price to the library.

It is essential for the manufacturer to have a good stock of lumber on hand. The best wood furniture can be made only from wood that is first air dried, then kiln dried, and finally allowed to anneal before it is cut up, fabricated, assembled, and finished into tables, carrels, and other items. As a result, it is necessary to have a sizable lumber pile, with wood under cover in various stages of drying, several modern dry kilns in operation, and space inside for kiln-dried wood to anneal or cure before it is rough-cut. The factory must have a controlled humidity level so that the wood does not pick up significant moisture before it is worked and finished. All this costs money and it follows that it is really not possible to build wood library furniture of the best quality in small factories or with modest capital. Further, it is essential to have good, sophisticated machinery available in order to maintain a sizable volume of manufacture of a consistent quality. These machines are enormously expensive, for instance, a programmable router or saw can cost $50,000 each, and such machines must be kept busy to return their investment. In other words, such machines are needed for volume and then must maintain volume to pay for themselves. These machines, although they are expensive, are less expensive than their equivalent in hand labor today, for the latter is not only more expensive but less dependable and often unavailable. Thus, manufacture of wood library furniture must be performed in sizable factories with a large inventory of wood, a full complement of expensive machinery, and a good pool of skilled labor—in short, a well-established, strongly capitalized enterprise.

There are manufacturers who produce, or actually assemble, wood furniture under much less optimum conditions and there is a market for their products where a low initial price is the most important consideration. Such firms, often small, assemble furniture from components such as self-edged laminate-covered particle-board panels and wood or metal leg assemblies purchased elsewhere. These adequately meet the needs of some libraries, but librarians/planners should not be under the illusion that they are purchasing high-quality wood library furniture. To confuse the issue still further, good manufacturers often use both particle board (in some panels, not usually load-bearing ones) and metal leg assemblies, the latter in special designs. Good wood furniture makers usually use some real wood elements, properly assembled with dowels and pinned in bushings and other sophisticated fasteners, while assemblers of less good furniture depend on wood screws and other less expensive and complicated fasteners for assembly.

Sanding and finishing are two elements of furniture manufacture that only the better manufacturers do properly. Proper sanding, particularly of curved or unsymmetrical surfaces, requires expensive machinery and hand work and high-quality finishing requires hand rubbing, which is a labor-intensive technique. Sanding should be done on all furniture surfaces, not just those that show. Proper sanding and finish application will be the most obvious hallmarks of the well-manufactured item of library furniture. Manufacturers of ordinary furniture will tend to use visible surfaces that need little or no sanding or finishing wherever possible, thus saving on these expensive and aesthetically pleasing surface treatments.

Wood seating, the second most important category of library furniture/equipment, is produced by still another group of firms. Wood seating is made by processes and machines quite different from those used for wood library technical furniture. The proper storage and treatment of the wood is even more important to chair manufacturers, for wood chairs must be assembled with all their wood elements in equilibrium (of same moisture content) or failure is imminent. Only a few firms have the equipment and the "know-how" to produce wood chairs of good quality. Along with stable moisture environment for the wood and adequate dry kilns using up-to-date techniques, it is essential that chair manufacturers have steam bending technology. If they do not, they are limited to straight-line designs or must saw curves for back posts or seat backs with the likelihood of fractures on grain lines. Chair manufacturers must also maintain upholstery shops as part of their operations. Chairs are almost never made in the same factory as library technical furniture or "case goods," and are seldom made by the same firms. When library furniture manufacturers offer chairs in their catalogs, the chairs are made by other firms such as Jasper or Gunlocke to designs and specifications prepared or approved by the manufacturers of library technical furniture. As a result of this practice, several library manufacturers may offer nearly identical chairs made by one manufacturer but sold under each firm's name with their own distinctive catalog numbers. This is not necessarily undesirable, for generally library furniture manufacturers will select chairs from manufacturers whose standard of quality is compatible with their own.

THE MANUFACTURE OF STEEL LIBRARY SHELVING

The manufacture of steel bookstacks is, of course, much different from that of wood library furniture and the differences among manufacturers are much more difficult to discern. Basically, the manufacturers of steel bookstacks produce very similar products in large volume and there is little opportunity for design variation to suit the desires of individual customers, unlike the manufacture of wood library furniture, much of which is of custom design. The differences between shelving manufacturers' products will be in basic designs (i.e., welded frame versus bolted-together or sway braced frame) or in final appearance, exemplified by quality of paint cover or roughness of corners or edges. There is probably not much to be gained by visiting the factories of steel shelving manufacturers in contrast to factories where wood furniture is fabricated. Seeing and comparing actual installations of different manufacturers will provide information regarding the relative quality of steel shelving lines. The way components fit together, obvious imperfections and durability of paint cover are the important factors to be considered in evaluating steel shelving installations. Most manufacturers of steel shelving are long-established firms who make other steel products, typically lockers or office filing equipment, along with shelving for libraries.

MARKETING FURNITURE AND EQUIPMENT TO LIBRARIES

There are almost as many approaches to marketing library furniture as there are manufacturers. No manufacturer produces wood furniture, chairs, and steel bookstacks and markets them directly to consumers. Library Bureau comes closest by manufacturing wood furniture and steel shelving in separate factories, but it makes no chairs. Its marketing operation covers most of the United States, but there are a few independent distributors who represent the firm in some regions. Gunlocke/Sjöstrom manufactures seating and library technical furniture in adjacent plants in Wayland, New York, but has no steel shelving capability and sells through a dealer network backed up by factory representatives. Estey makes only steel shelving and sells mostly through its own representatives, although there are a few dealers in "hard-to-cover" sections of the country.

Obviously the patterns of manufacturing and marketing vary greatly among companies. To help understand some of the terms we have just used, some explanation may be helpful. Salesmen or sales representatives, attempting to sell furniture or equipment, make direct contact with customers. They work for a manufacturer, a manufacturer's representative, or a dealer. Manufacturers, of course, make furniture or equipment. Manufacturer's representatives are usually not employed by manufacturers and sell several noncompeting lines on a commission basis. Frequently they work as one-man operations based in their homes, although some have offices. Dealers sell the products of a number of manufacturers, often competing ones, and buy merchandise from manufacturers which they then sell to customers after adding a mark-up to cover their expenses and make a profit. They often have a showroom and employ personnel to handle installation and service. Dealerships handling library goods are generally either (a) general office furniture houses that have one or more lines of furniture or equipment used in libraries (seating or steel shelving); or (b) firms specializing in the education or library market with a few lines, generally noncompeting, which they try to sell to this limited market. Those dealers specializing in the library or education market generally possess greater expertise and can often provide design or layout service, sometimes free, and sometimes only for a fee. Whether these services are free or not may depend on the likelihood of their getting the order and the size of the particular contract. Some manufacturers, both those who sell directly to customers and those who work through manufacturers representatives and dealers, also provide consultative and design service, which often are based on considerable knowledge and experience. When utilizing such services one must bear in mind that the provider has his own interest to consider, along with yours, and his recommendations will be based on selling his own product, which may not be entirely to your advantage. Nonetheless, although manufacturers' employees can rarely match the knowledge of library operations possessed by the librarian and consultant, their experience in working with so many other libraries can be most useful. An independent library furniture consultant can help to evaluate the validity of their recommendations.

Pricing

The prices purchasers pay for library furniture are, of course, a matter of great interest to prospective librarian purchasers. These prices are almost never firmly established nor identical for different customers. Prices are seldom published for general distribution, although this occasionally happens. When price lists are freely available, they frequently show additional discounts based on quantity, for obviously, costs of production go down as more identical items are produced and this can be reflected in prices. Very often, however, price lists are available only to selected buyers or designers, along with dealers, manufacturers' representatives and, of course, the manufacturers' own employees. The prices that do appear in such lists are often purely list prices, the full amount of which hardly anyone ever pays. The manufacturer then allows discounts from these prices to vendors or, if he sells directly, to customers. The vendor will take the price given him by the manufacturer, add a mark-up to cover his costs, plus a profit, and this will be the bid or selling price. The vendor will try to cover in this price his overhead, or cost of running his business, including rent, utilities, personnel costs, advertising, and other costs of operation. He must also include an amount of compensation for his sales representative who sells the job, which is usually some fixed percentage of the contract cost. Also, he must include a profit for the firm.

A typical furniture transaction might go like this: a customer requests a quotation for 200 tables to a specification that ABC Educational Furniture Company knows XYZ, Inc., a manufacturer of library furniture can meet. ABC looks on its current price list from XYZ, whom it represents, and sees that the list price is $300 per table. Since its discount on the total is 50 percent, it can buy these tables from ABC for $30,000. To determine a bid price, it adds on the salesman's commission (say 5 percent of $30,000, or $1500), their overhead (say 20 percent, or $6,000), and, since it expects the contract to be heavily contested, a modest profit (say 10 percent, or $3,000). The company often will have to install the tables, and if so, it must account for this additional cost by adding on an additional $2,000. Thus the bid price will be the total of these amounts, or $42,500.

If XYZ, the vendor, knows his business, he will have a good idea who his competitors for this job will be and will have a pretty good idea of what their bids will be. First, the specification will indicate which vendors will bid against them. Then, the way those vendors have bid on recent contracts, particularly those of a similar size, will often be indicators of how they will bid on the contract in question. Further, current information about potential competing vendors and their financial situations and the production load of the manufacturers they represent will assist in evaluating the competitive situation. A manufacturer who has empty space in his production schedule will frequently bid lower than he would like in order to keep his factory filled with work. On the other hand, a bidder who has had a succession of contracts where there was little or no profit possible will have to compensate by bidding higher. The time of year when delivery is desired can also be a factor in bid prices. So many installations are needed for school opening that a customer who needs furniture in January or February can sometimes get a more favorable price than the customer who has to have the job installed in August.

Occasionally manufacturers do not want a contract for some reason, perhaps because they have a full production schedule or because they do not want to make a particular item. They will therefore often bid very high so that they do not get the contract, instead of simply not bidding. Often, failure to enter a bid, especially when a customer expects it, can result in a disappointed librarian or purchase department dropping a vendor from its list of qualified bidders.

From all this, it is plainly evident that prices of library furniture, particularly wood furniture, vary greatly depending on such factors as how badly (or little) manufacturers want contracts, the time of year, how easy or hard the furniture is to produce, and how much manufacturers are concerned about future relations with the customer. When all the variables that can influence vendor's pricing are added to these factors, it becomes extremely difficult to detect patterns or consistencies in pricing.

Payment

A related matter here, and one seldom discussed, is that of payment. All the items on a fair percentage of larger contracts, for one reason or another, will not be delivered or installed at the same time. Or there may be one or more imperfect items which must be repaired or replaced. In such cases, librarians and purchasing agents sometimes delay making payment until the contracts are completed. And for that matter, some purchasers pay very slowly because of their own inefficiency or excess of paperwork. At least one state purchasing agency always has to pay more for anything it buys because of its reputation for slow payment. The buying library that pays quickly and makes partial payments for partial deliveries will get better bid prices and pay less for what it buys. Partial payment will help hold to a minimum the amount of capital, often borrowed at high interest rates, that is "tied up" when a manufacturer has already paid material and labor costs of furniture delivered but not yet paid for.

Sales representatives are the customary contact between the manufacturer or vendor and the buying library. They can be marvelous sources of information about their product and their industry. They also can be well informed about other libraries and librarians, and often function as traveling "newspapers." All this information can be most useful. They can also steal more time than a librarian may want to give. Librarians should be careful about this, but not be foolish enough not to want to see salesmen.

9
INTERIOR APPOINTMENTS AND SYSTEMS

INTRODUCTION

Earlier in this volume we pointed out that there was no intention of going over the same ground that Metcalf (1965), Ellsworth, and others had already covered in their works on library planning. This author's basic concern is to discuss the selection, evaluation, and procurement of furniture and equipment used in libraries. Most other aspects of planning library interiors were well covered by other writers, particularly in the 1960s during the boom in library building. However, there are some aspects of library interiors where there have been developments since earlier books on the subject or which, in this writer's view, require further treatment. Some developments in library interiors, new in the 1960s, have been with us long enough that they can now be better evaluated. And, of course, there are a few developments which are so new that earlier writers could not cover them. In this chapter, we will talk of some of these aspects, including environmental systems, materials and surfaces, transportation of people and materials, security, locational information, communication, and other aspects of library interior design and operation that contribute to a more functional and attractive building. In no case will we discuss any of these points exhaustively; in some cases a shelf of books would not exhaust these subjects. Rather, we will introduce each subject briefly and point out some particular problems, benefits, or applications for libraries.

ENVIRONMENT

Heating, Ventilating, and Air Conditioning (HVAC)

Until 20 years ago, there were almost no air-conditioned libraries. Since then, few libraries in the United States, even those located in the far north, have been built without air conditioning. Indeed, many older buildings, even some of our marble and granite monuments, have had air conditioning added for the comfort of the users and staff in the library during the hot summer months. Thus, many hundreds of libraries have for the last 20 years had facilities provided to add cooling air during the warmer months of the year. And yet, surprisingly, there are few libraries that report complete satisfaction with their air-conditioning systems. In fact, in the course of this writer's visits to many libraries in all parts of the country, there have been more complaints about air-conditioning system inadequacies or breakdowns than any other single functional problem. Reasons for such problems vary widely but it is clear that the design of completely successful HVAC systems is dependent on simplicity of system design and relatively simple and proven control systems, along with luck and perhaps even a little black magic. Library administrators should insist on separate balancing contracts and documented testing of the completed systems to assure that specified air volume at the proper temperature and humidity is provided before systems are accepted and paid for.

The proper distribution of conditioned air has many critical aspects. Openings for both supply and return air should be located where they do not affect furniture placement or function. Ceiling systems for air distribution seem to work best for libraries. There are on the market a number of integrated ceiling systems (Fig. 1), which can provide air supply and return in the same ceiling system with acoustic conditioning and lighting. Such systems can provide a large number of outlets in any space, thus cutting down on air velocities and volumes from individual diffusers, a frequent cause of excessive noise and drafts.

It is not possible to provide conditioned air at temperatures that will suit all building occupants. Different individuals have different comfort levels, and no system can please all. Most people working seated feel cool in an area where persons moving about will be comfortable. Some catering to individual preferences is possible in closed rooms if each has a thermostat and is zoned individually, but this is expensive initially and can consume more energy than dependence on fewer zones. If several closed rooms are in a single zone, thermostats should be placed in a "neutral" area. One office occupant who likes extremes in temperature and has the thermostat in his office or study can make life miserable for the occupants of adjacent offices.

Humidity control should be an element in any system of heating, ventilation, and air conditioning. Some humidity control is important to people, but seems even more important for the protection of library materials. Excessive moisture and lack of air movement are deadly to the paper used in most modern books. A relatively low humidity level of 30 to 50 percent will help book papers to endure and will not be objectionable to most occupants. There may be a minor problem with static electricity if carpet is not treated to ground and prevent static buildup. Humidistats should be placed in book storage areas, or areas with little air movement, to warn

FIG. 1 Integrated ceiling systems work well in reader/stack areas, providing evenly distributed conditioned air and light, along with acoustical treatment. State University of New York, Cortland, New York.

of humidity buildups. Exact humidity control seems not easy to achieve and it is best to avoid specifying any narrower humidity range than is essential for the health of library materials, users, and staff. It is also important that a high degree of filtration be a part of air-handling units. Airborne dust and dirt are extremely hard on books and add significantly to wear and tear on furniture and equipment, as well as increasing the cost of maintenance. Filtration must be designed into such systems and, most important, filters must be changed when they become dirty.

As mentioned earlier, HVAC systems seem prone to cause problems in a high proportion of installations. Certainly some are badly designed; however, all too frequently, poor maintenance and failure by personnel to understand a complex system are responsible for equipment failures. A modern HVAC system is very complex, utilizing mechanical, plumbing, and electrical components with which local engineering and maintenance personnel must be thoroughly familiar. A well-conceived, conscientiously carried out program of preventive maintenance is essential, as are good instrumentation and monitoring of mechanical components. Some larger institutions now use computer-based electronic monitoring systems which automatically keep track of the performance of critical valves, filters, and other parts of the HVAC system and notify maintenance personnel of impending problems before they become serious. Even the best-designed and -maintained systems will fail to operate properly at times. So that the library can remain open during such "down" times, it should be possible to (a) provide some air movement by operation of the ventilation section of system if it is not the part that is down; and (b) have operable windows that can be opened during such emergencies. However, windows should not be operable during periods when the system is working normally, or else the systems operation will be impaired and energy wasted; this can be managed by having windows operated by removable keys which are closely held and brought out only during emergencies.

Artificial and Natural Lighting

Other works have treated the subject exhaustively and this writer will not get very deeply into it. However, after visiting more than 200 libraries of every size, it is clear that many architects and planners continue to be unable to devise satisfactory lighting systems for libraries. They fail to light column lines, they use "nightclub" lighting in areas where close work with printed material is done, and they prevent flexible utilization of space by directional or concentrated area lighting. They frequently use lights that are very expensive to operate and that must be relamped frequently. In the name of aesthetics, they commit sins that make it difficult and expensive to rearrange functions. Since library operations and services are changing more rapidly today than ever before, it is essential that lighting systems be designed to provide good light levels that operate with modest expenditures of energy.

Until recently, fluorescent fixtures have provided the best quality and quantity of light for energy expended, but sodium vapor lamps are now suitable for some interior use and can be seriously considered for overall library use. The color temperature is much different from fluorescent, and the warmup time precludes their use for individual rooms. Earlier we pointed out the benefits of so-called integrated ceiling systems for even distribution of conditioned air. The same systems can provide well-distributed overall light for libraries. If the structural system leaves column lines that the overall system will not light properly, supplementary lighting must be added so that flexible use of library space is not precluded.

Too much light has been provided in many recently built libraries with attendant glare, excessive contrast, and reflections on table tops and screens of microform readers and visual aids. Fortunately, steadily increasing energy costs will prevent this problem in the future. Hopefully, architects will now concentrate on providing light of adequate quantity (between 50 to 70 footcandles) and of high quality distributed evenly throughout the library.

The era of glass-walled libraries seems to be past, and this is indeed sensible, considering the increased cost of energy. While nearly all libraries should have some fenestration, it should be held to the minimum necessary for aesthetic considerations and staff morale. Windows are responsible for heat loss, require perimeter heating to prevent condensation, and damage books and furniture finishes. Rare books and materials, especially, should never be exposed to the sun's rays. Wood finishes on furniture and upholstery will fade quickly if the sun shines directly on them. There are transparent films, among them one marketed by 3M Corporation, which can be added to existing windows to reduce radiational heating and can filter book-damaging rays.

When windows are specified, they should be the kind that provide filtration of the deleterious portion of the spectrum and should be so insulated that energy loss to the outside is greatly reduced. Whenever possible, windows should be facing north. Venetian blinds and draperies will assist in light control at times, but if these must be constantly in use, the window they cover should probably not have been there in the first place. Architects considering the use of windows in libraries should look at the possibility of using sun screens or overhangs to reduce direct sunlight. Windows on library perimeters often can be placed advantageously high, so that furniture placement and stack location are not adversely affected. A favorite device of architects is the use of skylights; however, all too frequently, they leak and should therefore be used with caution and carefully designed.

Noise

Most libraries have left behind the era when "shushing" the patrons is a time-consuming part of the librarian's work. There are not still in operation many monumental, "echo-chamber" libraries that have not adopted physical modifications to reduce noise transmission. And most newer libraries have been designed with noise suppression as an important consideration. Still, too many libraries, even newly constructed ones, are noisy enough that concentrated reading and study are difficult. Carpeting helps greatly, and should be used whenever possible. New or renovated libraries should have carpeted floors and acoustically paneled ceilings. Stack ranges or bays, used to separate reader areas into smaller areas, will reduce noise levels significantly. Backing made of acoustic material added to double-faced stack ranges will greatly reduce noise transmission.

Soft materials on walls, and use of soft-faced end panels on bookstacks will help even further. These measures should help to make any library quiet enough to suit users and staff.

INTERIOR MATERIALS

Floor Coverings

Ten or fifteen years ago, there was considerable controversy about floor coverings for library use, with some planners preferring so-called resilient floor coverings and others advocating carpet for new libraries. Today the carpet adherents have clearly won, and resilient floors are principally used in utility areas, lobbies, and restrooms. The evidence is clear to most planners that the initial greater cost of carpet is outweighed by its lesser cost of maintenance, along with its other advantages. Many of these are particularly critical in libraries, among them being that of noise reduction. Even those libraries that are unable to use carpet throughout will often make a strenuous effort to carpet traffic areas to reduce footfall noise. The color and warmth of carpet are also aesthetically important in libraries. Properly installed carpet is for walkers a safer surface than sometimes slippery resilient floors, and it is more comfortable to walk and work on and therefore a boon to staff.

There are, of course, problems in using carpet, and librarians should plan to compensate for them. Most carpets stain more easily than resilient floors and spots should be cleaned quickly before they have a chance to set. Wheeled traffic, common in libraries, operates with some difficulty over carpeted floors; this can be alleviated by using relatively low-pile carpet, at least in traffic areas and by using large wheels on trucks. Also, carpet in libraries should generally be applied by the direct glue-down method. This method uses no separate pad and the carpet backing is glued directly to the floor. This permits easier, more permanent, less expensive installation and reduces carpet resistance to rolling traffic. Some underfoot comfort and noise suppression is lost, but in neither is the loss significant. Resilient or other hard-surface floors should be used in utility and storage spaces, receiving rooms, and restrooms, and also in very heavy traffic areas leading outside the building.

Carpet for library use must be carefully selected to meet the needs of various library areas. Not only must carpet fabric (wool, nylon, acrylic, etc.) be correct for the application, but also the construction of the carpet must be carefully considered. Some carpets are suitable for luxury or prestige areas, others for heavily trafficked areas, still others for areas where color fastness and resistance to damage by wetting are important. Nearly all carpet manufacturers produce a wide range of carpets with different fabrics and methods of construction. They will classify their various carpets by the kind of use for which they are designed, and will be helpful in guiding in the selection of carpet that will best meet one's needs. No attempt is made to treat carpet comprehensively in this chapter; however, following are a few general observations.

Wool is still the finest fabric for high-quality carpet. It is probably not suitable for general use in libraries. Its increasing scarcity is causing prices to rise very high, and it does not wear quite well enough for general library use. However, for special collections areas or other luxury applications it is strongly recommended. Wool has the best overall appearance, the best resistance to soiling, and when it is soiled, cleans easily. It is not as durable as some artificial fabrics and has a high static level.

The acrylics have been deservedly popular for years. They have good color fastness and clean up easily. High-quality acrylics can look nearly as luxurious as wool; however, they have poor soil resistance and are easily resoiled. They are also less durable than some other fabrics.

Polypropylene is considered by some carpet authorities to be the fabric of the future. It is very durable, cleans easily, and resists staining. It does not look as attractive as do some other fabrics, and the range of available colors is not great.

Nylon is currently the fabric most suitable for general library use. It has always been the most durable carpet fabric and maintains its appearance well. It has suffered from a lack of luxurious appearance, from very easy soiling, and a high static level. In recent years, however, new forms of nylon have been developed that hide soil and look more attractive. Antistatic materials are now commonly added to better-quality nylons, and some varieties of soil-hiding nylon, such as Antron III, have built-in static reduction. A good-quality carpet of a material like Antron III is, at this stage of technological development, probably the best for overall library use, with its combination of good appearance, long wear, and reasonable cost.

When selecting carpet for library use, a number of considerations must be borne in mind. The amount of use is obviously a critical factor, as is the quality and quantity of required maintenance. It should be remembered that maintenance generally deteriorates with the passing of years. With the kind of use and abuse library carpet receives, solid colors, particularly light ones, are not a wise choice in traffic areas. Medium dark colors, particularly tweeds, will retain their appearance longer. Very dark colors are not good, for they show dust from foot falls. The pile depth of carpet used in library traffic areas cannot be deep or luxurious feeling because of the resistance caused to rolling traffic. However, the weave should be dense enough that the pile stands up in heavy traffic. There is fairly rapid change in carpet technology, so librarians will need to research fabric and construction at the time they are requesting carpet. Books such as the one by Shoshkes and Berkeley listed in the bibliography, will provide background material that will orient carpet specifiers to the subject. Articles in Contract, and other magazines dealing with commercial interiors will provide information on current developments. The book by Berkeley, published by the Library Technology Program, also gives helpful data on floor coverings other than carpet.

Walls and Wall Coverings

The kinds of walls and wall coverings used can be important to the function and long-lasting good appearance of library interiors. Today's library functions are changing rather rapidly; for instance, the new emphasis on instruction in many academic libraries is resulting in reorganization of space to provide for the needs of such programs. Those libraries with interior spaces divided by demountable partitions can easily rearrange these areas to provide for such new requirements. Of course, demountable partitions that extend from the ceiling can be added in most libraries, although these are usually not completely satisfactory with vaulted or coffered ceilings. Office landscape or free-standing partitions, suitably covered, can be used to separate spaces and create offices in any kind of library, but sound transmission is a problem. Concrete block (CMU) is a material frequently used for interior walls and need not be nearly as permanent as it looks. It can be put up or taken down with little difficulty, and with a little patching or paint, new spaces can be created. When closing off new spaces, if sound transmission is a critical factor, some kind of sound baffle should be placed at the wall line above the dropped ceiling. It is almost always wise to use relatively soft surfaces on new walls used to construct spaces.

Wall coverings in libraries have, until rather recently, been of hard surfaces, such as marble, painted plaster, metal, and concrete block. All these hard surfaces provide no help in noise reduction and, except for marble, are not easily maintained. Today's libraries require wall surfaces that absorb sound and are easily cleaned. All sorts of materials are being used as wall materials to help with these problems (Fig. 2). Cork, wall carpet, and draperies used for wall coverings all help reduce noise in special situations. Vinyl wall covering helps to some degree in noise reduction and greatly eases maintenance. It is easy to clean and difficult to deface permanently. Paint on plaster, metal, or cement block is not easy to keep clean, especially with the flat finishes favored by many architects. High-gloss paints are much easier to keep clean, as most marks can be sponged off this kind of surface. Wood paneling is occasionally used in libraries; it is relatively expensive but maintenance free and adds greatly to the beauty of the interior. The junction between wall and floor is often a problem area because maintenance equipment used on floors is sometimes struck against the wall at this level. A vinyl base or an extension of carpet 2 or 3 in. up the wall will help to avoid such problems.

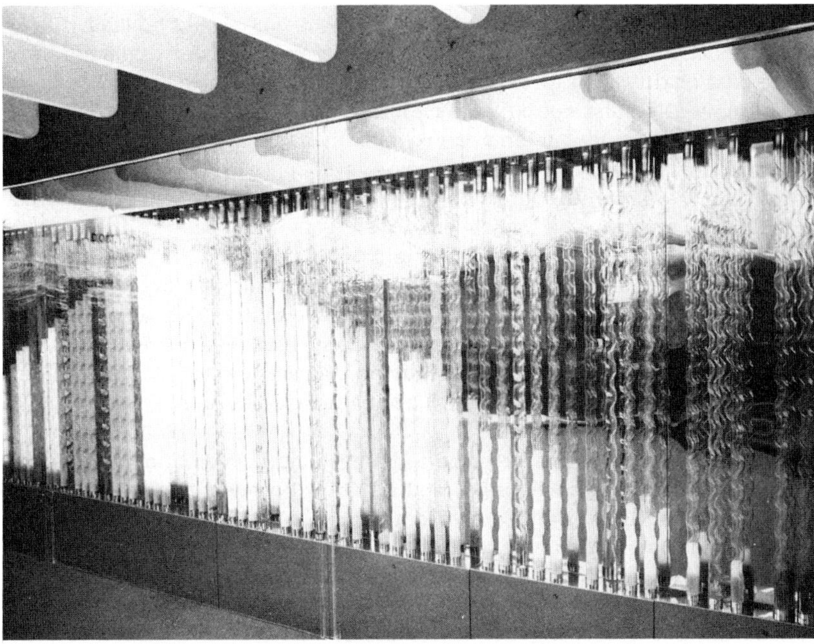

FIG. 2 Something different in wall covering—fluorescent tubes. Canadian Institute for Scientific and Technical Information, Ottawa, Ontario, Canada.

Windows and Doors

Modern air-conditioned buildings should, as stated earlier, have windows with operable sashes controlled by removeable keys, without elaborate mechanism for opening them. They should open out. They should be tinted to reduce glare and filter out harmful rays. Venetian blinds or draperies can be used for light control. For some installations, particularly where nonprint material is to be used by a group, a two-track drapery system, with one set for light diffusion and the other for exclusion of light is useful though rather expensive. Several new libraries have used a new system with thin venetian blinds sandwiched between two layers of glass. In at least one instance, a couple of these have failed and have been nearly impossible to repair. Librarians should be cautious about complicated systems, particularly around windows.

Interior doors are among the most heavily used objects in the average library, yet they are seldom noticed. Door surfaces and hardware are frequently the first parts of the library to become tired and worn looking, which, of course, invites carelessness and vandalism throughout the building. To forestall this, doors in heavy traffic areas should be clad with high-pressure laminate rather than finished wood. Hardware should be of the best quality with metal finishes that do not wear under the heaviest use. Door sills must not be a barrier to rolling traffic. Lights (windows) in or beside doors very often are problems because the desire for privacy on the part of occupants of closed rooms is in opposition to the need for library staff to know what goes on in such spaces. Some users, particularly in individual studies, are wont to cover the glass with posters, art work, newspapers, and other opaque materials to gain privacy. To counter this tendency, some librarians have specified large windows that are difficult to cover completely. Another solution is to use quite small windows and to insist that they remain uncovered for safety reasons. At Penn State the emergency evacuation procedure requires that windows in studies be left uncovered, and the lights (windows) are so small that no one feels too exposed to the view of passersby.

Exterior doors in libraries tend to be problems. Too often they are monumental in appearance, size, and weight. Frequently they are difficult for the weak or light in weight to use and impossible for users with some kinds of handicaps. Some of the most recently built libraries, including several in Canada, use electronically operated automatic doors that are activated by the weight of entering users on sensors under mats just outside the doors. These are of great assistance to readers handicapped in any way and, for all entering and leaving the library, are most pleasant to use. They apparently also cut down on loss of conditioned (heated or cooled) air, and seem to be relatively maintenance free.

Traffic patterns at entrance doors should be obvious, with signs clearly orienting users. Signs on doors should indicate "entrance" and "exit." Door hardware must be extremely hardy so that it holds up under the heavy load such doors receive. Some kind of rough-surfaced mat should be located just outside and/or inside the main entrance doors to remove as much foot-carried dirt or moisture as possible before the patron enters the library itself. It is also very useful to have sound-absorbing material in lobby or vestibule to quiet the noise of users' conversation as they enter the library.

AIDS TO USING THE LIBRARY

Directories and Graphics

In too many libraries it is difficult for the users to find their way, let alone use them successfully. Even librarians have often been heard to say that they find some libraries forbidding and confusing. Imagine then, the first-time nonlibrarian user's reaction to many of our more imposing libraries, if professionals find them somewhat intimidating. It is important to make lobby areas inviting and unconfusing, and to provide clear and adequate directory information.

The lobby can be simplified and made more inviting with partitions and lighting. Carpet and upholstered furniture will give a warmer appearance. Well-conceived, simple, attractive directory information is essential. There should be a changeable presentation listing names of departments, units, and functions and a dimensional presentation showing spatial relationship among departments. The latter should present the entire building in sections showing building floors with major functions and areas housed on them and floor plans for each floor showing in more precise detail what is housed on them. Many libraries have a list of staff members with their room numbers or location. This can be combined with the directory of departments and units or may form a separate directory. The ideal locations for the floor plans and directory are near the entrance and close to elevators or main stairs.

On each floor, adjacent to the elevators or main stairs, there should be (a) a sectional plan of the building; (b) a plan of the particular floor; and (c) a directory for that floor. Each elevator should contain a sectional plan of the building so that users are reminded of each floor's functions and holdings. In view of changes in function and location, it should be made sure that it is relatively easy to change sign lettering. In addition, in libraries of any size, up-to-date diagrams of the collection's location in stack areas should be placed liberally near and within stack areas as well as near the public catalog. Lettering in these will also need to be easily changed. While it is important that all directories and plans be revised and kept up-to-date relatively easily, it is quite essential that they be of the highest quality, well conceived and designed, well located, highly visible, and with lettering of high quality and consistent and distinctive style. Signs should be well lighted, and color and color-coding are often very useful elements. Originality and striking appearance are also important. Hopefully, the realization of all these criteria will result in directories and graphic presentations that are noticed, read, and understood by those using the library. Librarians should be ready for change and have on hand or permanently available additional letters of the same type face in appropriate sizes.

Closely related to building directories and reproductions of plans locating building functions is the use of signs and lettering throughout the library. These are extremely important for patrons trying to use libraries, particularly those housed in large and more complicated buildings. Very rarely do libraries have attractive, clear, and adequate graphics. In too many instances, signs are dirty or faded with ordinary-looking lettering in different styles. Frequently they are "invisible" to users because they lack distinction and are too wordy, or the print is too small. Signs should be used sparingly, for the more that are used, the less attention they all will receive.

Signs that are to be relatively permanent should be designed to be kept free of dirt, defacement, or other damage. They may be encased in plastic or glass, embossed or laminated, or in some way protected from becoming tired, bent, or faded. Temporary signs, necessary in the operation of any library, should be clean, bright, well designed and lettered, and protected by lamination or some transparent protective covering. Again, unless signs are few, very well done, clear in meaning, and well located, they will not be effective. Signs on counters or in cluttered areas are often missed. Rather, signs hanging from the ceiling or columns or above doors are more visible.

New or renovated buildings generally are designed by architects and designers, who should also be involved in design and specification of graphics and directories, if possible. Their taste and feel for space, along with knowledge of what materials are commercially available, will be of great value. Several recently built libraries, including those at the University of Denver and the University of Toledo have used a technique called supergraphics, which consists of very large letters or symbols, often affixed or printed in bright colors directly on walls and columns (Fig. 3). Obviously, their messages are necessarily short but such large letters can highlight locations such as "lending desk" or "copy service" from across a large room. This technique can be used effectively in refurbishing older libraries. When the University of Kentucky finished its recent addition, the older section of the library was refurbished and supergraphic arrows and signs were used quite effectively to direct users about this relatively confusing building. Many older libraries could make existing collections and services more comprehensible to their users with the design and implementation of a supergraphic sign and directional program.

Color and Decoration

Libraries built before 1950 were furnished in a relatively spartan fashion; however, the next 20 years saw great improvement in the appearance and aesthetic appeal of their furnishings. These two past decades have also seen heightened interest in the importance of color and the use of decorative articles in libraries. The introduction of carpet was a most important factor, for the presence of large floor surfaces in one or more colors meant that walls, columns, and furniture colors and finishes had to be coordinated, or the resultant interior might be very strange looking indeed. Color began blossoming in all kinds of libraries and the results were nearly always gratifying. Libraries became more inviting and less formal and many readers felt that this new atmosphere made their libraries more pleasant places to use, and that the less formal appearance and organization made them easier to use. Libraries, always considered to be showplaces on campus or in towns and cities, began to show interior appointments to match their often handsome exteriors. Chairs began to appear with upholstered seats and backs and steel bookstacks erupted with some amazing colors. Walls, columns, and doors began to be clad with bright colors.

FIG. 3 "Supergraphics" leading readers around the library are very effective. Penrose Library, University of Denver, Denver, Colorado.

Then, within the last few years, other decorative devices have begun to be used, particularly in new libraries. A number of new libraries have added galleries and areas for the display of works of art, both from libraries' own collections and those of invited exhibitors. Works of art are also often hung on library walls. Paintings and other artwork are fine additions to any library, contributing not only brightness and color, but also enhancing the library's role as a center of culture. Exhibit areas can be created in lobbies, corridors, or in open areas within public spaces. Free-standing panels are useful for hanging artwork and for defining space within gallery areas. Some special lighting to highlight individual works is especially useful. Systems of track lighting such as the Lightolier systems (Fig. 4) are admirably suited for this purpose, for they can use a variety of floodlights and spotlights along with "wall washers" to light such areas. Some recently built libraries have acquired works of art as part of the building budget plan. An outstanding example is the Canadian Institute for Science

FIG. 4 Library gallery with track lighting. The Pennsylvania State University, University Park, Pennsylvania.

FIG. 5 An unusual decorative object, created by an eminent quiltmaker. Canadian Institute for Scientific and Technical Information, Ottawa, Ontario, Canada.

and Technical Information (CISTI), the national science library of Canada in Ottawa, which has the largest complement of works of art in a new library that the author has seen. Here, along with paintings and sculpture, there are mobiles, an enormous quilt (Fig. 5), a display wall containing more than 300 items, and a plant-activated light display. While few libraries can match this kind of expenditure, nearly any library can manage to acquire some art and decorative objects with which to beautify it.

Another source of visual interest is the use of living plants, which has been adopted enthusiastically by many libraries recently (Figs. 6 and 7). Planters and plants are not expensive and they can be maintained by a professional nursery or by interested members of the library staff. Libraries of any vintage can greatly upgrade their environment by adding living plants. Plant suppliers will gladly advise on the best plants for a specific purpose, and there are a great number of books on the subject.

FIG. 6 Effective use of plants add greatly to the beauty of a library. Canadian Institute for Scientific and Technical Information, Ottawa, Ontario, Canada.

FIG. 7 Another beautiful interior with luxurious seating and living plants. Regent Square Branch, Jacksonville Public Library, Jacksonville, Florida.

TRANSPORTATION

The movement of people and things to and within the library is highly important to its efficient operation. As we pointed out in Chapter 1, the most heavily used sections of the library need to be as close to the entrance as is feasible so that the greatest mass of users has the least distance to travel into and out of the building. As a result, traffic routes and transportation facilities in remote parts of the library can be smaller and less elaborate. There are also significant advantages in planning traffic patterns for transportation of material so that the larger quantities of material (generally books) have shorter distances to travel. Librarians planning for movement of materials often think of books in process as their principal concern. Actually, books that must be reshelved after being returned from circulation are the major material load in most libraries and the traffic patterns between the circulation area and the stacks should be short and easily travelled.

And, of course, materials in process should flow efficiently from loading dock or mail room through processing and on to the shelves.

Elevators

Elevators have become especially important in library planning during the last few years because of the considerable number of high-rise or tower buildings built recently. Several newly completed libraries have reached more than 10 stories, and quite a number more reach between 4 and 10 stories. Libraries 2 stories high can manage with public elevators only for handicapped users, and libraries 3 stories high can manage with minimal elevator service, especially if the entrance is on the middle level. However, buildings 4 or more stories in height will need major elevator service.

Although elevators are expensive, lack of sufficient elevator service will greatly discourage use of the library. They should be concentrated in one location—locating single elevators in different corners of the building is foolish. They will get much better utilization, be less expensive, and back each other up when one is out of commission if located together. Generally, a separate freight or staff elevator is not necessary—there is not usually enough traffic generated for such an elevator. Rather, one of the group of elevators can be oversized, possibly with openings into receiving/mail rooms and processing or lending areas to facilitate handling of materials. This oversized elevator should be capable of being fitted with furniture padding when appropriate. Elevators should be fast moving and respond quickly to calls. Call buttons (outside) should light when pushed and it is important to have a floor locator (Fig. 8) at each elevator. This soothes the tempers of people who otherwise often become impatient when an elevator does not come quickly enough to suit them. Destination buttons inside the car should be lighted and have some directory information accompanying them. The walls and ceiling of the cab should be as impervious to vandalism as possible. Elevators will occasionally malfunction, sometimes with people in them. It is therefore essential that library personnel be made aware of such an emergency and the location of the car involved. This can be done by telephones in cars or by some other communication or alarm system. Some libraries are unwilling to have telephones in cars because of vandalism.

Other Transportation Devices

Escalators have been used in some libraries. They are considerably more expensive than elevators, but move many more people over limited distances than elevators. A serious handicap is the amount of floor space they occupy. However, for some applications, for instance between two floors with very

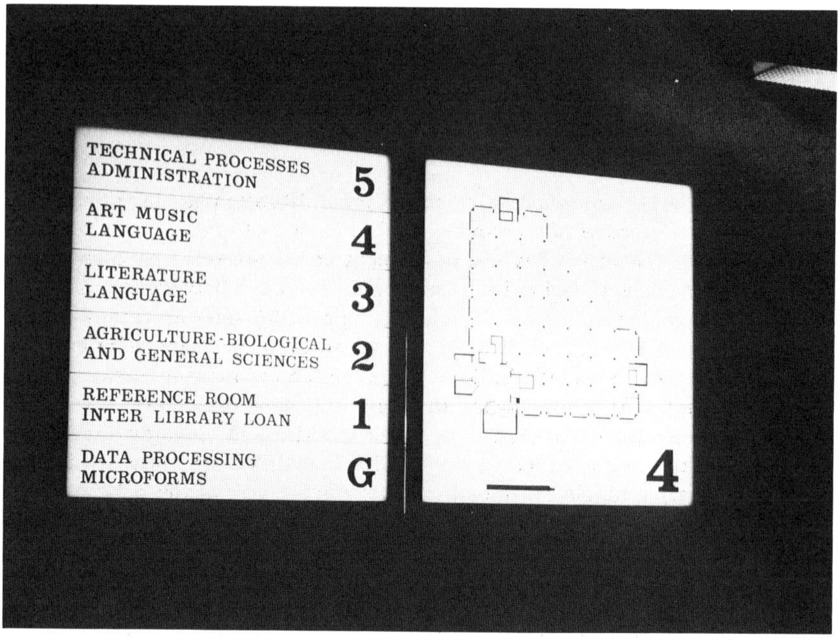

FIG. 8 Directory/map near elevator call buttons. The Pennsylvania State University, University Park, Pennsylvania.

heavy occupancy and considerable movement between them, they are ideal if one can afford the cost in money and floor area.

Conveyors, pneumatic systems for book calling, and booklifts are not as common as they once were, thanks mostly to the almost universal acceptance of the open-stack concept in libraries, at least in the United States. There seem to be some indications of a return to the closed stack because of the severity of book losses and damage and the increasingly high cost of stack operation. On the other hand, the costs of paging books are not to be contemplated lightly.

COMMUNICATION DEVICES

Adequate communication systems for spoken and written contact, both within the library and outside, are essential to library operation. Telephones will be the aural contact with the outside world and usually are the principal means of interior spoken communication. A private intercom system occasionally is used in intralibrary communication, usually for the sake of economy, the reason being that local service provided on telephone instruments requires so-called key phones that cost an additional monthly rental charge, which quickly equals the total cost of private intercom sets. All libraries have telephone service, though not all have the right amount nor all the features they need. Special telephones and features can greatly assist library service and operations, often at reasonable cost. Some examples are (a) "Speakerphones," instruments where several persons at one location can talk and listen to a called or calling party; (b) amplifying telephones for those with impaired hearing; (c) dataphones for data transmission; and (d) telephones that plug into jacks located in card catalog areas, whereby staff with catalog drawers at hand talk with patrons directly. Libraries with a large volume of long-distance toll calls should consider WATS (Wide-Area Telephone Service), an AT&T service that permits unlimited toll calls for a flat monthly fee.

Telephone service and private intercom systems constitute most of the aural communication used in libraries, although an occasional library will use public address systems and paging or signalling systems. Public address systems can be used to clear the building and to locate individuals, although the latter should be done sparingly or patrons will complain—and with justification. Systems using small pagers that staff can carry or signalling systems using quiet gongs or bells can alert staff members when they are needed. They can then go to a nearby phone to find out where and why their presence is required. Some paging systems use very small receivers (Fig. 9) that can be carried on a belt, use long-life rechargeable batteries, and receive actual voice communication. They are particularly handy for stack personnel who can be reached with instructions wherever they are.

In libraries, mail constitutes the overwhelming bulk of written communication, but there are other kinds worth noting. Teletype, i.e., typewritten communication transmitted over telephone lines, is used in interlibrary loan and other interlibrary communications. Telefacsimile, which is the transmission of almost any written or graphic communication over telephone lines, has many potential applications for libraries. Several library networks utilize telefacsimile to exchange copies of pages of library material. Flat page copy is placed in a transmitter at one library, a phone connection is made with the requesting library, and an exact copy of the page being transmitted is received on the telefacsimile machine at the receiving end. The quality of copy can be excellent and the system provides instant transfer of printed material between libraries, which in rare instances, is of great value to the library user. However, even though the cost of facsimile is less than it was 15 years ago, it is still expensive. The fixed costs for machine rental and telephone charges (if one has Wide-Area Telephone Service) are considerable, thus encouraging use to drive per-page costs down. On the other hand, the more telefacsimile is used, the higher total labor costs will be; thus reducing the attractiveness of high volume. However, telefacsimile does offer a practical way to transmit copies of text materials, which is not otherwise possible in current technology. Another

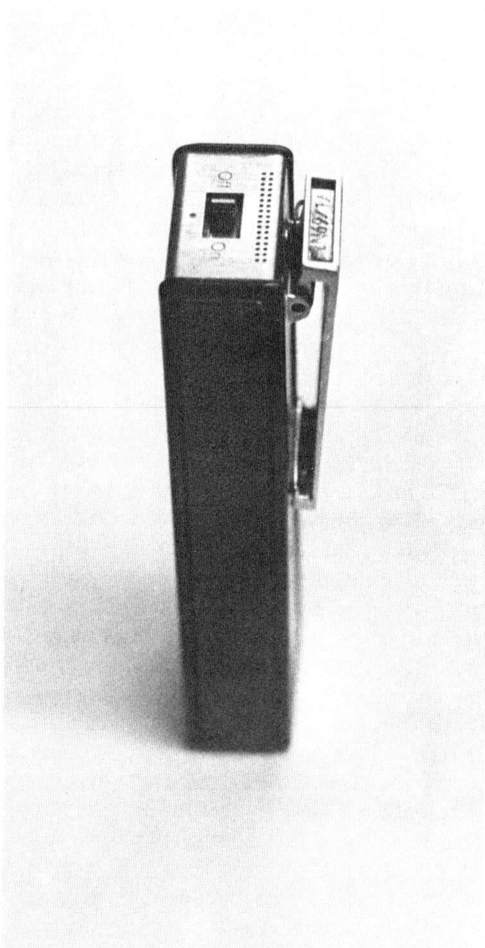

FIG. 9 This pager has one-way voice communication and is small and light enough to wear comfortably. The Pennsylvania State University, University Park, Pennsylvania.

less expensive form of telefacsimile transmits facsimiles of handwritten messages and can be used to retrieve materials from book stacks. One company manfactures a version of this called Telautograph.

LIBRARY SECURITY

In the last 20 years, maintaining the security of library materials has changed from a minor irritant to a major problem. Many libraries have discovered that they are losing more than one percent of their collections each year. Of course, recent trends—opening library stacks and making library collections more accessible—have contributed to making library materials less secure. Additionally, recent changes in building codes have required numerous emergency exit doors which offer more ways for book thieves to get out of buildings unobserved. Under most codes, such exits must use doors with so-called panic hardware or bars so that persons can always get out in case of emergency. In one library visited by the author, all such doors were locked at all times except in emergency when a switch operated from the lending desk unlocked these doors. Whether such a solution is possible depends on the local codes and regulations. When emergency exits must have panic bars, it is important to prevent casual use of these doors by appropriate signs and exit alarms. Both should be very obvious. The exit alarm used at Penn State for some years is a very noticeable, somewhat ugly, bright-red mechanical alarm which works like an alarm clock. It is difficult to use mistakenly an exit door so equipped. Some architects have specified more attractive, less obtrusive exit alarms, but these provide little or no deterence. Others have used systems that indicate illegally opened doors on an animated panel at the lending desk. This does notify library staff that a door has been misused, but, of course, too late to do anything about it. A few libraries have tried closed-circuit TV to watch remote doors and to discourage their unauthorized use. Some nonair-conditioned libraries have had problems with persons stealing books by throwing them out windows to confederates. About the only solutions here are to add air conditioning and lock the windows or, if windows permit, add screens.

Many libraries have found that many of their lost books have been carried out the front doors. Guards or door checkers help somewhat, but their effectiveness is limited. As a result, many libraries have recently added electronic book security systems whereby books are specially treated so that the system alarms and stops persons who try to leave the library with books not checked out.

All the currently available systems have a passage through which library users are guided with detection devices built into posts on either side of the passage (Fig. 10). Library books, not properly charged and passed through the passage, set off audible alarms in the system and lock exit gates or turnstiles and prevent the book thief from leaving the library. Systems currently marketed utilize either magnetic detection or radio response in their operation and are either of a bypass or full-circulation type. Bypass systems require at the exit desk the presence of a staff member who examines books handed to him by the patron, and passes them behind the sensing

FIG. 10 Electronic book-security system. (Gaylord/Magnavox.)

gate to the patron. Full-circulation systems, on the other hand, operate without library staff in attendance. They require books to be treated when circulated and detreated when returned. All these systems are expensive and the cost of treating even 10 percent of a large collection at about 10¢ per book is appalling. On the other hand, many libraries have been suffering library material losses of such magnitude that these expensive systems, even though not totally effective, pay for their initial cost in two to four years. As a result, they are now of great interest to librarians; many are being sold and several companies are marketing them aggressively.

In evaluating such systems for purchase, there are many factors to take into consideration and the decision to purchase a system, once made, is well-nigh irreversible. Thus the librarian contemplating such a purchase should research the field thoroughly and carefully consider the unique needs of the library. Bypass systems are somewhat more effective than full-circulation systems, but exits must then be staffed. With full-circulating systems, the confrontation with a violator may be more difficult than when a staff member is on duty right at the exit. Any of the systems has some failures; none is completely effective. Various shielding techniques have been tried by violators, some successfully. The matter of false alarms, that is when objects other than the treated book set off the system, is a potentially serious problem. There are questions about the suitability of magnetic systems with some forms of nonprint media. Another important factor to consider is the cost of processing the books and materials with the inserts characteristic of each system. Finally, in considering the companies offering the systems, it is essential to take into account their experience, financial responsibility, and reputation for honest selling and good service. Many libraries have had several years' operation experience with these systems and will be happy to share their experiences.

Control of egress from library doors is currently the primary security measure taken in libraries, but the need for security measures of all sorts seems to increase each year. Some libraries have uniformed guards or police on patrol, and vandalism and even arson have been problems in recent years for some libraries. Increasing use of vending and coin-operated copy machines, as well as change-making machines, results in more money in libraries to attract thieves. Many libraries now have safes, keep only minimum quantities of change in desks, and make frequent bank deposits.

Vandalism

Serious problems, such as vandalism, arson, and wanton destruction have become more common in libraries and will probably continue and even possibly increase. Library design in the future must give more attention to these matters and assure that the problems are minimized. Earlier in this chapter we mentioned the use of easily cleaned wall coverings, particularly in corridors and lobbies. Wall and panel surfaces in restrooms should be of materials that are not easily defaced. Walls in elevators seem to attract particularly the efforts of graffiti artists and should have surfaces that discourage their efforts.

Fire Protection

Closely related to security and vandalism problems are the questions of fire prevention, detection, and extinguishment. Several libraries have been severely damaged or destroyed by fires in recent years. Accidents leading to serious fires are rare, most recent fires have resulted from arson. Prevention is not easy, but libraries in high crime areas should consult with experts on the problem. Undoubtedly they will suggest locking off secluded areas, use of closed-circuit TV (real or simulated) and frequent patrols in less-travelled parts of the library. There are available book return units that deter introduction of dangerous or fire producing substances through their slots. Smoke or heat detectors, or both, are a must for early detection and location. Alarm pulls and hand extinguishers should be plentiful and easy to find. Annunciator panels near the main entrance where staff are aware of them should use warning lights keyed to locations in the building where an alarm has been pulled or heat or smoke detectors have discovered the signs of fire. Such a panel alerts staff and fire fighters to fire locations quickly, and avoids disastrous delays.

Extinguishing fires in libraries is a question that has caused much controversy. Many librarians argue, with reason, that water used to fight fires causes more damage to books than does the fire itself. Obviously, however, when a fire is well advanced, water is the only substance that will extinguish it. In libraries, the early detection of fire and extinguishment before it grows is the best response. This implies the necessity for a widely distributed extinguishing system that automatically fights fires while they are still small. Many insurers are insisting on automatic water-sprinkler systems in the libraries that they cover. Available are those that sprinkle only in the area where the fire is located and shut off automatically when smoke or fire is no longer detected. This feature permits a minor blaze to be put out automatically, but prevents sprinkling from continuing to operate throughout a weekend or vacation period. Still, there will almost certainly be some damage to library materials even with brief sprinkling. Carbon dioxide automatically released into an area is an extinguishing system occasionally used, but the safeguards to keep people out of the area being treated are serious problems. A gaseous substance called Halon in concentrations harmless to persons can be released into a small area when fire is present and will quickly put out fire. However, Halon is so expensive that it can only be used in special situations, or for very valuable collections.

Finally, it is essential that well-organized evacuation procedures be developed and practiced in libraries of any size. A library safety and security officer can be valuable in developing and executing good programs in these little considered, but critical areas.

BIBLIOGRAPHY

BIBLIOGRAPHIC NOTE

The literature on planning library buildings is voluminous. Books and journal articles have appeared in considerable numbers during the building boom years since World War II. Most aspects of library building planning, programming, and design have been covered exhaustively and a listing of pertinent titles would fill many pages. However, the subject of this volume—the selection, evaluation, and purchase of library furniture and equipment—has been touched only lightly in library literature and the books and articles that are available too often are not helpful because they have become outdated or are otherwise insufficient.

The large, general works on building planning, such as Metcalf (1965), and Wheeler and Githens (1941), discuss the subject of furniture and equipment; Metcalf, in particular, does so in some depth. The recent British work on the planning process by Godfrey Thompson (1977), offers some quite interesting approaches to the selection of furniture. There have been some useful monographs discussing special types of library equipment such as Hawken's (1960, 1962, 1975) notable works on microforms and photocopying and Gawrecki's (1968) discussion of compact shelving. One issue of Library Trends, under the editorship of Frazer Poole (1965), concentrated on library furniture and equipment; another, edited by Cassata, focused on book storage (1971). Berkeley (1968) and Shoshkes (1974) discussed floors and carpeting, respectively. Two little-known studies, alluded to in the text, are those of Holmes (1970) and Serig (1975).

But there is very little up-to-date material and there seems to be no point in listing all those works the author, for age or other reasons, found wanting. Those wishing the most recent information on these subjects should consult the two indexes, Library Literature and Library and Information Science Abstracts and search back as far as seems useful.

SELECTED BIBLIOGRAPHY

Berkeley, Bernard. (1968). Floors: Selection and Maintenance. Library Technology Project, American Library Association (LTP Publication 13), Chicago.

Cassata, Mary B., ed. (1971). Book Storage. Library Trends 19:287-395.

Gawrecki, Drahoslav. (1968). Compact Library Shelving (LTP Publication 14). Translated by Stanislav Rehak. Library Technology Program, American Library Association, Chicago.

Hawken, William R. (1975). Evaluating Microfiche Readers: A Handbook for Librarians. Council on Library Resources, Washington.

Hawken, William R. (1962). Photocopying From Bound Volumes; A Study of Machines, Methods and Materials. Supplements, nos. 1-3 (1963-1964). Library Technology Project, American Library Association (LTP Publication 4), Chicago.

Hawken, William R. (1960). Full-Size Photocopying. State of the Library Art, Vol. 5, pt. 3. Graduate School of Library Service, Rutgers, the State University, New Brunswick, N.J.

Holmes, Donald C. (1970). Determination of the Environmental Conditions Required in a Library for the Effective Utilization of Microforms. Association of Research Libraries, Washington, D.C.

Library and Information Science Abstracts. (1969-). Library Association, London.

Library Literature. (1876-). H. W. Wilson, New York.

Metcalf, Keyes D. (1965). Planning Academic and Research Library Buildings. McGraw-Hill, New York.

Poole, Frazer, ed. (1965). Library Furniture and Furnishings. Library Trends 13:385-524.

Serig, Dennis I. (1975). Seated Reading. An Observational Study. Unpublished thesis (M.S.). The Pennsylvania State University, University Park, Pa.

Shoshkes, Lila. (1974). Contract Carpeting. Whitney Library Design, Watson-Guptill Publications, New York.

Thompson, Godfrey. (1977). Planning and Design of Library Buildings, 2d ed., Nichols, New York.

Wheeler, Joseph L., and Githens, Alfred M. (1941). The American Public Library Building: Its Planning and Design . . . C. Scribner's Sons, New York.

APPENDIX A
SAMPLE SPECIFICATIONS

This appendix contains sample specifications for (a) general technical furniture; (b) steel bookshelving (bracket-type); and (c) seating, the three major groupings of library furniture that demand careful specification. They are each based largely on specifications used currently, or at one time, by one or more major manufacturers. The author has altered them somewhat to make them more precise, but not proprietary. They are intended to illustrate points made earlier, but not to be used verbatim. Specifications should always be tailored to the particular requirements for each unique situation; a competent consultant can assist with this. The comments below each specification are intended to emphasize some of the more important points.

SPECIFICATIONS: LIBRARY SEATING

General Specifications

Bidder's Qualifications

General: Bidder shall be or represent a long-established, thoroughly experienced, financially responsible concern, regularly engaged in the manufacture of specialized library seating.

Plant facilities shall be equipped with modern woodworking machinery to insure precision in mass production, operated by thoroughly trained and experienced personnel under qualified supervision. [Comment: These are general, but set tone for kind of vendor desired.]

Manufacturer is required to have sufficient lumber on hand at time of award to fabricate all furniture and seating herein specified. Such lumber shall have been air dried for a period of not less than 6 mo. at the point of manufacturing.

Materials and methods: All lumber shall be kiln dried on manufacturing premises to 5 percent moisture content and maintained at 5 percent moisture content throughout manufacturing process. Species of lumber shall be northern-grown whitesap hardrock maple, solid stock, for the study chairs. [Comment: Quality of lumber and its treatment prior to fabrication is extremely important. If properly air-dried lumber is not at hand, it is not easy to assemble. Possession of adequate lumber indicates responsible manufacturer. Proper moisture content essential for proper joining of chair components. Northern-grown woods generally superior to southern-grown due to greater toughness.]

Manufacturer is required to manufacture the frame and assemble it in one factory under one team of supervisors. [Comment: Greater assurance of quality when manufacturer fabricates frame elements, then assembles them.]

Factory visit: Successful bidder is to accept visit or visits from representative of using agency and must notify representative of using agency of production schedule so subsequent visits can be scheduled. [Comment: There are manufacturers of poor furniture who deliver their product with the knowledge that few libraries can or will return inferior merchandise. A threatened visit can discourage their bidding, and, if they do bid and receive a contract, a visit could prevent delivery of inferior merchandise.]

Bidder's Responsibility

Product design: Since the seating is an integral part of a new and modern library installation, the design and styling must be modern and equally aesthetic to that specified. The owner reserves the right to reject furniture if the design and styling is not deemed suitable for the purpose for which it is intended.

Bidders must state the name and location of factory or factories wherein the furniture will be manufactured and the number of years they have been manufacturing seating of this nature. Bidder must also submit with his bid a signed certificate that (a) the method of construction and materials are as specified; (b) finishes and upholstery materials are as specified. [Comment:

The first sentence aims to establish the identity, location and experience of the manufacturer. The signed certificate assures his intention to meet specifications.]

Construction samples: Each bidder shall submit three production samples of the study chair. Such samples must be submitted 10 days prior to bid opening, and must be approved by the owner prior to bid opening. Failure to submit samples as indicated shall disqualify vendor's bid, and his bid shall be returned unopened.

Two of the samples will fulfill a portion of the contract, the third will be destructive-tested and will be provided at the expense of the bidder. Intact samples will be returned to unsuccessful bidders. [Comment: It is reasonable to require three samples for large contracts of 300 or more chairs of a type.]

Deviations from specifications (other than those listed as unacceptable below) shall be indicated by the submission of detailed drawings, together with complete specifications, showing exactly what substitutions the bidder proposes to make. Any intent to substitute shall be clearly called to the owner's attention at the time the bid is submitted to facilitate comparison with original specifications. [Comment: Require bidders to describe and illustrate any alternates they propose to supply.]

Unacceptable deviations: Due to the special purpose and long years of continual hard use to which the furniture will be subjected, the following furniture types are unacceptable under these specifications:

1. A miscellaneous assortment of seating parts assembled by the dealers or agents will not be considered as meeting requirements of these specifications, as it is mandatory that furniture maintain harmony in design, materials, construction, and finish.

2. Chairs not manufactured with all curved parts being steam-bent from solid stock lumber.

3. Frame assembly using screws instead of dowel assembly, except at the corner blocks.

[Comment: All proscribed practices are characteristic of poor chair manufacture. For instance, curved frame elements that are sawed are weak and can fracture along grain lines; on the other hand, steam bent pieces are stronger than before they are bent.]

Installations: Each bidder shall submit with his bid a list of at least ten library seating installations where manufacturer has supplied similar furniture. Five of the installations must be 5 years old or older.

Warning of disqualification: This specification represents the minimum standard to which bidder is required to adhere. Since the manufacture of quality furniture depends to a large extent on experience, reliability, skill, and construction methods of the manufacturer, the owner reserves the right to accept or reject, in whole or in part, any or all bids, and to award the contract to other than the lowest bidder, if, in his opinion, his interest will be better served. The owner reserves the right to be the judge as to the competency of the bidders as defined above. The failure to comply with any of these instructions on the bidders part shall be sufficient to disqualify his bid. [Comment: A few manufacturers threaten legal action in order to bluff their way to contracts, claiming that it is impossible to prove that they will not meet specifications. This important section assures that the buyer has the right to reject bids without being required to document his objections.]

To insure truly comparative bidding, each bidder must base his proposal on the specifications, without deviations, unless such deviations comply with "Deviations from specifications" under "Bidder's Responsibility."

Successful Bidder's Responsibility

Guarantee: Each bidder shall guarantee the entire installation, as represented in his bid, against defect in material or workmanship for a period of 3 years. The successful bidder further guarantees to replace, without cost to the owner, any and all items that shall become defective within the above time, where the defect is clearly a fault of manufacture and not of misuse. [Comment: No manufacturer of good chairs should object to a 3-year guarantee. Other manufacturers may object.]

Sample Specifications: Study Chair

Lumber shall be select and better #1 and #2 whitesap hardrock northern maple (Acer Saccharum) and all lumber for exposed surfaces shall be free and clear of surface blemishes, mineral streaks, and sticker stains.

Lumber shall be air dried for a period of not less than 6 mo., then kiln dried in the kilns of the manufacturer who will subsequently fabricate it into the complete furniture. Moisture content of the lumber shall be reduced to 5 percent. Lumber shall be stored in an annealing area where the lumber shall be allowed to return to normal atmospheric temperature without reabsorbing moisture. [Comment: Species and origin of wood are important. Some so-called hardwoods are really too soft for use in seating.]

Glue for all joinery shall be animal hide glue, equal to a reading of "1" on the Peter Cooper scale. It shall be mixed fresh daily, cooked, and kept in heated glue pots. Dowels shall be of a diameter and length calculated to provide the best joints. They shall be compressed grooved, both spirally and longitudinally. They shall be of hickory or maple and shall be predried to 3-percent moisture content.

Finishing materials shall be the best of their respective kinds. Stain shall be pigmented, synthestain, guaranteed permanent. Sealer shall be a lacquer primer, 18 to 20 percent solids. Subsequent two coats shall be of the highest grade lacquer, applied hot, and of 27 to 30 percent solids. [Comment: Dowels properly dried and grooved are essential for good glue joints. The compressed grooves permit good glue coverage. Using dowels with slightly lower moisture content than surrounding surface insures that as moisture returns, the dowel will tightly fill the hole prepared for it, further assuring glue dispersion.]

Prior to finishing, all exposed surfaces shall be carefully sanded, all edges rounded, and corners broken. All exposed wood shall receive an application of the stain specified, dried, sanded, then a coat of sealer. After application of sealing lacquer specified on all exposed surfaces, sanded smooth, there shall be applied two coats of lacquer specified, with an interval of not less than 8 hours between coats of lacquer and a light sanding between coats. [Comment: Finish application and sanding done properly assure the feel and appearance of good seating.]

Glides shall be case-hardened steel with interior of resilient rubber.

Front posts shall be $1 \times 1\frac{3}{4}$ in. tapering to 1 in.

Back posts shall be steam-bent to pattern and finish $1 \times 1\frac{7}{8}$ in. at side rails.

Side rails shall be $3 \times 2\frac{3}{8}$ in. double-doweled to front posts and back posts.

Side stretchers $1 \times 1\frac{3}{16}$ in. shall be doweled to front and back posts and entire side assembly shall be flush-sanded and corners rounded to $\frac{1}{8}$-in. radius.

Front rail shall be double-doweled to seat and to front posts, flush-sanded with curve of seat, $1\frac{1}{16} \times 2\frac{1}{4}$ in. at front posts and $1\frac{7}{8}$ in. at center.

Back rail shall be $2\frac{3}{8} \times 1\frac{5}{16}$ in. with bottom edge shaped to same curve as front rail, screwed to bottom of seat with two (2) screws. Back rail shall have one dowel into back post and one dowel into side rail.

Cross stretcher shall be $1\frac{1}{2} \times \frac{3}{4}$ in. double-doweled to side stretchers.

Rear cross stretcher shall be $1 \times 1\frac{3}{16}$ in., doweled to back posts.

Seat shall be maple, $1\frac{1}{16}$ in. thick glued-up tongue and groove with top of seat shaped to a 52-in. radius.

Back rest shall be steam-bent to a 36-in. diameter, $5\frac{3}{4}$ in. wide at center, $\frac{3}{4}$ in. thick, joined to posts with three (3) dowels at each joint. Bottom of back rest shall be shaped to a curve.

Seat frame shall be reinforced with four hand-fitted corner blocks, $1 \times 1\frac{1}{2} \times 3\frac{3}{4}$ in., glued into position and held with two (2) screws.

Seat pitch and back pitch, and the included angle, shall be correct for a library study chair.

Overall width shall be $18\frac{3}{8}$ in. at bottom and $17\frac{3}{4}$ in. at top. Overall depth shall be $19\frac{1}{2}$ in., overall height $31\frac{1}{2}$ in. Seat depth shall be $15\frac{1}{4}$ in., seat height $17\frac{1}{4}$ in., height of back above seat $15\frac{1}{2}$ in.

Upholstered seat and inside back shall be upholstered with $1\frac{1}{2}$-in. latex slab rubber (medium density), with cover attached by blind tacking one side and applying a tack strip on the opposite side. Outside back shall have a double layer of wadding and cover applied same as inside back. No welts or gimps shall be used.

Upholstery shall be 3-oz-weight top grain leather. Upholstery colors to be selected after award.

SPECIFICATIONS: LIBRARY FURNITURE AND EQUIPMENT

General Specifications

Bidder's Qualifications

General: Bidder shall be or represent a long-established, thoroughly experienced, financially responsible concern, regularly engaged in the manufacture of specialized library furniture.

Manufacturer shall stock and maintain a constant inventory of specialized library furniture units and intermembering parts. [Comment: Most of the material under "Bidder's Qualifications" and "Bidder's Responsibility" is almost identical to that under seating with same comments.]

Plant facilities shall be equipped with modern woodworking machinery to insure precision in mass production, operated by thoroughly trained and experienced personnel under qualified supervision.

To insure proper control of lumber the manufacturer shall have available modern kilns of forced-circulation type. Lumber drying must be done at his plant or under his supervision. If done at a remote plant, the method of transportation must include humidity control.

Materials and methods: All material and hardware shall be the best of their kind, as hereinafter described. All construction and fitting shall utilize the best and latest-proven cabinetmaking practices known to the specialized library furniture industry.

Factory visit: Successful bidder is to accept visit or visits from representative of using agency and must notify representative of using agency of production schedule so subsequent visits can be scheduled.

Bidder's Responsibility

Product design: Since this equipment is to be an integral part of a new and modern library installation, where design and decorative aspects are as important as the quality of materials and construction, the design and styling must be identical to that specified.

Each bidder must submit with his bid cuts, photographs, or sketches for each item of furniture listed in these specifications under the "Schedule of Equipment," and must state the name and location of factory or factories wherein the furniture will be manufactured and years during which they have been manufacturing equipment of this character. Bidder must also submit with a bid a signed certificate that:

1. the method of construction and leg attachment are as specified. [Comment: Assembly with particular emphasis on method of leg attachment is almost essential if library furniture is to be durable.]
2. the method of finishing will include hand-applied penetrating oil, stains with excess removed from surface before application of sealer. [Comment: Hand application produces the finest finish on wood surfaces.]

Construction samples: Each bidder shall submit construction samples consisting of card tray, shelving unit, full-sized table corner showing top, method of leg attachment, leg ferrule, and leveler. Samples to be submitted at time and place requested by owner.

Deviations for specifications: No deviations are acceptable.

Installations: Each bidder shall submit with his bid a list of at least ten libraries where he has supplied similar equipment within the last 5 years.

Warning of disqualification: This specification represents the minimum standard to which bidder is required to adhere. Since the manufacture of quality furniture depends to a large extent on the experience, reliability, skill, and construction methods of the manufacturer, the owner reserves the right to accept or reject in whole or in part any or all bids and to award the contract to other than the lowest bidder, if, in his opinion, his interest will be better served. The owner reserves the right to be the judge as to the competency of the bidders as defined above. The failure to comply with any of these instructions on the bidder's part shall be sufficient to disqualify his bid.

To insure truly comparative bidding, each bidder must base his proposal on the specifications, without deviation.

Successful Bidder's Responsibility

Shop drawings: The successful bidder shall furnish to the owner, for correction and approval, shop drawings in duplicate as may be necessary to the proper conduct of the work. The bidder shall then make such corrections as are necessary and resubmit revised prints until a final approval is obtained from the owner.

Guarantee: Each bidder shall guarantee the entire installation, as represented in his bid, against defect in material or workmanship for a period of 3 years. The successful bidder further guarantees to replace, without cost to the owner, any and all items that shall become defective within the above time, where the defect is clearly a fault of manufacture, and not of misuse.

Service: Manufacturer must maintain a service department in the area where installation is located. Name and address of factory-trained representative must be given, to insure immediate service, should this be needed.

Material

Lumber

All wood to be selected from thoroughly air-seasoned stock, having a moisture content of 17 to 20 percent, then kiln dried to a moisture content of 5 to 6 percent, and allowed to cool and temper approximately 30 days before being milled.

Kiln drying to be done at the plant of manufacturer or under his supervision to insure proper moisture control. Lumber grading to be in accordance with grading rules of the National Hardwood Lumber Association. [Comment: Seasoned and dried wood is essential to good furniture.]

Exterior surfaces shall be selected northern hardrock maple, free of imperfections, carefully matched for harmonious color.

Interiors shall be hardwood, sound throughout, but unselected as to color. [Comment: Somewhat less durable hardwood is acceptable in interior.]

Plywood

Plywood shall be of water-resisting glue construction, and shall be of thickness and number of plies specified.

Exterior panels shall have face veneers to match adjacent woodwork. To be good one or two sides, as design of specific unit requires.

Face veneers shall be not of less than $\frac{1}{36}$ in. thickness and carefully selected and matched.

Interior panels where used for divisions, inside ends, and backs shall be clear and sound.

Flake board shall be 45-lb density, dry formed, three-layer panel material composed of wood flakes and synthetic resin adhesive that are bonded together in the presence of heat and pressure in a multiplaten press. The outside or face layers are composed of small wood flakes or particles. The center core is composed of larger wood flakes. All particles are cut from fresh timber to specified shape and thickness.

Plastic Laminate

A high-pressure plastic laminate, $\frac{1}{16}$ in. thick, which will not craze or crack and is not harmed by alcohol, fruit acids, boiling water, or temperatures up to 275°F. Top layer of this laminate is saturated with melamine resin, the bottom layer impregnated with phenol-formaldehyde resin, producing a tough and dimensionally stable covering. A backing sheet of this same material is always to be applied, to prevent the surface covered from warping.

Standard Compressed Fiber

This shall be a composition of compressed wood fibers, pressed by hydraulic pressure into homogeneous sheets. It shall have a tensile strength of 3500 lb/in^2, a shearing strength of 4500 lb/in^2, a specific gravity of 0.91 and a Rockwell Test of 40 to 45 using $\frac{1}{2}$-in. ball.

Glass

DSA Glass shall be of the best grade and used for glazing in bookcase doors where called for. Polished plate glass $\frac{1}{4}$ in. thick shall be used in display cases and sliding glass doors in bookcases.

Hardware

Hardware shall be of a matched modern design, constructed to meet the specialized requirements of functional library equipment. Material to be brass or bronze with a satin chrome finish. [Comment: The following items will generally be purchased from other suppliers. The manufacturer must be certain that these components are of the highest quality.]

Drawer and cupboard pulls shall be a rounded-bar-type design. Pulls shall be secured to drawer head, etc., with machine screws.

Hinges shall be $2\frac{1}{2}$ bullet-tip tight pin, with wings not less than $\frac{1}{16}$ in. thick. Doors under 4 ft in height to be fitted with one pair of hinges, over 4 ft with $1\frac{1}{2}$ pair of hinges.

Locks shall be of the heavy-duty cylinder type with eight tumblers, consisting of two sets of four tumblers, locking in opposite barrel splines. Noses of locks to be finished satin chrome to match other hardware. Keys are of nonduplicable style, double-bitted with three serratures. Locks for sliding doors to have similar mechanism. Locks for wood sliding doors to have a throw bolt to lock into strike on other door.

Leg glides shall be furnished on all tables, leg bases, and chairs. For tables and leg bases the glide shall be of brown Bakelite, 2-in. diameter, with swivel-type stem, having a knurled knob permanently fastened to the stem for ease in adjustment. $\frac{1}{2}$ in. adjustment shall be provided.

All chairs shall have $1\frac{1}{8}$-in. diameter cushion glides, except the low swivel chairs, which have casters.

Levelers shall be adjustable, and shall be provided on all desk legs.

Elbow casters shall be of a heavy cast-metal design with cast strike plate. Catches shall be provided in convenient position on left-hand door of all double-hung doors. Doors $6\frac{1}{2}$ ft high on bookcase units shall be equipped with 4-in. surface bolts with keeper plates at top and bottom.

Friction catches shall be provided on all swinging doors and shall be of rubber-roller spring-type.

Drawer stops shall be provided on drawers not equipped with extension slides to prevent accidental removal, and shall be semiautomatic type, cadmium-plated, securely fastened to drawer back. Stops to have convenient finger lever for voluntary removal of drawer. No stops required on card trays.

Drawer extension slides shall be heavy-duty-type, furnished where called for on legal and letter file drawers and drawers equipped with removable card trays.

Shelf standards (for adjustable shelves) shall be aluminum flush-recessed-type $\frac{3}{4}$ in. wide and shall provide adjustment on $\frac{1}{2}$ in. centers by use of metal clips. The clip slots shall be numbered for ease in aligning clips.

Note: An acceptable alternate method utilizes holes bored 1 in. on center in vertical rows, which receive metal support pins that carry weight of loaded shelves.

Construction

In general, all technical library equipment must utilize the best cabinet-making practices and constructions. Dimensions of stock are to be maintained accurately, and $\frac{3}{4}$ in. work shall be a minimum thickness, unless otherwise specified. All joints shall be mortised and tenoned, all work securely glued and blocked. Exposed surfaces shall be entirely free from machine marks and evenly sanded for finish. All glue used shall be the best-quality water-resistant glue, having the greatest possible resistance to moisture. All table tops, shelving parts, and parts of freestanding items shall be of selected hardwood construction, thickness as specified, assembled into component units by the electronic high-frequency edge-bonding process. [Comment: This section describes good practice standards in the industry and any good manufacturer should meet them.]

Finish

All exposed wood surfaces shall be thoroughly hand-sanded to remove traces of machine or mill marks before finishing. A transparent wiping stain shall be hand-applied, and when penetration is complete shall be hand-rubbed clean, so that no film of excess stain remains to destroy the adherence of the finish coats. All surfaces shall receive a coat of sealer and exposed surfaces are to be hand-sanded before first coat of water white catalytic finishing material is applied. After proper drying time, this coat shall be hand-sanded and recoated. The final coat is left to cure 16 hours, then working surfaces are hand-rubbed to a satin-smooth finish.

All unexposed surfaces shall receive one seal coat and one final coat.

The resulting finish is to have sufficient elasticity to resist atmospheric changes and shall successfully withstand the testing of finishes. [Comment: Different manufacturers will vary in the way they apply finishes and this section describes a very high-quality method. Nothing much less elaborate than the process described here will produce a good finish.]

Sample Specifications for Individual Items

Reading Tables (72 in. long 48 in. wide)

Table top shall be $1\frac{1}{4}$ in. full thickness of five-ply solid lumber-core panel construction covered with plastic-laminate suede finish and all edges of top covered with $\frac{3}{8}$ in. thick solid concealed band. [Comment: A table this size should have a lumber-core top.]

The underside of the top is to have metal bushings embedded in it to receive the leg plates. Metal-threaded bushings are to be inserted with a power tool, borings to receive the threaded bushings shall be same diameter as shank of bushing providing maximum holding strength between the screw threads and core of table top. A shadow strip is to be applied on underside of table top along all sides, set in $\frac{3}{16}$ in. from edge of top. Bottom edge to be rounded to protect chair backs.

Legs are $2\frac{1}{4}$-in. minimum square solid maple with two trim lines cut the entire length of leg. Top of leg to be fitted with $\frac{1}{4}$-in. thick steel mounting plate, permanently fastened with $\frac{5}{16}$-in. diameter machine bolt engaging concealed edge bushing.

The mounting plate shall be $\frac{1}{4}$-in. thick steel, black epoxy, $6 \times 4\frac{1}{8}$ in. having seven holes bored and counterbored for attaching of legs and stretcher. A triangular plate, 6 in. long bent to an L-shaped angle, shall be welded to the fastening plate, forming a truss stabilizing the leg and stretcher member to the table top.

End rails between legs are $3\frac{5}{8}$ in. wide, $1\frac{3}{8}$ in. thick, permanently attached, and are fastened to top with six machine bolts engaging threaded anchors in table top. Shakeproof washers shall be used under heads of machine bolts. [Comment: The length of this section reflects its importance. The method of leg attachment must be carefully specified to assure the table's continued stability and durability.]

Two reinforcing center stabilizers, V-shaped, are fastened to underside of top with twelve sheet-metal screws and eight screws to end aprons. Bottom of leg to be fitted with adjustable glide, 2 in. in diameter. The end rails are an integral part of the structure of the table and tables without this construction feature will not be considered. [Comment: The reinforcing stabilizers (keels) help to support the table top and prevent its sagging in the middle. They should be secured at the end to provide the table structure with maximum stability.]

Table, rectangular: 72 in. wide × 48 in. deep × 29 in. high.

Table, rectangular: 36 in. wide × 24 in. deep × 29 in. high as above, but legs to be 2 in. square.

Table, rectangular: 60 in. wide × 36 in. deep × 29 in. high as above, but apronless and with four round turned splayed legs with 4 in. stainless steel ferrules and 2 in. diameter adjustable glide.

Table, round: 48 in. in diameter, similar in construction to above rectangular table (36 × 24).

Table, reference: 8 ft wide × 24 in. deep × 42 in. high with four call-slip aluminum racks each side (special).

Table, top only: 72 in. wide × 33 in. deep × $1\frac{1}{4}$ in. thick without legs or aprons mounted between card catalog cases with $\frac{1}{8}$ in. aluminum angles.

Index table, double-faced: Triple-tier 96 × $47\frac{3}{4}$ × $64\frac{1}{2}$ in. high overall. Working surface 96 × $65\frac{3}{4}$ × 29 in. high, each side shelf unit to be $93\frac{3}{8}$ × $16\frac{1}{4}$ × $35\frac{1}{2}$ in. high with two shelves each side, and two interior and two end divisions $16\frac{1}{4}$ × $35\frac{1}{2}$ in. high. Base shall have $2\frac{1}{2}$ in. square leg each corner with integral bend rails 6 in. screwed to longitudinal stretcher 6 in. wide using 6 × $1\frac{1}{2}$ × $\frac{3}{16}$-in. aluminum angles. Clear book height between shelves shall be 14 in. and construction shall be such as to render table free from sag or vibration (special).

Index table, double-faced: Double-tier otherwise as above one shelf each side.

PENNSYLVANIA STATE UNIVERSITY LIBRARIES
SAMPLE BOOKSTACK SPECIFICATION

Scope

This specification covers shelving and accessories to be used for metal library shelving (bookstacks). The basic units, sizes, color, etc., shall be as listed on the material schedule of the bid invitation.

General Conditions

Proposal

Bids for stack construction and the correlated work under this contract will be accepted only from those regularly engaged for the past 10 years in the manufacture and installation of similar equipment. [Comment: While years of experience do not guarantee a quality product, they do guarantee a number of installations that enable the prospective buyer to evaluate the product.]

Commercial-grade or case-type shelving will not be considered as meeting this specification. [Comment: All prospective bidders shall be bidding on the same product.]

The owner or architect will not consider a bid being responsive if the manufacturer of the equipment being bid has reneged on previous contracts with the owner, or has a history of repeated nonperformance elsewhere. [Comment: There are manufacturers of library shelving whose installations have often been not satisfactory to their purchasers. It should be possiblé to disqualify the bids of such bidders on the basis of consistent poor performance.]

Should any bidder intend to vary from the details of construction specified hereinafter, he shall furnish with his bid complete specifications and detail drawings showing exactly what he proposes to furnish and shall call attention to the details that vary from these specifications to aid the owner in checking same for consideration.

Notice to Bidders

Each bidder, before submitting proposal, shall examine all drawings relating to this work and shall become fully informed as to the extent and character of the work required, and its relation to other work in this building. No consideration will be granted for any alleged misunderstanding of the materials to be furnished or work to be done, it being understood that the submission of a proposal is an agreement to all items and conditions referred to herein, or indicated on the accompanying drawing. [Comment: It is important that the bidder thoroughly understand what he is bidding for and the conditions that will prevail at the installation site, so that there is no possibility of misunderstanding his responsibilities.]

Visit to the installation: Each bidder, in order to validate his bid offering, must make arrangements with the library director to have a representative visit the site to inspect all aspects of the project. Layout drawings will be available for inspection. At the time of such visit the representative will receive from the director a letter indicating the date and name of the representative who visited the installation. This letter, signed by the director, must be attached to the bid offering or such offering will be considered incomplete. [Comment: This visit will give additional assurance that there be no misunderstanding of responsibility by the vendor. These precautions are suggested because there have been a fair number of instances of serious problems arising from such misunderstandings.]

Delivery time: Each bidder shall state with his offering the amount of time required to complete the installation following approval of shop drawings. It will also be necessary for each bidder to indicate how soon, after award of a contract, shop drawings will be supplied to the library. Bidders will not be permitted to plead "hardship" should job conditions, after receipt of bid offering, not be as anticipated at the time of preparation of the offering. Bidders shall be prepared to install shelving in building according to schedule furnished by the library.

1. Number of days required to furnish shop drawings after award of a contract: ____________________.
2. Number of days required to complete installation after approval of shop drawings: ____________________.

(Failure to answer the above questions may result in bid disqualification). [Comment: Misunderstandings about delivery schedules are very common when purchasing steel shelving. A performance bond can be helpful, but these are not possible for some buyers and are difficult to enforce. A clear understanding about delivery schedules with written agreement is essential.]

Samples: Each bidder must deliver to the library prepaid, and prior to the date of bid opening, the following samples: One 9-ft-long range of units complete with all shelves, end panels, and carpet pins. Sample range shall be representative of the type of bookstacks and the various types of shelves and accessories required by the library. Units to be completely assembled at the library by the vendor no later than 3 working days after bid opening. Samples submitted will be subject to a complete examination and review and a complete evaluation through destruct- or nondestruct-testing. Failure to have samples delivered and assembled as specified will render the bid incomplete and be grounds for rejection. [Comment: While all bidders should have their sample on hand for the bid opening, actual erection is necessary only for those bidders most likely to receive the award after the bids are tallied. The erected sample will enable those evaluating bids to see whether the most likely awardees indeed meet the specifications.]

On-site changes: The library reserves the right to make on-site changes in the location of stacks and accessories, if required. Ample notice will be given to avoid delay in work. [Comment: In almost every instance, the library will need to make minor changes at the time of installation. This should be possible without problems and additional cost unless extra materials and work are involved. Interior dimensions will seldom be exactly as planned, so minor adjustments and changes are almost inevitable. And, of course, librarians and others change their minds during the long planning/construction process and it should be possible to rearrange shelving to meet their needs.]

Delivery: Anticipated completion date of the building is ________________. No deliveries will be accepted before that date. All deliveries shall receive prior approval. The successful bidder shall be on hand to receive and accept his equipment from the carrier and provide all handling to the final location in the building. There shall be no COD shipments with respect to equipment or cost of transportation. The library will provide freight and passenger elevators for contractor's use. Crating materials and other trash resulting from the installation work shall be removed from the premises daily. No accumulation of trash shall be permitted. [Comment: Deliveries often seem to arrive at the most inopportune time. Advance notification will avoid such problems and allow the library to have personnel on call to assist with unloading, clear receiving rooms, etc. While the manufacturer or vendor is responsible for the delivery, local personnel will often be needed to help.]

Damage or loss: The contractor shall assume the responsibility for loss or damage to the merchandise through the period of installation. Any damage caused to the premises or property by the contractor shall be repaired at the expense of the contractor.

Installation: Equipment shall be uncrated, set up, and anchored to walls, as necessary. All accessories and fittings shall be completely assembled and installed. Installation shall be done under the supervision of a competent installation superintendent regularly employed by the contractor. Installation equipment to be used in the building shall be approved by the library director. Upon completion of installation by the contractor, equipment shall be tested for proper function and operation in the presence of authorized personnel of the library. All adjustments necessary for proper operation shall be made and equipment cleaned and left ready for use.

Shop drawings: The contractor shall furnish to the library director and the architect for their correction or approval shop drawings in duplicate, as many as may be necessary to the proper conduct of the work. The contractor shall make any corrections and resubmit revised prints until final approval of shop drawings is obtained from the library director and architect. [Comment: Here is the final opportunity to clear up misunderstandings and to be sure that you will get what you need from the vendor. These should be checked carefully and corrections requested as needed.]

Workmanship: The workmanship shall be of the best quality throughout. All fitting, welding, and flanging operations shall be done in a workmanlike and neat manner. Bolts shall have rounded or hexagonal nuts and hexagonal heads. Exposed portions of uprights, shelves, etc. that come in contact with shelved material shall have smooth surfaces to prevent abrasion.

Guarantee: The metal shelving contractor shall guarantee the entire installation against any defect in material or workmanship for a period of 1 year, dating from time of acceptance of work. Contractor shall replace any work proven defective, immediately upon notification in writing, at anytime within the period covered by this guarantee without expense to owner.

Materials

Sheet metal: The sheet steel forming the various parts of the work shall be of the grade best suited to the individual work. In general, sheet steel shall be metallic furniture stock, cold- or hot-rolled, reannealed and full-pickled, or equivalent. All gauges shall be manufacturers' standard.

Hardware: All label holders shall be formed aluminum to display 5 × 3 in. labels. Final finish of hardware shall be of a heavy coat of an approved lacquer.

Type of Stack

Bidders under these specifications shall base their quotations on what is known as the bracket-type bookstack construction, wherein shelf-supporting members consist of a central column only, supporting the adjustable shelf in cantilever fashion. The bookstacks shall be of unit construction, wherein each unit of stack, including top or tie channel, base shelf, adjustable shelves, and all parts of only one unit can be removed from any bookstack range without disturbing other bookstack units in the same range. The frame of each section of shelving may consist of two uprights bolted together by top spreaders and bottom spreaders or shelves (initial section in a range), or one upright-bolted to top spreaders and bottom spreaders or shelves which are bolted to the second upright in an existing initial shelf section (additional unit in a range of shelving or each section of shelving may consist of two uprights welded together by top and bottom spreaders (see illustrations on page 145).

Column-base brackets shall extend continuously from face to face of the stacks to provide maximum stiffness for supporting columns. Bookstack columns shall be correctly spaced by unit-type base shelves at the bottom of each section or by bottom spreaders and by unit-type inverted tie channels (top spreaders) over the tops of stack columns. [Comment: The use of continuous-base brackets is important to the structural integrity of bracket-type shelves. They should always be requested.]

Finish

Each shelving part shall be sent through a multistage automatic washing and phosphatizing machine where the metal is thoroughly washed to remove all dirt and oil and insure maximum efficiency in the application of the phosphate coating, which is subsequently sealed or set with a final chromic acid rinse, followed by complete drying in a dry-off oven to insure a completely dried surface before paint application. When dry, the part shall receive a finish spray coat of marproof enamel and shall be baked for 9 min at a mean temperature of 325° F. The painting operations described shall be performed with the use of automatic equipment.

Note: This is a typical finish-stage procedure based on one manufacturer's practice. Other finish processes will differ in detail without necessarily being inferior to this practice. The written specifications for finishing supplied by any manufacturer of library shelving will indicate good practice. All too often, the final results indicate lack of adherence to his own standards. A check of recent installations by different manufacturers will give the best indications of their current practices and success in meeting their own specifications.

Finish-Test Requirements

The following are one manufacturer's standards:

Color must match manufacturer's color plate and there must be no excessive fading and discoloration when exposed for 24 hours to GE-S-1 sunlamp at a distance of 10 in.

Gloss: 55 min.-60 max. reading when measured on Gardner 60-degree Glossmeter.

Marproofness: The finish must withstand a 4-lb weight falling through 20 in. onto a $\frac{5}{8}$-in. diameter round-nosed punch that is in contact with test plate, the latter being placed over a $\frac{5}{8}$-in. diameter hole in the base plate. There must be no flaking or cracking of the paint film (Gardner Impact Tester or equivalent).

Water immersion: Must withstand 200 hours of immersion at room temperature without showing signs of softening or blistering.

Salt spray: Must withstand 100 hours of 20-percent salt spray. Rust creepage or loosening of paint not to exceed $\frac{1}{8}$-in. creepage from "X" line, tested with masking tape (ASTM method B-117-62).

Abrasion resistance (tentative): Weight loss of paint must not exceed average of 165 mgs/1000 cycles on the Taber Abraser using CS-10 wheels and 1000 g load. A minimum of three tests to be conducted.

Note: The Durometer hardness of the CS-10 wheels must be within an 80 to 85 range at time of test.

Alkali resistance: Three percent sodium hydroxide at room temperature. A shallow well made of clay is filled with the solution. After 4 hours, sample is rinsed and there should be no signs of pimpling or blistering.

Flexibility: Finish must withstand 180° bend around $\frac{1}{4}$-in. diameter Mandrel without cracking, flaking, or loss of adhesion.

Uprights

These descriptions of upright systems indicate the practice of two leading manufacturers. Both provide uprights that perform satisfactorily. Other manufacturers use other approaches that are equally valid.

Manufacturer "A"

Uprights shall consist of three types, i.e., initial uprights, wall uprights, and double-faced intermediate uprights.

Initial uprights: Shall consist of two pieces, inner upright and end upright. The inner upright shall be made in a C-shape of 16-gauge steel 2 in. wide across the web having $\frac{15}{16}$-in. flanges and $\frac{1}{2}$-in. return flanges. The $\frac{15}{16}$-in. flange shall be perforated with rectangular slots vertically on 1-in. centers. The slots shall be $\frac{1}{4}$- by $\frac{5}{8}$-in. These slots shall receive the hooks and safety lugs on the shelf brackets. Every fifth and sixth slot shall be clearly marked for convenience during installation and adjustment of shelves. Intermembering holes, for sway braces, tie channels, and particularly for attachment of plate base brackets, shall be located in the web of stack uprights to develop full strength for the connection of these members.

The outer upright shall be made in a C-shape of 18-gauge steel and shall be so designed to intermember with the inner upright. There shall be no punching or slotting in this upright except for the slots used to receive the label holder. The dimensions of this upright shall be 2 in. across the web, $1\frac{3}{4}$ in. across the flanges, and $\frac{1}{4}$-in. across the return flanges. The return flanges shall be perforated to accept the connection of the range finder.

Wall uprights intermediate: This upright shall consist of two uprights as described for the inner half of the initial upright.

Double-faced intermediate: This upright shall consist of two uprights as described for the inner upright initial plus a 3-in. wide web stiffener of 13-gauge steel which passes through the upright from the top of the base bracket to a point $82\frac{3}{4}$ in. high or to within $7\frac{1}{4}$ in. of the top of the uprights. These three items shall be spot-welded together securely at intervals of approximately 12 in. The spacing between the upright halves produced by the web stiffener shall provide a slip joint for the insertion of the base brackets.

Manufacturer "B"

Upright columns must be approximately $2\frac{1}{2} \times 2\frac{1}{2}$ in. tubular design with sufficient right-angle bends so as to provide for minimum deflection when loaded—95 lbs per shelf on only one side (90-in. high section with seven shelves). Channel-formed uprights must have full-height vertical fillers so as to close the open edges and equal tubular uprights.

Tie Channels (Top Spreaders)

Tie channels shall be made of 16-gauge steel and shall be formed $2\frac{1}{8}$ in. wide, with legs extended downward over upright tops. Tie channels shall be box-formed with ends double punched for attachment to upright webs. Tie channels are not to be continuous but are to extend between uprights to facilitate removal of any unit of bookstack without disturbing other units of the same range.

Sway Braces

Double-faced ranges shall be supplied with diagonal sway braces, put in between the uprights to prevent longitudinal sway of the stacks. Sway braces shall be $\frac{1}{4}$-in. diameter rods, hooked into the stack uprights and provided with turn buckles to provide takeup so that uprights will be held vertical.

Strut Channels

Where ranges require extra lateral bracing, strut channels shall be provided. Strut channels shall be made from 16-gauge steel formed $1\frac{1}{2}$ in. wide, with upturned legs 1 in. high. Strut channels shall run at right angles to the stack ranges and shall be spaced on about 9-ft centers. Struts shall be firmly bolted to the upright tie channels.

Bracket Shelves

The shelves shall each be made of one piece of minimum 19-gauge steel formed at both front and back with three 90° bends (to receive wire book supports and clip shelf label holders), making a hollow square in section and having the edges slightly rounded. Ends of shelves shall be turned down at 90° to form proper connection to the end brackets. This formation gives maximum strength without excess weight and without too thick an appearance. The front face of the shelf shall be $\frac{13}{16}$ in. thick. Shelves shall be designed to carry a uniformly distributed load of 40 lbs/ft^2 without deflection in excess of $\frac{3}{16}$ in. Adjustable shelves for standard sections shall measure $35\frac{1}{2}$ in. clear between shelf brackets.

Brackets

Plate brackets for ends of book shelves shall be 16-gauge steel with neatly angled front edge with outward-turned flange. Brackets shall be $7\frac{1}{8}$ in. high and extend over the full depth of the shelf. All exposed edges shall be deburred. Brackets shall be properly and securely fastened to the shelves by interlocking lugs formed at the bottom of each bracket. The back edge of each shelf bracket shall be provided with a notched hook and a neatly rounded safety lug. Bracket hooks shall intermember with perforations in the stack uprights, and each hook shall be reinforced with an elongated indenture. Bracket lugs shall also intermember with upright perforations and shall be properly designed to prevent unintentional lifting of shelf assemblies and to prevent lateral movement of the shelves. The outward-turned flange of the bracket gives appearance of thickness and prevents knifing of the books when they are placed on the shelves.

Closed bases shall be made of 19-gauge steel channel formed 3 in. thick. Ends of closed bases shall be formed down to intermember with clips on base brackets.

Base brackets shall be made of 13-gauge steel. The bottom edge should be formed with a 1-in. wide flange to distribute the weight of the upright section over a large area of the floor. The front edges of the base brackets shall have neatly angled corners. All exposed edges shall be deburred to eliminate any possibility of scuffing or tearing of the books.

The base brackets shall be attached to the uprights with $\frac{3}{8}$-in. diameter machine screws. The intermediate base brackets shall have two lugs formed in a Z-shape to support the base shelf. The end base brackets will not have any lugs projecting beyond the outside of the base brackets on the exposed ends of a range.

End Panels

Metal: It should be noted that practice differs here; this section describes a good end panel but others are quite satisfactory.

Closed ends (end panels) shall be of two-piece construction for double-faced stacks, consisting of two wide panels. For wall stacks, each closed end shall consist of a single wide panel. Each wide panel shall be C-shaped in cross section, made from 19-gauge steel, formed $1\frac{3}{4}$ in. thick, with square corners at both exposed edges of each panel. Panels shall be completely interchangeable at either end of wall stacks and/or double-faced stacks. Each panel shall be fitted with an individually formed 5 × 3-in. aluminum label holder with satin finish. The top of each closed-end assembly shall be fitted with 14-gauge steel reinforcing angle, securely attached to stack upright sections. Each wide panel shall be fastened at two points to the reinforcing angle at the top and fastened at two points to the base bracket at the bottom of each end upright.

Wood and high-pressure laminates: Wood end panels shall be of five-ply construction. All woods used in the construction shall be selected from thoroughly air-seasoned stock free from imperfections of all kinds and perfectly air and kiln dried. All exposed woods shall be of northern hard birch or maple, fine grained, selected for uniformity of texture, figure, and grain. All veneers for any one end shall be obtained from the same flitch. No veneers shall be less than $\frac{1}{28}$ in. in thickness. No rotary cut or peeled veneer shall be allowed on exposed surfaces. Core stock shall be of good core-stock material with tight glue joints. The bonding agent used to glue up the core stock and for bonding the veneers to the core shall be water-resistant resin adhesive, which will retain practically all of its strength when occasionally subjected to thorough wetting and drying. End pilasters shall be of solid wood $\frac{13}{16}$-in. thick rabbeted and securely glued to the five-ply end. Ends shall be fastened to steel shelving with a metal channel.

High-pressure-laminated plastic end panels shall have high-density particle-board core, self edged on all edges. Backing sheet, neutral color, on back surface. Thickness shall be $\frac{3}{4}$-in.

APPENDIX B
LIBRARY BUILDINGS VISITED (1960-1976)

ALABAMA

University of Alabama, Birmingham
University of Alabama, Tuscaloosa

CALIFORNIA

Chabot College, Hayward
Foothill Junior College, Los Altos Hills
Mount San Antonio College, Walnut
Stanford University, Stanford
University of California, Berkeley*
University of California, Davis
University of California, Los Angeles
University of California, Riverside
University of California, Santa Cruz

COLORADO

Air Force Academy, Colorado Springs
Boulder Public Library, Boulder
Colorado College, Colorado Springs
Colorado State University, Fort Collins
University of Colorado, Boulder*
University of Denver, Denver

CONNECTICUT

University of Hartford, Hartford

DELAWARE

Delaware State College, Dover
Wesley College, Dover

*Visited more than one library at this location.

FLORIDA

Florida Atlantic University, Boca Raton
Florida Southern University, Lakeland
Florida State University, Tallahassee
Florida Technical University, Orlando
Jacksonville Public Library, Jacksonville*
Jacksonville University, Jacksonville
Tampa Hillsborough Public Library
University of Florida, Gainesville
University of Miami, Coral Gables
University of North Florida, Jacksonville
University of South Florida, Tampa

GEORGIA

Columbus College, Columbus
Emory University, Atlanta
University of Georgia, Athens
Wesley College, Macon

ILLINOIS

Aurora College, Aurora
Chicago Public Library, Chicago
John Crerar Library, Chicago
Mundelein College, Chicago
Northwestern University, Evanston
University of Chicago, Chicago
University of Illinois, Chicago
University of Illinois, Urbana*

INDIANA

Ball State University, Muncie
Concordia College, Fort Wayne
Notre Dame University, Notre Dame
Purdue University, Lafayette
University of Indiana, Bloomington*

KANSAS

University of Kansas, Lawrence*

KENTUCKY

University of Kentucky, Lexington

LOUISIANA

Louisiana State University, Baton Rouge
Tulane University, New Orleans
University of New Orleans, New Orleans

MARYLAND

Anne Arundel Community College, Arnold
Johns Hopkins, Baltimore
Loyola Notre Dame, Baltimore
Towson State College, Towson
University of Maryland, College Park*
U.S. National Agricultural Library, Beltsville

[Maryland]
U.S. Naval Academy, Annapolis*
Washington College, Chestertown

MASSACHUSETTS

Amherst College, Amherst
Boston Public Library, Boston
Boston University, Boston
Clark University, Worcester
Episcopal Theological Seminary, Boston
Hampshire College, Amherst
Harvard University, Cambridge*
Radcliffe College, Cambridge
Salem State College, Salem
Southeastern Massachusetts University, North Dartmouth
Tufts University, Medford
University of Massachusetts, Amherst
University of Massachusetts, Boston
Williams College, Williamstown

MICHIGAN

Detroit Public Library, Detroit
Flint Junior College, Flint
Grand Valley State College, Allendale
Henry Ford Community College, Dearborn
Oakland University, Bloomfield Hills
University of Michigan, Ann Arbor
University of Michigan, Dearborn
Wayne State University, Detroit

MISSOURI

St. Louis University, St. Louis
University of Missouri, Columbia
Washington University, St. Louis

NEW HAMPSHIRE

Dartmouth College, Hanover
Phillips Exeter Academy, Exeter
Plymouth State College, Plymouth
University of New Hampshire, Durham

NEW JERSEY

Princeton University, Princeton
Stockton State College, Pomona

NEW YORK

Columbia University, New York
Cornell University, Ithaca*
Hamilton College, Clinton
Hofstra, Hempstead
New York Public Library (Central), New York
New York University, New York
State University of New York, Binghamton
State University of New York, Cortland
State University of New York, Fredonia
State University of New York, Oneonta
State University of New York, Oswego
Syracuse University, Syracuse
Wells College, Aurora

NORTH CAROLINA

Davidson College, Davidson
Duke University, Durham
East Carolina College, Greenville
Mars Hill College, Mars Hill
North Carolina State University, Raleigh
Pembroke State University, Pembroke
Salem College, Winston-Salem
University of North Carolina, Chapel Hill*
University of North Carolina, Charlotte
University of North Carolina, Greensboro
University of North Carolina, Wilmington
Wake Forest University, Winston-Salem
Winston-Salem State University, Winston-Salem

OHIO

Bowling Green State University, Bowling Green
Kent State University, Kent
Oberlin College, Oberlin
Ohio Northern University, Ada
Ohio State University, Columbus*
Ohio University, Athens
University of Akron, Akron
University of Dayton, Dayton
University of Toledo, Toledo
University of Youngstown, Youngstown
Wright State University, Dayton

OREGON

Lewis and Clark College, Portland
Mount Angel Abbey, St. Benedict
Portland State University, Portland

PENNSYLVANIA

Altoona Public Library, Altoona
Beaver College, Glenside
Bethel Park Public Library, Bethel Park
Bethlehem Public Library, Bethlehem
Bloomsburg State College, Bloomsburg
Bryn Mawr College, Bryn Mawr
Bucknell University, Lewisburg
Carlow College, Pittsburgh
Carnegie Library of Pittsburgh, Pittsburgh*
Carnegie Mellon University, Pittsburgh
Chatham College, Pittsburgh
Cedar Crest College, Allentown
Chester County Library, West Chester
Clarion State College, Clarion
Dickinson College, Carlisle
Drexel University, Philadelphia
Duquesne University, Pittsburgh
Eastern Baptist College, St. Davids
Edinboro State College, Edinboro
Erie Public Library, Erie
Free Library of Philadelphia, Philadelphia*
Gannon College, Erie
Gwynedd-Mercy College, Gwynedd Valley
Haverford College, Haverford
Harrisburg Area Community College, Harrisburg

[Pennsylvania]
Harrisburg Public Library, Harrisburg
HRB-Singer, Inc. Library, State College
Indiana University of Pennsylvania, Indiana
Juniata College, Huntingdon
Keystone Junior College, LaPlume
Kings College, Wilkes-Barre
Kutztown State College, Kutztown
Lackawanna Junior College, Scranton
Lafayette College, Easton
La Salle College, Philadelphia
Lehigh County Community College, Schnecksville
Lehigh University, Bethlehem*
Lincoln University, Lincoln University
Lock Haven State College, Lock Haven
Lycoming College, Williamsport
Mansfield State College, Mansfield
Marywood College, Scranton
Mifflin County Library, Lewistown
Millersville State College, Millersville
Montgomery County Community College, Blue Bell
Muhlenberg College, Allentown
Philadelphia Community College, Philadelphia
Point Park College, Pittsburgh
Pottsville Public Library, Pottsville
Reading Public Library, Reading
Robert Morris College, Pittsburgh
St. Francis College, Loretto
St. Vincent College, Latrobe
Scranton Public Library, Scranton
Shippensburg State College, Shippensburg

[Pennsylvania]
Somerset Public Library, Somerset
State Library of Pennsylvania, Harrisburg
Susquehanna University, Selingsgrove
Swarthmore College Library, Swarthmore
Temple University, Philadelphia
Thiel College, Greenville
University of Pennsylvania, Philadelphia*
University of Pittsburgh, Pittsburgh
University of Pittsburgh, Titusville
University of Scranton, Scranton
Ursinus College, Collegeville
Warren Public Library, Warren
Widener College, Chester
Wilkes College, Wilkes-Barre
Williamsport Public Library, Williamsport
York College, York
York Public Library, York

SOUTH CAROLINA

Baptist College, Charleston
Claflin College, Orangeburg
Clemson University, Clemson
College of Charleston, Charleston
Francis Marion College, Florence
University of South Carolina, Columbia*
Voorhees College, Denmark
Winthrop College, Rock Hill
Wofford College, Spartanburg

RHODE ISLAND

Brown University, Providence*

TENNESSEE

Austin Peay State University, Clarksville
Fisk University, Nashville
Joint University Libraries, Nashville
University of Tennessee, Knoxville

VERMONT

Bennington College, Bennington
Green Mountain College, Poultney

VIRGINIA

College of William and Mary, Williamsburg
University of Virginia, Charlottes-ville
Virginia Wesleyan, Norfolk

WEST VIRGINIA

University of West Virginia, Morgantown
West Virginia Wesleyan College, Buckhannon

WISCONSIN

Beloit College, Beloit
University of Wisconsin, Madison
University of Wisconsin, Milwaukee

DISTRICT OF COLUMBIA

Georgetown University
George Washington University
Library of Congress

CANADA

Canadian Institute for Scientific and Technical Information, Ottawa, Ontario
McGill University, Montreal, Quebec
Ryerson Polytechnic Institute, Toronto, Ontario
Trent University, Peterborough, Ontario
University of Guelph, Guelph, Ontario
University of Toronto, Toronto, Ontario
York University, Toronto, Ontario

INDEX

ISBN 0-8247-6900-7